bright sky press

2365 Rice Blvd., Suite 202 Houston, Texas 77005

10   9   8   7   6   5   4   3   2   1

Library of Congress Cataloging-in Publication Data

Chemerka, William R.
The music of the Alamo: from 19th century ballads to big-screen soundtracks /
by William R. Chemerka and Allen J. Wiener.
p. cm.
Includes bibliographical references and index.
ISBN 978-1-933979-31-1 (jacketed hardcover : alk. paper) 1. Alamo (San Antonio,
Tex.)—Songs and music—History and criticism. 2. Patriotic music—United States—History
and criticism. I. Wiener, Allen J., 1943- II. Title.

ML200.9.C56 2008
781.5'99—dc22   2008014227

Book and cover design by Tutu Somerville, Cregan Design
Printed in China through Asia Pacific Offset

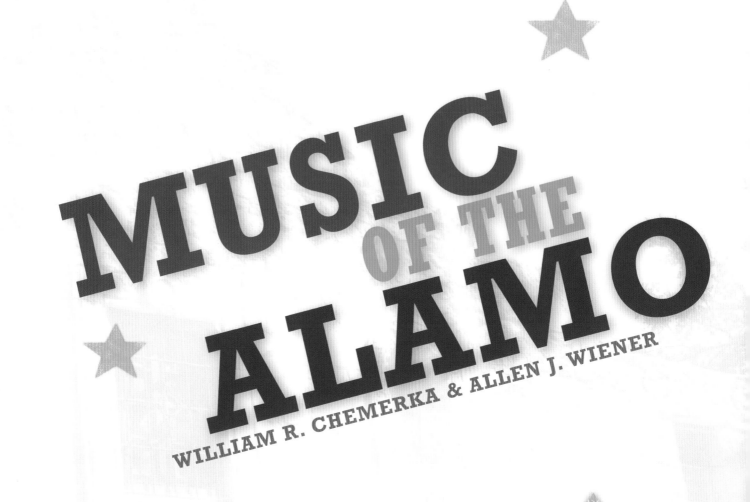

MUSIC OF THE ALAMO

WILLIAM R. CHEMERKA & ALLEN J. WIENER

b
bright sky press

HOUSTON, TEXAS

 # DEDICATIONS

To my wife, Kathy, who has seen me through it all.

ALLEN J. WIENER

To my wife, Deborah, for her support and inspiration.

WILLIAM R. CHEMERKA

MUSIC
OF THE ALAMO:
FROM
19TH CENTURY
BALLADS
TO BIG-SCREEN
SOUNDTRACKS

TABLE OF CONTENTS

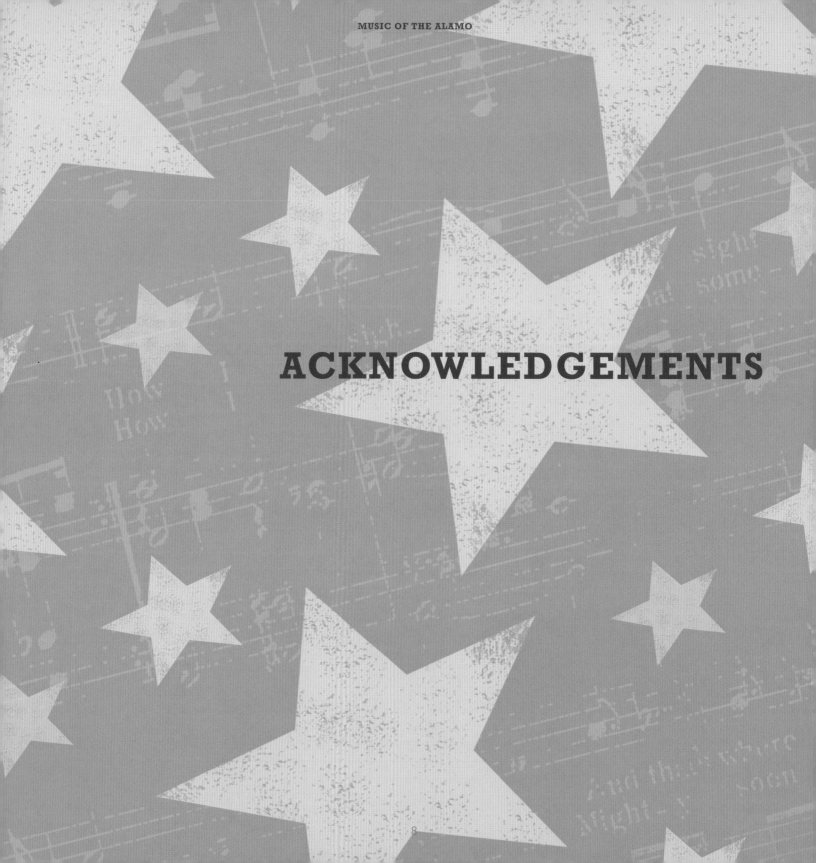

ACKNOWLEDGEMENTS

We both have long held an interest in the Alamo, which led us to this search for the ways in which it has been remembered in song. In that search, we crossed paths with many experts, professionals and good friends who showed kindness and support in helping us on our way.

The staff at the Daughters of the Republic of Texas Library at the Alamo has been particularly helpful over the years. Our thanks to Elaine Davis, Martha Utterback, Charles R. Gamez, Debra Bryant, Warren Stricker, and the Library staff.

The assistance and resources of the Library of Congress cannot be overstated. Our particular gratitude is extended to Todd Harvey in the Library's American Folklife Center and to the staff of the Library's Music Reading Room.

Members of The Alamo Society were generous with their time as they examined their collections of Alamo records, sheet music and related collectibles in an attempt to locate specific titles. Thanks to J. Matthew Hurley, Jerry Laing, John Berky, Texas-Bob Reinhardt, and Frank Thompson. Invaluable contributions were made by Dave Lewis, Paul DeVito, Ken Sutak and Dr. Murray Weissmann.

We sincerely appreciate the generosity of several contemporary musical artists who allowed us to share their pre-recorded songs about the Alamo and Davy Crockett: Dean Shostak and Alamo Society members Carl Peterson, K. R. Wood, Tony Pasqua and Mike Boldt. Mike also co-produced and engineered this book's accompanying CD.

Help on various song title searches was also provided by Stephanie Levine, Al Stefanowicz, Cynthia Levine, Bob Stefanowicz, Bill Jentz, Mike Powers, Tom DeVoe, Brian Cheney and the late Jerry Hadley.

We are very grateful to Sherry Bond, President of Vidor Publications, Inc.; Stephen Suffet; Bernard J Taylor and Siebahn Gallagher (www.bernardjtaylor.com) for graciously granting permission to quote lyrics from songs.

Special thanks to Alamo Society members Jim Boylston, Tom Kailbourn, Rocky Edwards, Kevin Hendryx, Paul Scheineman, Gerard Martinez and Terry Friend for their help.

Thanks also to Caitlin Von Schmidt, Bob Reece, Robert Jahn, Peter Menta, Mat Kastner, Jim Luft, Cynthia Fabian, Alan Leatherwood, Jimmy C Carpenter, Ray Herbeck, Jr., Joey Berkley, Justin "Bumper" Reeve, Gil Prather, Mike Petee, Billy Edd Wheeler, O. J. Sikes, Mark Guerrero, Rosie Dyer, Charles Briggs (University of California Berkeley Folklore Archive), Betty Anderson (Alamo Defenders Descendants Association), Lisa A. Struthers (Albert & Ethel Herzstein Library, San Jacinto Museum of History), Philip Hutchinson, Jerry Robbins (the Colonial Radio Theatre on the Air), Ken Laing, The Kingston Trio Place; Norm Friedlander, Paul Vidal (Moulin du Seigneur), Bill Dean-Myatt, Dennis J. Vetrovec (Cunningham Memorial Library, Indiana State University), Ralph Bukofzer (I Am...I Said, A Fan of Neil Diamond website, www.iaisnd.com), Jackie Kaspersin (Dynamic Recording and 1st Audio USA), Derek Sivers (CD Baby), Craig Moerer Records, Out-Of-Print Records, Memory Lane Records, Flipside Records and Collectables, Folk-Legacy Records Inc., Texanna Records, Frank Scott (Roots & Rhythm), Chris Dunkley, Sally Koch, Dwight Adair, Karen Bippert, Sandy Paton, Tom Hinders, Jim Berg, Jeff Hause (Comedy on Tap website), Marilyn P. Fletcher (University of New Mexico), Dennis, Kimberly and Zephyr Goza (The Act!vated Storytellers), Laura Huber (Blue Sky Vinyl Records), Bob Koester (The Jazz Record Mart), Mary Adamic (Disney Publishing Worldwide), Gary Helsinger (Universal Music Publishing), Doug Johnson (Webster Music) and Jonathan Belott (Hal Leonard Corporation).

Of course, we are particularly grateful for the generous contributions made by Fess Parker and Phil Collins. Fess Parker, star of Walt Disney's *Davy Crockett, King of the Wild Frontier*, wrote the Foreword, and the award-winning vocalist-instrumentalist-composer Phil Collins wrote the Introduction.

We appreciate the support and encouragement that Rue Judd, Ellen Cregan, and the staff of Bright Sky Press provided to us.

Finally, thanks to all the artists who created the wonderful music that we have chronicled.

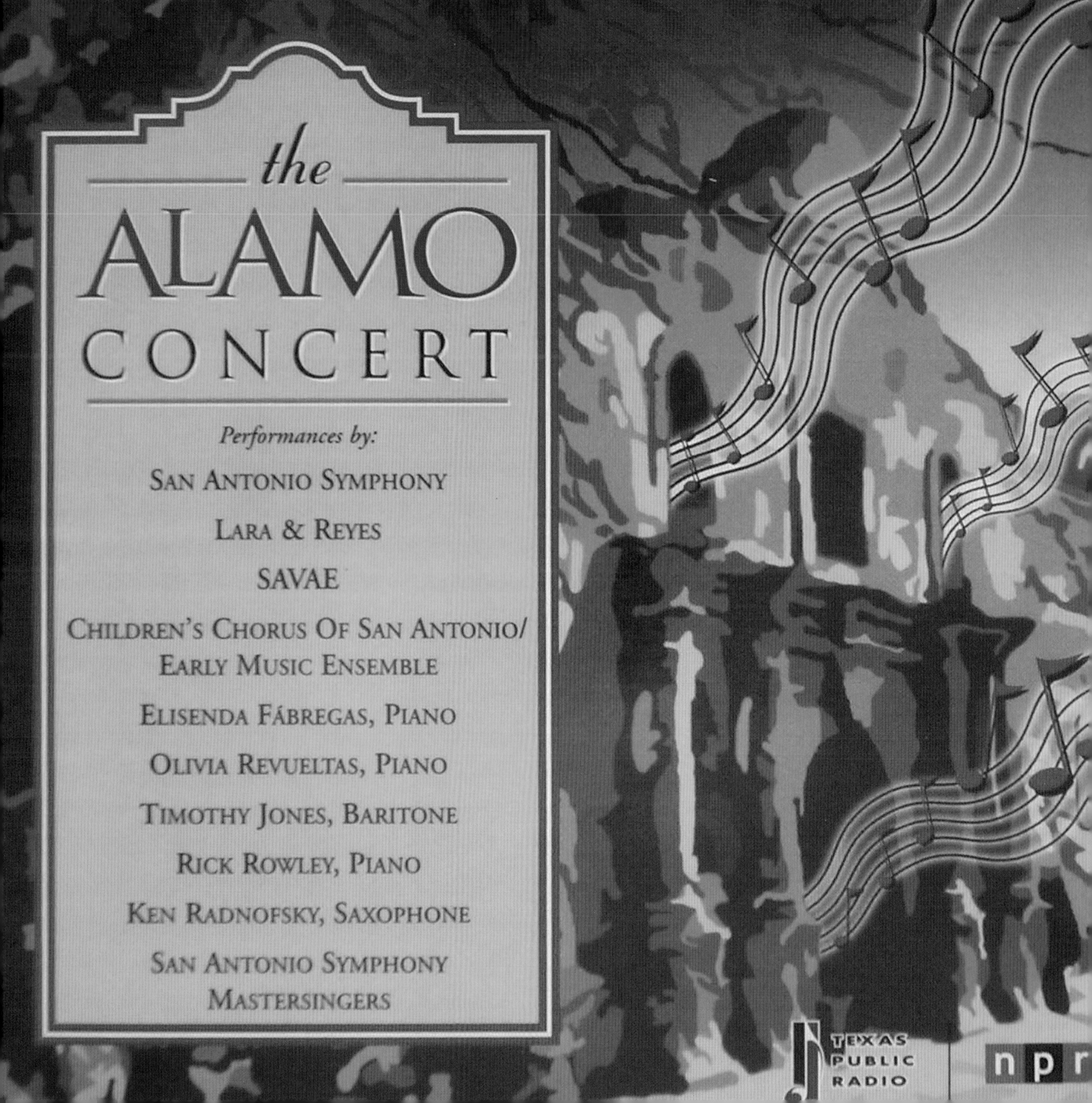

the ALAMO CONCERT

Performances by:

SAN ANTONIO SYMPHONY

LARA & REYES

SAVAE

CHILDREN'S CHORUS OF SAN ANTONIO/
EARLY MUSIC ENSEMBLE

ELISENDA FÁBREGAS, PIANO

OLIVIA REVUELTAS, PIANO

TIMOTHY JONES, BARITONE

RICK ROWLEY, PIANO

KEN RADNOFSKY, SAXOPHONE

SAN ANTONIO SYMPHONY
MASTERSINGERS

TEXAS PUBLIC RADIO

npr

FOREWORD
BY FESS PARKER

Music has been an unusual thing in my life. I am surprised how important it's been to me. As a boy growing up in Texas, I participated in singing patriotic songs with my grade school chums. I later became familiar with songs performed by W. Lee O'Daniel's Light Crust Doughboys, and Bob Wills and the Texas Playboys. And by the 1940s, like everyone else, I was well aware of "Deep in the Heart of Texas."

As an adult I never had the experience of singing until after my tour of duty in WWII. At The University of Texas, I sang 2nd tenor in the University Sing-Song competition between fraternities. Then, later, I had the good fortune to hear a concert by Burl Ives, who inspired me to learn American folk songs.

In my first meeting with Walt Disney, who was interviewing me for the role of Davy Crockett, I sang a song which I had written called "Lonely." This led to a personal contract with Walt Disney and two weeks later I made my first recording for Disney: "The Ballad of Davy Crockett." That song became a favorite of its time, sold millions of records and subsequently created the Walt Disney music publishing and record companies.

In 1954, I sang a song during the making of the "Davy Crockett at the Alamo" television episode. The song, "Farewell," was based on a poem Davy Crockett supposedly wrote. I later sang "Farewell" at the Hollywood Bowl in 1955, accompanied by 200 performers: the 100-voice Roger Wagner Chorale and the Los Angeles Symphony Orchestra. The explanation for such an extravagant accompaniment is that it was Walt Disney Night at the Hollywood Bowl, just weeks prior to the opening of Disneyland. I have appeared five times at the Hollywood Bowl where I also sang "The Ballad of Davy Crockett" in 1955 and again 50 years later in 2005.

Due in large part to the recordings I made at Disney Studios, along with song and dance appearances on television variety shows, I had the pleasure of appearing in a production of "Oklahoma" in 1963. I could never replace Howard Keel, but I was his substitute for that season. But that pretty much ended my musical career on stage; however, in the 1960s I was under contract with RCA during the Daniel Boone show and recorded for that label.

Music entered my life on a much more profound level upon my marriage to Marcella Rinehart in 1960. Marcella was a professional singer when I met her, and we recently celebrated our 48th wedding anniversary. For the past eight years, we have both been singing each Thursday evening with friends and guests at our small Wine Country Inn and Spa in Los Olivos, in Santa Barbara County, California.

Music has been, and continues to be, incredibly important in my life, and if you are reading this book, I expect you have the same interest and passion that I do. I am grateful for my 21-year friendship with Bill Chemerka. He and his co-author, Allen J. Wiener, have been intrigued by the Alamo for many years. I'm thankful that there are people like Bill and Allen, who care about the musical history of the Alamo and make sure we don't forget it.

Enjoy!

Fess Parker

INTRODUCTION
BY PHIL COLLINS

You are holding a fascinating book in your hands.

I consider myself a lifelong Alamo "freak." By that I mean that I have been living the story since I was a child of six. Reason being that I happened to grow up at a time when Walt Disney's "Davy Crockett" movies, starring Fess Parker, were out and I became that character.

I became Davy Crockett. I thought I was the only one. Wrong! I even won a few talent contests singing "The Ballad of Davy Crockett." I thought that was the first and only song about Davy Crockett. Wrong again!

Wrong, because the bad news started filtering through: there were MILLIONS of other kids like me, all obsessed with Crockett and the Alamo. It also seems from reading this book that there were hundreds of Crockett songs written way before Fess Parker was born.

I finally got over that disappointment though, and in 1960, when I saw the John Wayne movie, *The Alamo*, I thought I'd died and gone to heaven. Not only was it a great historic and romantic take on the story, but THE MUSIC!

The music was courageous, it was sad, it was patriotic. It was everything I wanted it to be. I sought out the album, but in England it was difficult to find. So I just went to see the movie over and over again.

In my view the music score written by Dimitri Tiomkin stands up just as wonderfully today as it did back then. "The Green Leaves of Summer" still sounds as hauntingly beautiful as it did when it first appeared. Tiomkin wrote many memorable Hollywood themes including *It's a Wonderful Life*, *High Noon*, *The Guns of Navarone*, and *The Fall of the Roman Empire*.

Likewise, the newest Alamo movie directed by John Lee Hancock has some wonderful musical themes. Carter Burwell's music captured the feel and tension that must have been surrounding those men in March 1836.

But this is all just the tip of a gigantic iceberg. When I read through this book I found hundreds of pieces of music inspired by, or linked to, the Alamo and its heroes. Some of it hokey, some of it very un-PC for today. However, some of the lyrics read like modern day Rap. "Pompey Smash," for example, is like Rap from the 1800s.

Although many of the ditties refer to Crockett, there is also a healthy smattering of songs that refer to Travis and Bowie and others. In some ways it's strange that Crockett was THE person that captured the public's imagination even at the time. True, he had been a politician, but the USA is vast and at that time news traveled very slowly, yet he was generally the one eulogised in songs.

It appears as if the first noted Crockett reference in song was 1835 with a March called "Go Ahead" (a favourite Crockett saying).

Also in the 1830s was a songbook, something that seems a relatively recent idea but is obviously not! Called "Davy Crockett's Free and Easy Song Book," it was reissued after the Battle to include songs about Crockett's bravery. Also, for the trainspotters out there reading this, there was a song called "The Alamo, or the Death of Crockett," which was written to the tune of an old English pub song. This tune later became used for the "Star Spangled Banner!"

I hope you don't think that I KNEW all this! I only found out through reading this book.

As time has worn on, I have become a serious Alamo buff and a collector of all things Alamo. Hence, the invitation to write the introduction to this book.

I tip my coonskin hat big time to Bill Chemerka and Allen Wiener as writers and researchers for this book. They have done a remarkable job searching out the songs and ditties prior to the Alamo Battle and the years following it. A vast undertaking, judging by the contents.

"Go Ahead"...read and enjoy.

Phil Collins

14

THE MUSIC OF THE ALAMO:

FROM 19TH CENTURY BALLADS TO BIG-SCREEN SOUNDTRACKS

AUTHORS' INTRODUCTION

The story of the famous Siege and Battle of the Alamo has been told in prose, poetry, art, film, and staged productions for over 170 years.

And it has been told in song.

For thirteen days in 1836, a small band of Texian and Tejano defenders, including Davy Crockett, William B. Travis, and Jim Bowie, stood their ground inside the Alamo against an overwhelming Mexican force commanded by Gen. Antonio López de Santa Anna.

In the predawn darkness of March 6, 1836, Santa Anna's *soldados* assaulted the Alamo. With the Mexican musicians playing the *degüello*, the signal for no quarter/death, nearly 2,000 Mexican infantrymen, some carrying scaling ladders and crowbars, rushed the Alamo's outer defenses. Within a half-hour, the walls were breached and scaled. The Texians regrouped inside the fortress's inner rooms. The Mexicans turned some of the Alamo's artillery pieces on the occupied rooms and destroyed the doors. In the smoke-filled darkness, Mexican soldiers poured into the rooms where some of the fiercest hand-to-hand fighting took place.

Some of the defenders managed to escape the Alamo. Manuel Loranca of the Mexican Dolores Cavalry regiment noted that "Sixty-two Texians who sallied from the east side of the fort were received by the lancers and killed." Inside the Alamo compound, a few defenders were captured but Santa Anna ordered them summarily executed.

The Mexican Army also defeated Texian units at San Patricio, Agua Dulce, and Refugio. Following his surrender to General José Urrea, Colonel James W. Fannin's command at Goliad was massacred, although some managed to escape the slaughter.

Finally, on April 21, 1836, Sam Houston's army defeated Santa Anna at the Battle of San Jacinto while a makeshift military band of several fifers and a drummer played the song "Will You Come to the Bower?" During the memorable battle, many Texians shouted "Remember the Alamo!"

The valiant struggle of the gallant garrison would resonate around the world in the decades that followed until the word "Alamo" became synonymous with courage under adversity.

It was inevitable that such an heroic stand would find its way into song and it was not long before poets, minstrels, troubadours and show people created musical works of every kind that were inspired by the Alamo. From 19th century folk ballads, minstrel show tunes and orchestral marches to more recent pop chart hits, children's songs, theatrical productions, classical suites and big-screen film scores, every generation has heard melodies that helped them "Remember the Alamo!"

This book traces the many and varied musical interpretations of the Alamo and its heroes and illuminates various periods of American musical history. Musically, the Alamo has been cast in patriotic songs, comic ditties, romantic tunes, satirical works and classical compositions. Frequently, the music of the Alamo has said more about the contemporary times of the writers and musicians than Texas' thirteen days of glory in 1836.

Even before the small Texian force took refuge in the Alamo, its most cherished hero, Davy Crockett, had become a national celebrity. By 1834, Crockett had been elected to Congress

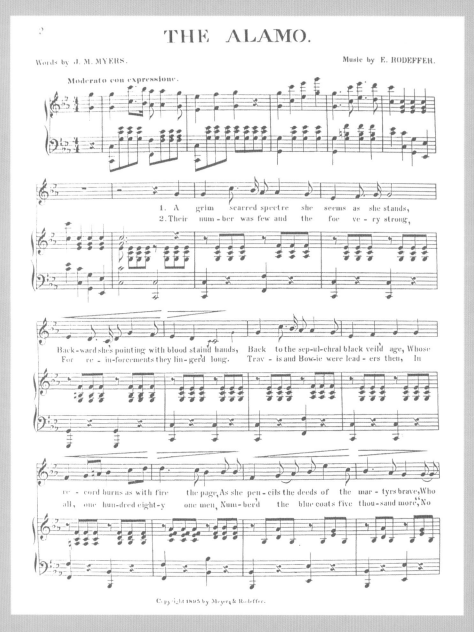

Countless songs have appeared under the title "The Alamo;" this 1895 offering by Mrs. Jennie Myers and Miss Ella Rodeffer may be the first.

three times, published a best-selling auto-biography, and concluded a highly success-ful tour of northeastern states. Songs were already being written about him in his life-time, including some made popular on the minstrel stage and in songbooks. Those minstrel songs, performed by white musi-cians in black-face makeup, represented the racist mindset of many Americans at the time, but sometimes also contained political satire and commentary.

Songs were written in the immediate after-math of the battle that reflected American disgust at the slaughter of the Alamo's defenders, joy over the ultimate Texan victory at San Jacinto, and an unhealthy dose of anti-Mexican racism. They also glori-fied Americans associated with the Texas war for independence, while demonizing the Mexicans, particularly Mexican general and dictator Santa Anna.

These songs became the soundtrack for the Mexican War a decade later, a war that also spawned new songs about the Alamo and its storied martyrs. Such music uni-formly glorified the Texan defenders and voiced outrage at Mexican barbarity, under-scored by a desire to possess the continent. Although many Americans objected to the Mexican War, the vast majority supported the war effort; in fact, many were encour-aged by some of the most vitriolic songs about the war. Music from this early period reflects the predominant attitudes on these

The Alamo story has been converted into staged musicals, including the 1999 production *Liberty! The Siege of the Alamo.*

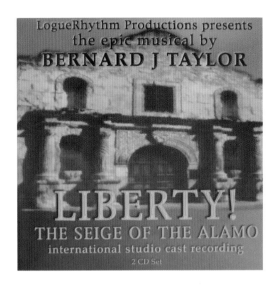

issues at the time and offers an often unflattering glimpse of early Americans who found themselves on the cusp of expansion, in the vanguard of "Manifest Destiny," and formed their views of Native Americans, Africans and Hispanics in that volatile, often bitter environment.

New war cries were set to music about the Alamo during later conflicts, even as older ones were dusted off yet again. One song, for example, reminded listeners to "strike the harp for those who fought for freedom long ago at San Jacinto." Such songs were good propaganda, casting enemies in an evil light, while rallying public support for war efforts.

But the Alamo also inspired songwriters in times of peace. In the early 20th century, tunesmiths frequently set romantic encounters in the shadow of the old fortress-turned-shrine, a most puzzling location for such rendezvous. One tune recalled how someone met their "love in the Alamo when the moon was on the rise."

In the second half of the century, pop culture dominated Alamo music, particularly in movies and on television, never more so than during the mid-1950s "Crockett Craze," which was set off by Walt Disney's "Davy Crockett" television mini-series. By 1955, few Americans did not know "The Ballad of Davy Crockett" by heart and quite a few artists from other countries recorded the song in a variety of languages. Nearly one hundred recordings of the ubiquitous "Ballad of Davy Crockett," penned by George Bruns and Tom Blackburn, would appear in the decades that followed.

Hollywood kept up the pace with the 1960 release of John Wayne's epic film *The Alamo.* The film's musical score, composed by Dimitri Tiomkin, included four songs co-written with lyricist Paul Francis Webster, including the Oscar®-nominated "Green Leaves of Summer."

Nor does there appear to be any serious decline in the use of the Alamo by songwriters. The new century already has seen the publication and recording of more songs about the Alamo and its legendary heroes.

Songs about the Alamo tell us something important about the people who wrote them, the public that responded to them, and the times in which they were written. Music inspired by the Alamo has been woven throughout the nation's popular culture since the battle smoke drifted away from the old abandoned mission. It has reflected the mood of the country in good times and bad, through rallying battle cries, innocuous love songs, and popular movie themes. It has been played in venues as diverse as concert halls and honky-tonks.

Although it has been employed for many purposes, much of this music has, indeed, helped generations remember the Alamo and preserve its place in the country's history and popular culture.

Crockett pictured on a bear hunt in an 1830s
edition of *The Crockett Almanac*.

THE EARLY 19TH CENTURY

In Texas 'cause I go for a crack.
Onwards march through prairie wide,
With rifle slung and knife in pocket,
Victory sits on freedom's side,
Three cheers for Houston and Davy Crockett!

"The Yankee Volunteer"

EARLY DAVY CROCKETT SONGS

Songs about the Alamo, its heroes and the Texian victory at San Jacinto began to appear almost before the battle dust had settled over the old mission-fortress. From the beginning a disproportionate number of Alamo songs would focus on or mention David Crockett, the most famous, celebrated and beloved Alamo martyr.

Even before he traveled to Texas in 1835, Crockett had been celebrated in song, on stage and in literature, usually as a fictional, larger-than-life character. Eventually, the real Crockett would be eclipsed in the public mind by his fictional counterpart "Davy" Crockett, a half-horse, half-alligator backwoodsman, who could leap mountains, wade rivers, or ride a comet.

As early as 1827, when he won his first term in Congress, Crockett's image as a rural wild man, who could "whip his weight in wildcats," had already begun to spread beyond his native Tennessee. In truth, Crockett was partly responsible for the rise of this fictional image, since he had adopted it during his political campaigns. It helped endear him to voters, who

were both amused and reassured that he really was one of them, one who understood their world and would represent them well. Even as he traveled to Washington, newspapers printed rumors that he was making his way there by wading the Ohio River while toting a steamboat on his back.

By the early months of 1831, Crockett had become so familiar a figure that a successful play, *The Lion of the West* by James K. Paulding, which was modeled after him, was produced in New York. Its protagonist, Colonel Nimrod Wildfire, played by James Hackett, was a raw and rugged backwoodsman from Kentucky, who was recently elected to Congress, a clear reference to Crockett. Wildfire personified the then-popular image of the backwoods brawler, boaster and "ring-tailed roarer." In the play, Wildfire refers to himself as a "screamer," a term that summarized all of those traits. The play helped to create the animated image of Crockett as a bold frontiersman, hunter, comic and clever trickster. In a moment of truly high drama, where life and art met head-on, Crockett attended a performance of the play in Washington, during which he was wildly applauded.[1]

In 1833 the first Crockett biography, *The Life and Adventures of Colonel David Crockett of West Tennessee*, written by James Strange French, was published. The book was an immediate success and a second printing was rushed to booksellers, now re-titled *Sketches and Eccentricities of Col. David Crockett of West Tennessee*. The book emphasized the exaggerated Crockett in vignettes showing, for example, his ability to bring down game with no more than an irresistible grin.[2]

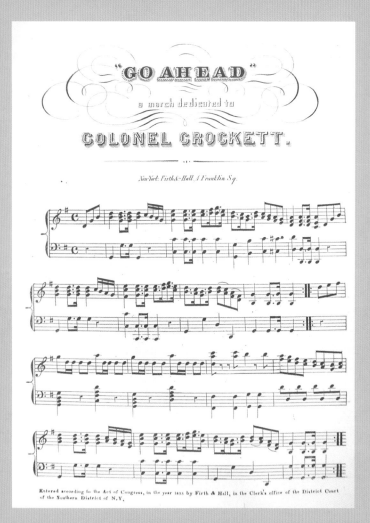

A series of *Crockett Almanacs* began a long run in 1835, which portrayed Crockett as the wild man of the backwoods and became immensely popular, despite the publications' increasingly racist and violent quality. The almanacs, which were published until 1856, also contained stories about other outrageous frontier personalities, assorted tall tales, recipes, and homemade remedies.

It was, thus, no surprise that Crockett would also find himself mentioned in popular songs of the period. "'Go Ahead' — A March Dedicated to Colonel Crockett," also called "The Crockett Victory March," appeared in 1835, but was probably an older tune simply re-titled to capitalize on Crockett's notoriety. Its actual date of origin is not certain. Crockett himself was probably aware of it and may have heard it performed.

The Crockett legend received a musical boost from songs performed in minstrel shows, which became popular in the United States in the 1830s. These were crude impersonations of black musical and dance forms, combining a savage parody of black Americans with an ironic affection for African-American culture.

"Zip Coon" and "Pompey Smash," two minstrel songs of the period, specifically mention Crockett. These were older songs that had undergone periodic changes in lyrics that reflected current events, political issues and national personalities. In that sense, minstrel songs like "Zip Coon" kept up with the times by reflecting names and events that the public was likely to recognize. As Crockett's fame grew, various performers added verses about him that found their way into printed sheet music and songsters. The lyrics were subsequently added to many popular song collections of the period which included suggested tunes to which they might be played. Several editions of a songster called *Crockett's Free and Easy Songbook* appeared in the 1830s, possibly during Crockett's lifetime. Although it is doubtful that he was involved in the publication of the book, or that he realized any income from the use of his name, by 1839 the collection included several songs about Crockett and the Alamo.

Publication of *Sketches* encouraged Crockett to pen his own autobiography, *A Narrative of the Life of David Crockett of the State of Tennessee*, in 1834. The book was a huge success and catapulted Crockett into the national spotlight. He undertook a successful tour of northeastern states the same year to promote the book. Wherever he went, he was wined, dined, toasted and honored. *An Account of Colonel Crockett's Tour of the North and Down East* was then published in 1835 under Crockett's name, but ghost-written by William Clark from Crockett's notes and speeches. The book documented the tour and was heavily laced with Whig Party political sentiments. By 1837, Crockett's autobiography was in its 24th edition.

"Zip Coon," or "Old Zip Coon," may date from as early as 1815, and was played to the tune of "Turkey in the Straw," which had previously been called "Natchez Under the Hill." It may have derived from the ballad "My Grandmother Lived on Yonder Little Green" which had originated from the Irish ballad "The Old Rose Tree." The song was performed with lyrics, but also became a staple in fiddle repertoires, especially in the South. Early versions included verses about Andrew Jackson's victory over the British at New Orleans in 1815. By the 1830s, when it appeared in *Crockett's Free and Easy Songbook*, new verses that mentioned Crockett had been added which acknowledged his status as a national figure.

At least three people claimed authorship of the song: George Washington Dixon (mentioned, but not credited as the composer, on the earliest sheet music), George Nichols, and Bob Farrell. All three were early blackface performers of the piece. Farrell was actually called "Zip Coon" and Crockett saw him perform the song in a Nashville theater in February 1834, taking the opportunity to wave his hat to the adoring crowd.[3] Authorship will probably never be settled, at least partly because verses were added and deleted with the passage of time by different performers to mirror contemporary popular culture and news.[4]

"Zip Coon" addresses political issues and, while it recognizes Crockett's backwoods eccentricities and unique brand of politics, casts the Tennessean as a potential agent of political change in Washington as a partner for Zip Coon, an outsized African-American counterpart to Crockett. Versions of "Zip Coon" that do mention Crockett may date from as early as 1833, but the earliest sheet music for the song is dated 1834 and was published by Thomas Birch as "Zip Coon, a Famous Comic Song, as sung by All the Celebrated Comic Singers, with wonderful applause, Composed and arranged for the Piano Forte." No composer is listed. One version includes the following stanza, which suggests that Crockett had developed presidential ambitions. Indeed, in 1833, the Mississippi State Convention asked Crockett for permission to offer him as a candidate for the presidency, but Crockett declined. Here,

"Zip Coon" suggests that he, not Crockett, is better presidential timber, but that Crockett (spelled "Crocket") would make a suitable partner as Vice President.

> Now mind what you arter, you tarnel kritter Crocket,
> You shant go head widout old Zip, he is de boy to block it,
> Zip shall be president, Crocket shall be vice
> An den dey two togedder, will hab de tings nice.

Another version, published in the 1839 edition of *Crockett's Free and Easy Songbook*, includes two different verses about Crockett, which may date from several years earlier:

> Dat tarnal critter Crockett, he never say his prayers,
> He kill all de wild Cats, de Coons and de bears,
> And den he go to Washington to make de laws,
> And dere he find de Congress men sucking deir paws.
>
> If I was de President of dese United States,
> I'd suck lasses candy and swing upon de gates,
> An does I didn't like I'd block em off de docket,
> An de way I'd block em off would be a sin to Crockett.[5]

These two verses do not appear in the 1834 sheet music and may be from a later or alternate version of the song. It was common for more than one writer or performer to publish his version of a song, thus different versions may have been in circulation simultaneously. The Crockett verses are very brief and have the look of words that were slipped into the already-existing song, after Crockett had become well-known. Whatever the actual chronological order of the different versions, they clearly show a growing recognition of Crockett as a national figure, both in folklore and politics in the early 1830s.[6]

Another revision clearly comes from Crockett's later years in Congress, when he opposed President Jackson's attack on the Second Bank of the United States. Jackson opposed the bank because he thought it was an unconstitutional, monopolistic tool of the wealthy. Although Zip may have found Crockett an acceptable running mate, he seems to side with Jackson on the Bank issue:

I tell you what' sa goine to happen now very soon,
De United States bank will be blown to de moon,
Den all de oder bank notes will be mighty plenty,
An one silver dollar will be worth ten or twenty.

O glory be to Jackson, for he blow up de Banks,
An glory be to Jackson, for he many funny pranks,
An glory be to Jackson, for de battle of Orleans,
For dere he giv de enemy de hot butter beans.

In contrast to "Zip Coon," "Pompey Smash," another anonymous minstrel song from the period, portrays Crockett as the Nimrod Wildfire-like backwoodsman, brawler, and weaver of tall tales, a characterization that was beginning to take shape. It contains none of the Crockett political references found in "Zip Coon," but, like Zip, Pompey Smash is a bold African-American character who is able to match wits and strength with Crockett. Several versions of "Pompey Smash" appeared in print. The first known publication of it appeared in the 1846 volume *The Negro Singer's Own Book* under the title

"Pompey Smash—The Everlastin and Unkonkerable Skreamer." A year later it was published in England in *Lloyd's Ethiopian Song Book*. Eventually racial stereotypes and Negro vernacular were eliminated as the song grew in popularity and its title would eventually evolve into "Davy Crockett," but the basic elements in the lyrics remained.[7]

The song may date from the early 1840s since a parody of it, "Pompy O' Smash," appeared in 1844. It makes no mention of Crockett, focuses on courtship, spells the protagonist's name "Pompy," and is played to a noticeably different Irish tune, an arrangement that reflected the growing mid-19th century Irish population in the United States. The tune is, however, blatantly racist and contains many derogatory stereotypes.[8]

"Pompey Smash" included some twenty verses that related Pompey's adventures, many of which did not involve Crockett. Like "Zip Coon," verses involving Crockett were added as the Tennessean became more widely known and were partly derived from the 1833 book *Sketches and Eccentricities*, particularly its depiction of Crockett's attempt to "grin" a squirrel into submission only to find that he's been grinning at a pine knot that looks like a squirrel. When Pompey finds this rather amusing, Davy is angered and the two engage in a brutal and inconclusive fight. These verses clearly come from the growing fictional image of "Davy," not from Crockett's actual life. Indeed, few songs about Crockett reflect the real man and most instead memorialize the legendary character. The song later borrowed adventures taken from the popular *Crockett Almanacs*, but with Pompey replacing Crockett.[9]

Although the minstrel shows eventually ended, "Pompey Smash" survived in written and recorded form, almost always under the title "Davy Crockett," attesting to the Tennessean's lasting appeal. Versions were found throughout the United States, many of them handed down through oral tradition with various lyrics. Several non-commercial field recordings were made in the early 1900s and commercial recordings soon followed. Some versions included verses from both "Zip Coon" and "Pompey Smash" and at least one version of "Pompey Smash" was titled "Zip Coon." The 1846 edition of *The Negro Singer's Own Book* includes a version that casts Zip as a foe of Pompey's. Pompey himself would reappear in other songs, like "My Polly Ann," an 1864 ditty that relates a romantic encounter, but does not mention Crockett. The Crockett-related lyrics in the original 1846 version speak for themselves:

Now I'll tell you 'bout a fight I had wid Davy Crockett
Dat haff hoss, haff kune, an haff sky rocket,
I met him one day as I go out a gunnin,
I ax him whar he guine, an he say he guine a kunein,
Den I ax him whar he gun, and he say he got nun,
Den I say, Davy, how you guine to hunt widout one.

Den says he, Pompey Smash, just come along ob Davy
An I'll dam soon show you how to grin a koon crazy
Well, I follow on arter, till Davy seed a squirrel,
Settin on a pine log, eatin sheep sorrel,
Den he stop rite still, and he gin for me to feel,
Says he, Pompey Smash, let me brace agin your heel.

I stuck out my heel, an I brace up de sinner,
An den Davy gun to grin hard for his dinner,
But de critter didn't move — nor didn't seem to mine him,
But seem to keep a eatin, and neber look behine him.
At lass, Davy sed, he ralely must be dead,
For I seed de bark fly all 'bout de kritter's head.

Den we boph started up, de truth to diskiver,
An may de debil roast ole Pompei Smash's liber,
If it wa'nt a great not, 'bout as big as a punkin,
Saz I, kurnel Davy, does you call dis skunkin.
Heah! Heah! Heah!!!
Den sez he, you black kaff, now I tell you doan laff,
If you do I'll pin your ears back, an bite you in haff.

I throde down my gun, an I drop my amynishin,
Sez I, kurnel Davy, I'll cool you ambishun,
He back both his years, an puff like a steamer,
Sez he, Pompey Smash, I'm a Tennessee skreemer,
Den we boph lock horn, an I tink my breph gone,
I was neber hug so close, since de day I was born.

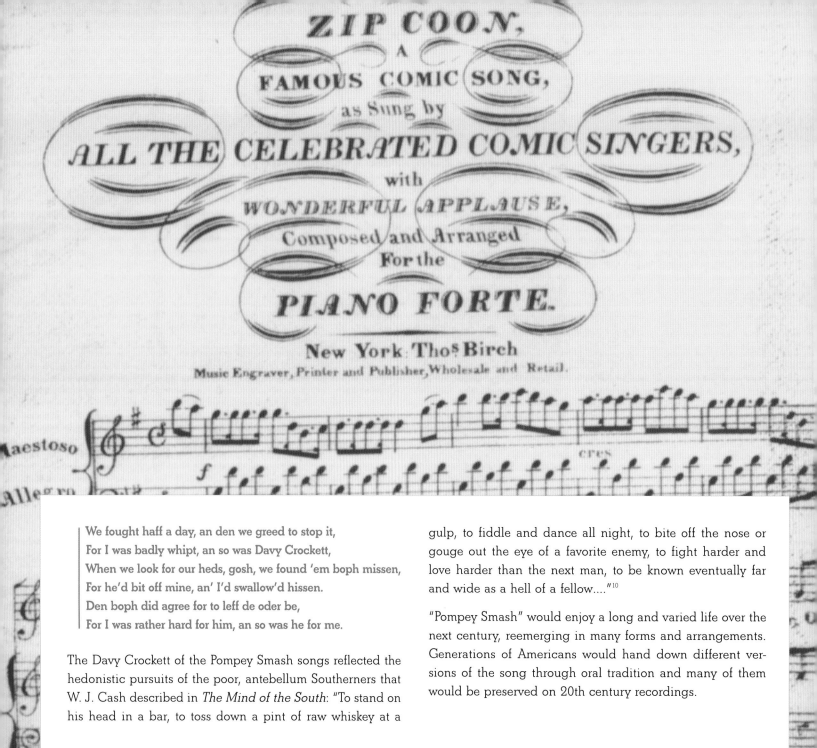

We fought haff a day, an den we greed to stop it,
For I was badly whipt, an so was Davy Crockett,
When we look for our heds, gosh, we found 'em boph missen,
For he'd bit off mine, an' I'd swallow'd hissen.
Den boph did agree for to leff de oder be,
For I was rather hard for him, an so was he for me.

The Davy Crockett of the Pompey Smash songs reflected the hedonistic pursuits of the poor, antebellum Southerners that W. J. Cash described in *The Mind of the South*: "To stand on his head in a bar, to toss down a pint of raw whiskey at a gulp, to fiddle and dance all night, to bite off the nose or gouge out the eye of a favorite enemy, to fight harder and love harder than the next man, to be known eventually far and wide as a hell of a fellow...."[10]

"Pompey Smash" would enjoy a long and varied life over the next century, reemerging in many forms and arrangements. Generations of Americans would hand down different versions of the song through oral tradition and many of them would be preserved on 20th century recordings.

Crockett appeared in other minstrel songs as well. "Jim Crow" included the following verse:

> Dey say South Carolina is a fool,
> and as for Johnny C. Calhoun,
> He'll be worse dan Davy Crockett,
> when he tried to fool de coon.

"Gumbo Chaff" and "Dinah Crow's Abolition (or, The grand rumpus at the Bowery Theatre)," both use the then-familiar phrase "a sin to Davy Crockett."

THE TEXAS REVOLUTION

Alamo songs were being written almost as soon as the Texas Revolution was won. Many of them were written as poems, without music, and appeared in published form with suggested melodies to which they might be played. The earliest of these songs urged Americans to drop whatever they were doing and rush to the aid of the valiant Texians. The songs reflected a developing national belief in what came to be known as Manifest Destiny, the near-religious doctrine of the 1840s that assumed that the United States was destined to possess all the land of North America, from the Atlantic to the Pacific. Mexicans were seen as cruel, tyrannical, evil interlopers who had to be driven from Texas, even though the territory belonged to them. However, many Texas revolutionaries supported the idea of remaining part of Mexico, albeit under a more democratic federal government. Such facts did not get in the way of a good song aimed at stirring up passion for American expansion.

Long before the Mexican War in the 1840s, the proposed annexation of Texas, westward expansion, and the Oregon dispute with England aroused public sentiment. Most Americans supported Texas independence, but there were sharp divisions regarding its annexation. Much of that dispute centered on Texas' certain status as an additional slave state. There was, nevertheless, growing support for westward expansion and a belief in the inevitability and, for many,

the divine right of the United States to extend its territory across the continent. England was opposed to U.S. expansion, largely due to fear of growing American power and the threat to its claim on the Oregon territory. Some songs of the period reflect U.S. resentment toward England and its expressed sympathy toward Mexico.

"The Yankee Volunteer," which appeared in the 1839 edition of *Crockett's Free and Easy Songbook*, refers to earlier American history, including the battles of Lexington, Bunker Hill and Andrew Jackson's victory at New Orleans. Two additional stanzas, mentioning Santa Anna, Sam Houston and Davy Crockett may well have been added following the outbreak of the Texas War. They make no mention of the Alamo or Crockett's death, but praise him and Houston for their bravery in volunteering (both did, after all, come from Tennessee, "the volunteer state"). The song sounds like a recruiting poster for the war, rather than a memorial for its martyrs, suggesting that it preceded the fall of the Alamo:

> The Southern hunter drain'd his cup.
> And slung his rifle over his back,
> "I guess my dander's riz right up,
> In Texas 'cause I go for a crack"
> Onwards march through prairie wide,
> With rifle slung and knife in pocket,
> Victory sits on freedom's side,
> Three cheers for Houston and Davy Crockett![11]

"All for Texas! Or, Volunteers for Glory!," which appeared in the 1848 *Rough and Ready Songster*, is quite similar and also appears to date from the Texas Revolution. It, too, seeks to rally American men of various professions to Texas' cause and, like "The Yankee Volunteer," offers "Three cheers for Houston and Davy Crockett!"

> Come, rouse boys, rouse, with spirits gay,
> Your valiant hearts, and boldly come
> In Texas' cause to march away,
> And volunteer all to follow the drum.

Liberty's songs in a foreign land,
Claims our rifles' potent aid,
Then join together, hand in hand,
And off to Texas — who's afraid?

The song even features a physician who vows to use his medical skills to battle the forces of Santa Anna:

I've not been afraid grim death to meet,
So I'll take the lancet and follow the drum.
I'll physic the Mexicans day and night,
And give 'em a dose of powder and pill,
I'll phlebotomize 'em if I can't fight,
And draw some blood if I can't kill.

A few of the songs were simply older marches that had been re-titled, such as "The Texian Grand March," which probably predated the war, but later appeared with a cover picture showing Santa Anna surrendering to Sam Houston on April 22, 1836, a day after the battle of San Jacinto. Perhaps the oldest song associated with the Texas Revolution is "Will You Come to the Bower?," an old Irish song that was played by Texians during that battle, which also inspired other songs, including "San Jacinto."

"San Jacinto" dates from 1836 and was reportedly written only two days after the Texian victory by an unidentified "gentleman who was in the battle." It was certainly written long before the Mexican War, although it also appears in the *Rough and Ready Songster*, indicating that it was resurrected to rally Americans to the war with Mexico. It glorifies the battle that secured Texas independence on April 21, 1836, and does not mention the later war. Although the song casts the victors as brave heroes, it acknowledges the carnage of the battle and the terrible price the Mexican soldiers paid that day. The battle, which lasted only about 18 minutes, quickly turned into undisciplined butchery by the vengeful Texians, who were not content to merely rout the Mexicans but determined to punish them for their slaughter of the Alamo and Goliad defenders. Despite pleas from Sam Houston and others to break off the

attack, the Texians went on shooting and bayoneting Mexicans long after they had attempted to surrender or simply ran away, many of them pleading "Me no Alamo!" Despite this, the song claims that the Mexicans met with "Texian Chivalry." The following verses are representative of the song.

On San Jacinto' bloody field,
Our drum and trumpets loudly pealed,
And bad a haughty tyrant yield
To Texian Chivalry.

Santa Anna travelled far to see
What men could do who dare be free,
In spite of Spanish musketry
Or Mexican artillery.

The boldest sons of Mexico
Have learned to fear a freeman's blow,
And dread the shout of "Alamo!"
From Sons of Liberty.

Similarly, "The Alamo or the Death of Crockett," written by Robert T. Conrad and sung to the tune of "The Star Spangled Banner," dates from 1837. Although it, too, appears in the *Rough and Ready Songster*, it had been included in much earlier songsters as well. Crockett biographer Constance Rourke described the song as one of the more popular reactions to the news of Crockett's death at the Alamo. A copy of the song was reprinted in Walter Blair's book *Davy Crockett: Legendary Frontier Hero*, which noted that it appeared in the 1837 edition of *Crockett's Free and Easy Song Book*, although Charles Wolfe says it was first published in the 1839 edition. It was often sung onstage and was considered a hit when it first appeared. In 1841 the song was performed at John Potter's Old Stable Theater in Memphis and was greeted by wild applause. Conrad, a politician and poet, had served as mayor of Philadelphia and an official of the Pennsylvania Historical Society. He published two books of poems, authored a play and served as editor of *Graham's Magazine*. Conrad had been a strong supporter of Texas independence, and his ode to Crockett is heartfelt. Its inclusion in the later songster suggests

"ROUGH AND READY SONGSTER"

Arm for the battle, the battle, the battle,
   And drive Mexican proud invaders afar;
Our young child of freedom is calling, is calling,
   For aid against a phrenzied and merciless foe,
Then onward for Texas, with valor appalling,
   Let vengeance and freedom be dealt in each
      blow.

To field freemen, freemen, freemen,
   The bold foe now threatens fair Liberty's star,
Arm for the battle, the battle, the battle,
   And drive Mexico's proud invaders afar.

Come wave high the banner, the bright starry
   banner,
   Your hearts will take fire at the Red White
     and Blue,
Quick, launch forth your thunder, your thun-
   der, your thunder,
   With Liberty's stars ever valiant and true,
Then shall the foemen, recoiling, recoiling,
   Retreat to his cavern, or sink to his grave,
And his boasting be silenced forever, forever,
   As freedom's bright stars o'er Texas shall wave
     To the field freemen, freemen, freemen, &c

TEXAS, THE YOUNG TREE OF FREE-DOM.

TUNE.—"*Harry Bluff.*"

Wake, sons of Columbia, by sea and by land,
With your arms crush the foe and his proud daring band,

46

Fair Texas the sappling of Liberty's tree,
Is grafted for e'er in the hearts of the free;
Ere Mexican's tyrants shall strike at its root,
Or with foreign aid strive to plunder its fruit,
To her fair injured land with your arms nobly
   fly,
And swear by our union to conquer or die,
   For Texas, the young tree of freedom.

Beneath the broad shelter of Liberty's vine,
Her fair spreading branches now tenderly twine,
And our proud eagle flapping his wings o'er each
   bough,
Screams "death to the hand that shall dare harm
   her now;"
On our heaven born flag her bright star we have
   wove,
It gleams with the light freedom sent from above,
Then on to the field by its dear holy light,
And sweep the proud foe from the soil of our
   right
   For Texas the young tree of Freedom.

REMEMBER THE ALAMO.

BY T. A. DURRIAGE.

TUNE.—"*Bruces Address.*"

When on the wide spread battle plain,
The horseman's hand can scarce restrain,
His pampered steed that spurns the rein,
      Remember the Alamo.

47

ROUGH AND READY SONGSTER.

When sounds the thrilling bugle blast,
And "charge" from rank to rank is past,
Then, as your sabre-strokes fall fast,
      Remember the Alamo.

Heed not the Spanish battle yell,
Let every stroke he give them *tell*,
And let them fall as Crockett fell.
      Remember the Alamo.

For every wound and every thrust,
On pris'ners dealt by hands accurst,
A Mexican shall bite the dust,
      Remember the Alamo.

The cannon's peal shall ring their knell,
Each volley sound a passing bell,
Each cheer, Columbia's vengeance tell,
      Remember the Alamo.

For it, disdaining flight, they stand,
And try the issue hand to hand,
Wo to each Mexican brigand !
      Remember the Alamo

Then boot and saddle ! draw the sword :
Unfurl your banner bright and broad,
And as ye smite the murderous horde,
      Remember the Alamo.
48

BEUNA VISTA.

SAN JACINTO.

On San Jacinto's bloody field,
Our drum and trumpets loudly pealed,
And bade a haughty tyrant yield
    To Texian Chivalry.

Our chieftain boldly led the van,
His sword grasped firmly in his hand,
And bade us tell the Mexican
    To think of Labordia.

'Twas evening, and the orient sun
Into his bed was moving on,
When our young heroes rushed upon
    The might of Mexico, &c.

Santa Anna travelled far to see
What men could do who dare be free,
In spite of Spanish musketry
    Or Mexican artillery.

The boldest sons of Mexico
Have learned to fear a freeman's blow,
And dread the shout of " Alamo!"
    From Sons of Liberty.

'Twas cheering to a Texian eye,
To see Sant' Anna's legions fly,
From Texas' dreadful battle cry
    Of death or victory!

The carnage ceased, in triumph then
Proudly shone the Texian star,
And vengeance on her conquering car
    Reposed most quietly.

The flag of battle we unfold,
                                          Hurrah.

United in a holy band,
For God, and for our native land.
                        Hurrah, hurrah, hurrah.

THE DEATH OF CROCKETT.

TUNE.—"*The Star Spangled Banner.*"

To the memory of Crockett fill up to the brim!
  The hunter, the hero, the bold Yankee yeo-
    man!
Let the flowing oblation be poured forth to him,
  Who ne'er turned his back on his friend or
    his foeman.
    And gratefaul shall be,
    His fame to the free;
Fill! fill! to the brave who for Liberty bled—
May his name and his fame to the last—*Go
    ahead!*

When the Mexicans leaguered thy walls Alamo!
  'Twas Crockett looked down on the war-
    storm's commotion,
And smiled, as by thousands the foe spread be-
    low,
  And rolled o'er the plain, like the waves of
    the ocean.
    The Texans stood there—
    Their flag fanned the air.
    And their shot bade the foe try what free
    men will dare.

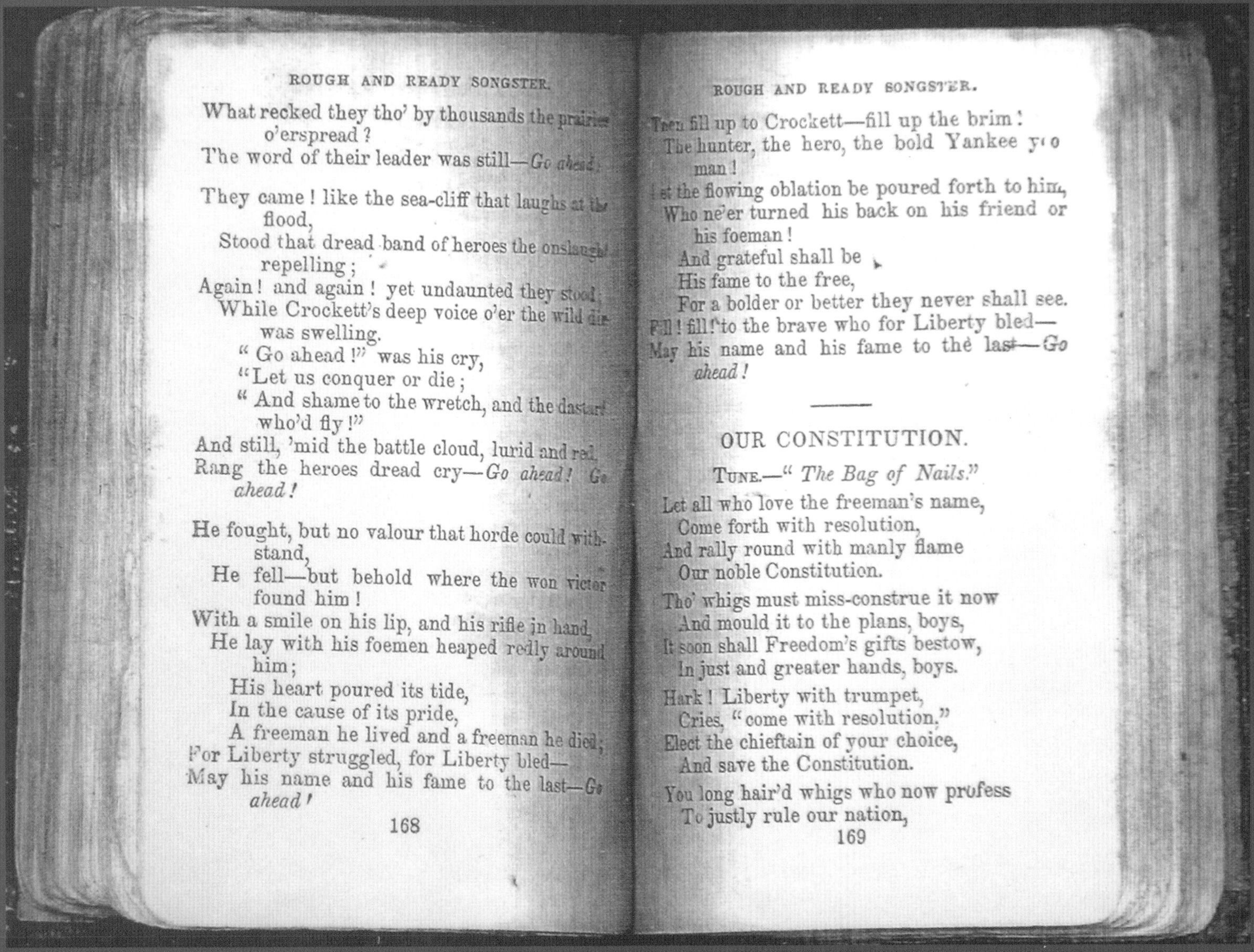

What recked they tho' by thousands the prairie
    o'erspread?
The word of their leader was still—*Go ahead!*

They came! like the sea-cliff that laughs at the
    flood,
    Stood that dread band of heroes the onslaught
    repelling;
Again! and again! yet undaunted they stood,
    While Crockett's deep voice o'er the wild din
    was swelling.
    "Go ahead!" was his cry,
    "Let us conquer or die;
    "And shame to the wretch, and the dastard
    who'd fly!"
And still, 'mid the battle cloud, lurid and red,
Rang the heroes dread cry—*Go ahead! Go
    ahead!*

He fought, but no valour that horde could with-
    stand,
    He fell—but behold where the won victor
    found him!
With a smile on his lip, and his rifle in hand,
    He lay with his foemen heaped redly around
    him;
    His heart poured its tide,
    In the cause of its pride,
    A freeman he lived and a freeman he died;
For Liberty struggled, for Liberty bled—
May his name and his fame to the last—*Go
    ahead!*

168

Then fill up to Crockett—fill up the brim!
    The hunter, the hero, the bold Yankee yeo-
    man!
Let the flowing oblation be poured forth to him,
    Who ne'er turned his back on his friend or
    his foeman!
    And grateful shall be
    His fame to the free,
    For a bolder or better they never shall see.
Fill! fill! to the brave who for Liberty bled—
May his name and his fame to the last—*Go
    ahead!*

OUR CONSTITUTION.

TUNE.—"*The Bag of Nails.*"

Let all who love the freeman's name,
    Come forth with resolution,
And rally round with manly flame
    Our noble Constitution.

Tho' whigs must miss-construe it now
    And mould it to the plans, boys,
It soon shall Freedom's gifts bestow,
    In just and greater hands, boys.

Hark! Liberty with trumpet,
    Cries, "come with resolution."
Elect the chieftain of your choice,
    And save the Constitution.

You long hair'd whigs who now profess
    To justly rule our nation,

169

that, even during the decade following independence, many Americans regarded Texas as rightfully belonging to the United States in the belief that it was the country's Manifest Destiny to possess and rule the entire continent.

> To the memory of Crockett fill up to the brim!
> The hunter, the hero, the bold Yankee yeoman!
> Let the flowing oblation be poured forth to him,
> Who ne'er turned his back on his friend or his foeman.
> And grateful shall be,
> His fame to be free;
> Fill! fill! to the brave who for Liberty bled
> May his name and his fame to the last — *Go ahead!* [12]

Crockett was again the subject of "Go Ahead," an anonymous tribute to him and his motto, "Be always sure you're right, then go ahead," which appeared with other Crockett-related songs in the 1839 edition of *Crockett's Free and Easy Song Book.* It is a rather graphic ode to the bloody Alamo battle and the violent end met by its defenders, and a far cry from the 1950s children's ditty "Be Sure You're Right (Then Go Ahead)," written and recorded by Fess Parker and Buddy Ebsen, co-stars of the Disney "Crockett" television series. Instead, it is a solemn, dirge-like ode to the battle and Crockett's steady movement from home to Texas, to battlefield and a bloody death.

> The fatal conflict rose,
> Hot grew the deadly fight!
> By hundreds fell their foes,
> And with a tiger's might
> 'Mid fiery bolt and burning rocket
> Hard fighting to the last, brave Crockett
> Cried, 'GO AHEAD!'
> The last he said
> When fell his head
> Among the dead! [13]

Tribute to Crockett also was paid in the 1839 fiddle tune "Colonel Crockett: A Virginia Reel" written by George P. Knauff. It has remained in fiddle repertoires to this day, albeit

A fanciful sketch of Crockett literally speaking from the stump during one of his backwoods campaigns.

under many different titles. It was recorded by Captain M. J. Bonner, under the title "The Gal on the Log," and by the Carter Brothers and Son, as "Jenny on the Railroad;" it also has appeared under the title "The Route."

The Alamo would remain a staple for songwriters who would continue to single out Crockett for special praise among all of the mission-fortress's defenders. His adventures, both real and legendary, would provide raw material for tunesmiths from minstrel stages to Hollywood screens. And he continues to inspire musical memorials.

[1] B. A. Botkin, ed., *A Treasury of American Folklore* (New York: Crown, 1944), 4-5, suggests that Crockett may not, in fact, have provided the inspiration for the play. He cites an exchange of letters between Paulding and Crockett in which the playwright denies any intention to lampoon or caricature the congressman, and Crockett replies by accepting the explanation. But those letters clearly refer to suggestions that Paulding's characterization of Crockett was a negative one; Paulding assured Crockett that such was not the case. Paulding never said that Crockett had inspired the Wildfire character, at least in part. Nonetheless, the press and public made the connection and the image of Wildfire was later used as the cover of an 1837 Crockett almanac. In fact, Paulding solicited stories about Crockett from contacts in Washington that he wanted to use in the play. Actually, only a portion of the play was performed the night Crockett attended, when *The Lion of the West* was one of a number of plays that constituted a special benefit performance.

COLONEL CROCKETT DELIVERING HIS CELEBRATED SPEECH TO CONGRESS.

A sketch of Crockett "entertaining" the House of Representatives, from an 1844 edition of *The Crockett Almanac.*

2 James Atkins Shackford, a Crockett biographer, speculated that the book had been written by Matthew St. Claire Clarke, Clerk of the House of Representatives (1822-1833).

3 *Philadelphia Courier:*, March 3, 1834.

4 *Folk Music of England, Scotland, Ireland, Wales and America* website (http://www.contemplator.com/america/turkeyis.html; from http://www.contemplator.com/folk.html; and from http://www.csufresno.edu/folklore/ballads/RJ19258.html

Website: *The Traditional Ballad Index* Copyright 82006 by Robert B. Waltz and David G. Engle. California State University, Fresno; also see *Collection of Popular American Songs* website

http://www.stephenfostersongs.de/Amsong59.htm.

5 In 19th century slang, the phrase "sin to Moses" and later "sin to Crockett," after the frontiersman's name, had become known throughout America. The phrases simply meant that something was so extraordinary that it would shame Moses or Crockett by exceeding even their legendary exploits.

6 Publishing sheet music at that time was similar to manufacturing and selling recorded music today. Sales of sheet music constituted considerable income to whoever held the copyright for the sheet music. Since minstrel songs like "Zip Coon" were of unknown origin, with unknown composers, they were in the public domain and fair game for anyone who wanted to publish sheet music for the song.

7 See Charles Wolfe, "Davy Crockett Songs: Minstrels to Disney" in Michael A. Lofaro (ed.), *Davy Crockett: The Man, the Legend, the Legacy, 1786-1986* (Knoxville: University of Tennessee Press, 1985); and Wolfe, "Crockett and Nineteenth-Century Music" in Michael A. Lofaro & Joe Cummings (eds.), *Crockett at Two Hundred: New Perspectives on the Man and the Myth* (Knoxville: University of Tennessee Press, 1989). Wolfe speculates that a reference to Halley's Comet and Andrew Jackson's battle with the Second Bank of the United States may date the song from 1833-34. He also notes that the *Negro Singer's Own Book,* the songster in which it first appeared, was a compilation of songs from earlier years. Wolfe also mentions that the song's reference to Crockett grinning the bark off a tree first appeared in *Sketches and Eccentricities of Col. Crockett of West Tennessee.* However, that does not necessarily date the song from that period, since the story could have been incorporated into the song at any time after 1833, although Wolfe makes the baseless suggestion that *Sketches* may have somehow been inspired by "Pompey Smash."

8 "Parody" did not necessarily carry the same connotation at that time that it does today, suggesting a comical lampooning of an original song. In the 19th century the term also referred to a new song being set to an older tune or, in this case, a rewriting of the lyrics, thus indicating that even earlier variations of "Pompey Smash" existed. A copy of the original 1844 "Pompy O' Smash" sheet music is found in the Lester S. Levy Collection of Sheet Music, part of Special Collections at the Milton S. Eisenhower Library of the Johns Hopkins University, available online at http://levysheetmusic.mse.jhu.edu/index.html.

9 *Crockett Almanac* publishers Turner & Fisher also published a version of the song in *The Negro Singer's Own Book,* 1848. See Wolfe, "Davy Crockett Songs," and "Crockett and Nineteenth-Century Music"; Wolfe estimates that at least twenty-two folk variations of "Pompey Smash" were cataloged in the United States during the 20th century.

10 W. J. Cash, *The Mind of the South* (New York, 1941), 52.

11 Wolfe, "Crockett and Nineteenth-Century Music," 88.

12 Ibid., 85-86. Wolfe also cites *Gibson County Past and Present,* Frederick M. Culp and Mrs. Robert E. Ross (Trenton, Tenn.: Gibson County Historical Society.

13 Ibid., 87.

THE MEXICAN WAR

If Mexy, backed by secret foes,
Still talks of taking you, gal,
Why, we can lick 'em all, you know,
An' then annex 'em too, gal

"Uncle Sam to Texas"

IT WAS INEVITABLE that songs written earlier about the Alamo and the Texas Revolution would reemerge during and after the Mexican War of 1846-1848. The war, after all, had broken out largely over U.S. annexation of Texas, which had been an independent republic for a decade, but whose citizens had favored annexation almost from the beginning. Indeed, there were leaders of the Texas Revolution, including Sam Houston, who had taken on Gen. Santa Anna's army at San Jacinto in 1836 with an eye toward ultimately joining the United States. Mexico, of course, resisted annexation just as adamantly.

The initial fighting was over land which both the Republic of Texas and Mexico claimed. On January 13, 1846, U.S. President James K. Polk ordered Gen. Zachary Taylor's army to cross the Nueces River and move on to the Rio Grande. On April 25, Mexican troops crossed the Rio Grande and attacked Taylor's force. Despite the obvious provocation by Taylor, Polk proclaimed after the battle that "American blood on the American soil" had been shed. A decade after the Battle of the Alamo, war had returned to Mexico.

New songs also were written during the Mexican War, typically demonizing Mexico, especially Santa Anna, who had once again found himself at the head of its army, and glorifying the Alamo, the Texian Revolt and it heroes. Some of the tunes were created by American soldiers themselves as they marched through Mexico, perhaps composed on tin whistles. New songs of the period, as well as older ones, found their way into songsters, which printed only the words to the songs and suggested older, familiar tunes to which they should be played. A number of marches, without words, were also published during the period with titles that commemorated the battles and heroes of the Mexican War or, to a surprising degree, dealt with Santa Anna.

Images of the Alamo and the Texas war were used in many songs to rally support for the war in the United States, where it was not universally popular (Congressman Abraham Lincoln was among the war's critics, and Ulysses S. Grant, who served in the war, later referred to it as "one of the most unjust ever waged on a weaker country by a stronger"). Many of the songs conjure images of Mexico as a dangerous and even evil threat and urged Americans to fight it with as much determination as the Alamo defenders had shown. John H. Hewitt, a prolific songwriter and arranger of the period, wrote several Alamo-related songs, including "The Alamo: Song of the Texan Ranger" in 1846, which is typical, as seen in the song's first verse:

> Our chargers, impatient are pawing the ground,
> As they hear the last bugle of reveille sound;
> Mount, mount! To your saddles, the rifle is slung,
> And the "lonely star" flag to the wild breeze is flung.
> Let the knife do its duty — it has slept long enough,
> Its point will get blunt, its steely cheeks rough;
> It thirsts for the blood of the Mexican herd
> 'Th Alamo! th' Alamo! th' Alamo! remember the word!

"Yankees Light the Fires Bright," by an unknown author, was one of several Alamo-related songs that appeared in the 1848 *Rough and Ready Songster*, but it appears to date from a year or two earlier since its lyrics clearly seek to rally Americans to join the fight against Mexico. Constance Rourke referred to this song in her 1934 biography, *Davy Crockett*, as an example of many songs written about the Tennessean and the Alamo in the years following the battle. The *Songster* suggests that the song be played to the tune of "Gray Goose," which Rourke describes as "an old and lively frolic tune." It is also one of the few Alamo songs to mention James W. Fannin, the commander of Presidio La Bahia in Goliad, where an even larger Texan force was brutally executed on Santa Anna's orders on March 27, 1836. However, the song misspells Fannin's name. Typical verses include:

> Remember gallant Crockett's bones
> Have found a glorious bed there.
> Then tell them in your thunder tones
> No tyrants' feet shall tread there.
>
> Remember where brave Fanning fell,
> With thirty gory gashes,
> And swear to ring the tyrant's knell,
> Ere they insult his ashes.
>
> Chorus:
> Come gather east, come gather west,
> Come around the Yankee thunder,
> Break down the power of Mexico,
> And tread her tyrants under.

An even more direct connection to the Alamo is found in "Remember the Alamo" by T. A. Durriage, which shows a strong taste for revenge on those who slaughtered the Alamo garrison. It also clearly expresses the degree of anti-Mexican feeling among Americans and, rather than portraying Mexican forces as an army, refers to it as no more than a "murderous horde." Texans, no doubt, especially would have responded to such demonization and a cry for revenge on forces led by Santa Anna, even a decade after the Alamo fell. Indeed, Texans had never felt entirely secure in their claim to independence from Mexico, which had never recognized the Republic of Texas. More than one cross-border skirmish had occurred between the nations since the Battle of San Jacinto.

"Remember the Alamo" also first appeared in the *Rough and Ready Songster*, which suggests that it be played to the Scottish tune "Bruce's Address." Carl Peterson includes the original lyrics, played to the traditional Scottish tune "Hey Tuttie Tattie"/"Scots Wha Ha'e" on his 2001 CD *Scotland Remembers the Alamo*. A completely different adaptation by Rich Gehr and Terry Gilkyson, in a more modern, uptempo acoustic arrangement, typical of 1960s folk recordings, was released in 1960 on the LP *Remember the Alamo*, with altered lyrics sung by Gilkyson and the Easy Riders. Dean Shostak included about a minute of the melody only, to the same tune used by Peterson, as part of his medley "The Legend of Davy Crockett" on his 2002 CD *Davy Crockett's Fiddle*.

> "Remember the Alamo" (T. A. Durriage)
>
> When on the widespread battle plain
> The horseman's hand can scarce restrain
> His pampered steed that spurns the rein,
> Remember the Alamo!
>
> When sounds the thrilling bugle blast
> And "Charge!" from rank to rank is passed
> Then as your saber strokes fall fast
> Remember the Alamo!
>
> Heed not the Spanish battle yell,

Let every stroke we give them tell,
And let them fall as Crockett fell.
Remember the Alamo!

For every wound and every thrust
On prisoners dealt by hands accurst,
A Mexican shall bite the dust.
Remember the Alamo!

The cannon's peal shall ring their knell,
Each volley sound a passing bell,
Each cheer, Columbia's vengeance tell.
Remember the Alamo!

For if, disdaining flight, they stand
And try the issue hand to hand.
Woe to each Mexican brigand!
Remember the Alamo!

Then boot and saddle! Draw the sword!
Unfurl your banners bright and broad,
And as ye smite the murderous horde,
Remember the Alamo!

Manifest Destiny, sometimes called "manifest desire," appeared in print for the first time in 1845 in "Annexation," an essay written by John L. O'Sullivan and printed in the *Democratic Review*. It was "Our manifest destiny [to] overspread the continent allotted by providence for the free development of our yearly multiplying millions," wrote O'Sullivan. Manifest Destiny also included the belief in Anglo-Saxon superiority over newly conquered peoples and an extension of slavery into the new territories. "Make way, I say, for the young American Buffalo" and "extending the area of freedom" were popular expressions of the day. Others, however, questioned bold expansionism. William E. Channing, the Unitarian abolitionist, warned Congressman Henry Clay that the nation must abandon "this vile sophistry" that supported the idea that "the mixed, degraded race of Mexico must melt before the Anglo-Saxon."

Manifest Destiny transcended legal and political fine points,

as well as history, and provided a convenient justification for U.S. conquest of land occupied by other nations. Here, "The Alamo or the Death of Crockett," written a decade earlier, is used to cast the war with Mexico as a continuation of his fight, this time to secure Texas for the United States. It features abbreviated passages from Crockett's well-known motto: "Be always sure you're right, then go ahead."

When the Mexicans leaguered thy walls, Alamo!
'Twas Crockett looked down on the war
    storm's commotion,
And smiled, as by thousands the foe spread below,
And rolled o'er the plain, like the waves of the ocean.

They came! like the sea-cliff that laughs at the flood,
Stood that dread band of heroes the onslaught repelling;
Again! and again! yet undaunted they stood,
While Crockett's deep voice o'er the wild din
    was swelling,
"Go ahead!" was his cry,
"Let us conquer or die;
"And shame the wretch, and the dastard who'd fly!"
And still, 'mid the battle cloud, lurid and red,
Ran the hero's dread cry — *Go ahead! Go ahead!*

Even before Texas was annexed, songwriters were stirring up expansionist sentiment. "The Song of Texas," an anonymous composition from around 1844 played to the tune of "Lucy Neale," makes no reference to the Alamo or the Texas war, but clearly shows U.S. sentiment regarding westward expansion, the concept of Manifest Destiny and support for the annexation of both Oregon and Texas. Indeed, James Polk won the 1844 presidential election by advocating a confrontational stand against Britain on the Oregon question. Great Britain had claims on the Oregon Territory; in fact, both the United States and Great Britain had maintained a joint occupation of the area since 1818.

"Our title to the country of Oregon is clear and unquestionable," said Polk in his inauguration address. "Already our people are preparing to perfect that title by occupying it with their wives and children." Sample verses from "The Song of Texas" include:

In Liberty's pure laws, now,
Uncle Sam and I are one,
and I will aid his cause, now,
For sister Oregon.

With Freedom's fire prolific,
We'll clear our rightful bound,
From Atlantic to Pacific
Is Uncle Sam's own ground.

The whole shall yet be free,
The whole shall yet be free,
And Uncle Sam shall have it all
In peace and Liberty.

Despite the Manifest Destiny theme that underscored "The Song of Texas," Polk was not eager to endorse the expansionist "Fifty-four forty or fight" slogan which proposed that the United States go to war with Great Britain over land as far north as 54°40'. But other songs added lyrical justification for American expansionism.

"Uncle Sam to Texas," an anonymous ditty sung to the tune of "Yankee Doodle," takes on England, in the form of "Johnny Bull," as well as Mexico in rallying Americans to the cause of Manifest Destiny. England feared American expansion and growing power and disputed the Oregon territory with its former colony. The song suggests that Britain also was secretly backing Mexico in the war. The lyrics ridicule both

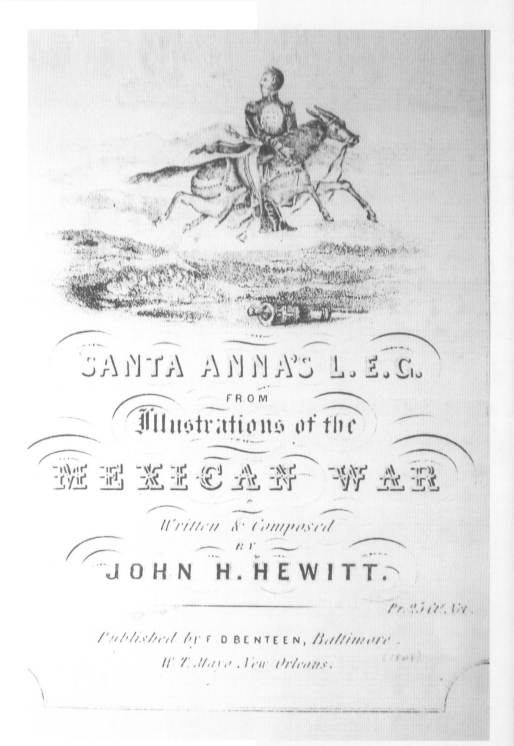

SANTA ANNA'S L. E. G.

FROM

Illustrations of the

MEXICAN WAR

Written & Composed
BY
JOHN H. HEWITT.

Pr. 25 cts. Net.

Published by F. D. BENTEEN, Baltimore.
W. T. Mayo, New Orleans.

countries, belligerently express support for President Polk and certainty in the righteousness of the U.S. cause, promising inevitable victory, not only over Mexico, but ultimately "all creation!"

> My overseer, young Jimmy Polk,
> Shall show you all my nieces,
> And then the cabinet we'll smoke
> Until our eagle sneezes;
> If Johnny Bull's fat greedy boys
> About our union grumble,
> I'll kick up such a tarnal noise
> 'Twill make 'em feel quite humble.
>
> If Mexy, backed by secret foes,
> Still talks of taking you, gal,
> Why, we can lick 'em all, you know,
> An' then annex 'em too, gal;
> For Freedom's great millennium
> Is working Earth's salvation,
> Her sassy kingdom soon wi come,
> Annexin' all creation.

Diplomacy rather than military action ultimately settled the Oregon question. A negotiated agreement with Great Britain in 1846 determined that the 49th parallel would mark the boundary between the United States and Great Britain. The 285,580 square miles that the United States acquired would one day evolve into the states of Oregon, Washington and Idaho, and sections of Montana and Wyoming.

SANTA ANNA

Gen. Antonio López de Santa Anna is, of course, best known as commander of the Mexican forces at the Siege and Battle of the Alamo in 1836. The general was later defeated at the Battle of San Jacinto on April 21, 1836, where he was captured by Sam Houston's Texian forces. Ironically, the Mexican commander was later invited to the White House by President Andrew Jackson and permitted to return to Mexico. In 1836 he was both commander of the army and president of his country. He would later rise to and fall from power in Mexico several times. During the Mexican War, songwriters would repeatedly make sport of Santa Anna, who ironically became the subject (or perhaps the target) of more songs from the period than Sam Houston.

Although other songs do not focus on Santa Anna, many of them mention him in passing, always casting him as the eternal villain. The Mexican dictator was perfect for the role since he was demonized as the vicious murderer of Davy Crockett, William B. Travis, James Bowie, other Alamo defenders and the garrison at Goliad. He was the living tyrant of an earlier war who was again leading the Mexican army, and no target could have been more inviting or convenient, at least to song writers of the period.

The Battle of Buena Vista was fought on February 23, 1847, the eleventh anniversary of the beginning of the Alamo siege, and pitted 14,000 Mexican troops under Santa Anna against a U.S. force of 5,000 under Zachary Taylor. Using heavy artillery, Taylor's men turned back the larger Mexican army and the battle ended at nightfall when the Mexicans retreated. Buena Vista quickly inspired the publication of songs marking the battle, particularly marches dedicated to Taylor or celebrating his victory.

"Santa Anna's March" is an anonymous 1847 instrumental "As played by the Bands of the Mexican Army on the field of Buena Vista the night previous to the battle," according to the sheet music arranged for the piano forte by William Ratel. The sheet music claims that, "This beautiful air was brought on by some Kentucky Volunteers having heard it played by the Mexican Bands at Buena Vista while on sentry duty." It was published in Philadelphia by George Willig, and in Lexington, Kentucky, by Bodley & Curd.

The same tune was published again in 1847, also under the

title "Santa Anna's March," with the note: "To which is added a popular melody composed on the battlefield of Buena Vista by an American officer;" arranged for Miss Mary-Ann Fitz Gerald by W. C. Peters. This sheet music is identical to that for the Ratel arrangement and may simply have been rearranged for Ms. Fitz Gerald. Peters published another arrangement of the same tune under the same title in 1850.

"Buena Vista," published anonymously in 1847 in *Songs of the People Volume 1*, makes typically derogatory reference to Santa Anna:

> That day heard Santa
>   Anna boast,
> Hurrah! hurrah! hurrah!
> Ere night he'd vanquish
>   all our host,
> Hurrah! hurrah! hurrah!
> But then the braggart did
>   not know
> That Taylor never yields
>   to foe!
> Hurrah! hurrah! hurrah!

The Mexican dictator also inspired the instrumental "Santa Anna's Retreat," another anonymous title from 1847. It was not an original tune, having first been played by the British, and having appeared under the titles "Johnny Cope," "Shay's March," "Quick March," "Nights of Gladness Quadrille," and "Spring Old-Time, Breakdown." It was not unusual for older tunes to be renamed, often with titles that referred to contemporary events.

Fiddler Henry Reed apparently learned it from his mentor, Quince Dillon, who had been a fifer in the Mexican War. Reed reportedly told musicologist Alan Jabbour that the tune was used by Santa Anna's army in retreat from the Americans, which is what Dillon must have told him, but Jabbour thought it more likely that the Americans had played it because of its British origins. Jabbour transcribed the tune from a performance by Reed.[2]

Throughout his roller-coaster career Santa Anna had found himself in and out of power several times and was even once exiled from Mexico. One of his "comebacks" occurred during a brief war between Mexico and France, some-

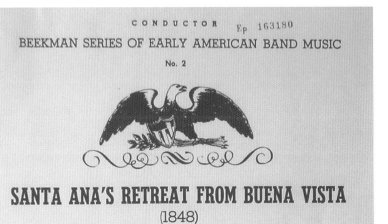

CONDUCTOR   Ep 163180

BEEKMAN SERIES OF EARLY AMERICAN BAND MUSIC

No. 2

SANTA ANA'S RETREAT FROM BUENA VISTA
(1848)

STEPHEN COLLINS FOST[...]
ARRANGED BY ROBERT L. LEI[...]

FULL BAND
Instrumentation as follows: (one copy of each unless otherwise spec[...]

Condensed Conductor Score	1st & 2nd Horn[...]
Flutes & Piccolos in C (4)	3rd & 4th Horn[...]
Oboes 1-2 (2)	1st B♭ Cornet ([...]
E♭ Clarinet	2nd B♭ Cornet [...]
1st B♭ Clarinet (4)	3rd B♭ Cornet [...]
2nd B♭ Clarinet (3)	1st Trombone
3rd B♭ Clarinet (3)	2nd Trombone
E♭ Alto Clarinet	3rd Trombone
B♭ Bass Clarinet	Baritone (Trebl[...]
Bassoons 1-2 (2)	Baritone (Bass [...]
1st E♭ Alto Saxophone	Basses (3)
2nd E♭ Alto Saxophone	String Bass
B♭ Tenor Saxophone	Timpani
E♭ Baritone Saxophone	Percussion (3)

Separate Parts

Conductor's Condensed Score ....
Extra Parts, each ....

BEEKMAN MUSIC, INC.
Sole Distributor in U.S.A. and Canada
Theodore Presser Co., Bryn Mawr, Pa.

Santa Ana's Retreat From Buena Vista

STEPHEN C. FOSTER
Arranged by Robert L. Leist

times referred to as "The Pastry War." The minor conflict began, surprisingly enough, when a French pastry cook living in Tacubaya, Mexico, claimed that some Mexican army officers damaged his restaurant. While defending his country from the French, the Mexican leader was badly wounded and lost a leg, after which he was fitted with a cork replacement.

During the U.S. war with Mexico, the Mexicans were so soundly defeated at Cerro Gordo that Santa Anna hurriedly fled the scene without his costly private carriage and personal belongings, which included his cork prosthesis. The Americans subsequently claimed that they had "captured" the dictator's artificial leg.

Santa Anna's lost limb gave rise to several songs that focused on the cork appendage. Most comical and memorable is "The Leg I Left Behind Me," an anonymous ditty sung derisively by U.S. troops to the tune of "The *Girl* I Left Behind Me," and first published in 1848. The final verse has Santa Anna lamenting that, in the future, he would be able to view the captured leg only on display.

> But should that my fortune be,
> Fate has not quite resigned me
> For in the museum I will see
> The Leg I Left Behind Me.

John H. Hewitt, who had written "The Alamo: Song of the Texan Ranger," joined in the leg-pulling with "Santa Anna's L.E.G. from Illustrations of the Mexican War," also from 1848. The song is full of puns that make great sport of Santa Anna's defeats, retreats and, as the title suggests, his lost cork leg.

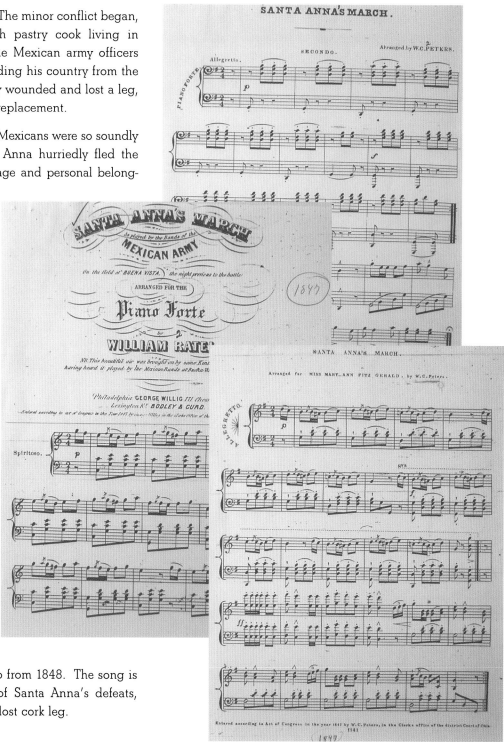

Who gallops so fast o'er your distant plane,
On a sweat-foaming mule with a slack-en'd rein
'Tis the "undying" hero, he's moving a peg,
To let the world know he has sav'd his last leg.

Chorus (repeats twice after each verse):
Ha, ha, ha, ha, yonder he goes
Whither, oh whither nobody knows,
Ha, ha, ha, ha, yonder he goes
Whither, oh whither nobody knows.

He's come off Scott-free, for he never would quail,
So, in saving his bacon, he's giv'n leg bail,
For, see in his carriage in quiet repose,
Lies the left leg of greatness without any toes.

To the Mexican nation of glory bereft,
Her patriot leader a leg-a-cy left;
But the Yankees perceiving the *right* one had gone,
Took the *left* — and the hero acknowledged the *corn*.

He made a *faux-pas* at old Vera Cruz,
At Sierra Gordo Scott stepped in his shoes,
But long may he live to stand on one peg,
And keep up a running account with his leg.

We like to see heroes who'll fight on their stumps,
They can do all their dancing without any pumps;
And, tho' he's not dead — as he oft wish'd to be;
Yet, I have been singing his last L.E.G.

"Santa Anna's Retreat from Cerro Gordo," also inspired by the battle, was an instrumental march published in 1847 by W. C. Peters in Louisville, and by Peters Field & Co. in Cincinnati. The song's sheet music cover claims that the song originated on the battlefield "...taken from a celebrated Scotch melody as performed by the American Bands on that occasion." There are two phrases in the sheet music, which do not appear to be lyrics, but rather points in the music that are intended to reflect particular embarrassment to Santa Anna, who loses both his artificial leg (which is wood here, rather than cork) and his hat. The lines appear toward the end of the piece ("Santa Anna loses his wooden leg," and a few bars later "Santa Anna loses his Mexican Hat"). The march appears to have been written in the field by soldiers during the war to be played on a tin whistle.

A slightly different arrangement of the march was published by J. L. Peters in 1851 in Missouri and was rearranged and published again in 1885 by William Cumming. That version retains the lines referring to Santa Anna's leg and hat and also claims that the march was composed and arranged by Cumming, and "Revised and improved by L. P." The claim that Cumming composed it is an exaggeration, at best, since the sheet music notes Peters' 1851 Missouri copyright for the song, thus making Cumming's contribution nothing more than a new arrangement of the tune, which had actually originated on the battlefield. In fact, all three published versions are the *same* and originated with the first 1847 publication. "Uncle Sam and Mexico," also from the *Rough and Ready Songster*, played to the tune of "Old Dan Tucker," makes derisive reference to Santa Anna's leg in lyrics written in the racist faux Afro syntax that was common in minstrel songs of the time (see "Pompey Smash" and "Zip Coon"). The final verse not only immortalizes Santa Anna's lost limb, but also throws in mention of little-remembered Mexican Lieutenant Colonel Pedro de Ampudia, who commanded the artillery at the Alamo. Ampudia survived the Texas Revolution and was promoted to general in chief of the Mexican Army of the North on the eve of the Mexican War:

Since Texas cut off Sant' Anna's peg
We'll *Amputate* Ampudia's leg,
An' so his carcass de air don't spoil,
We'll boil it in his own hot oil.

Ampudia fought in the battles of Palo Alto and Resaca de la Palma. He surrendered Monterrey to General Zachary Taylor on September 23, 1846, and later fought at the Battle of Buena Vista in February 1847.

'Way Down in Mexico," from 1847 or 1848, was collected by John Lomax early in the 20th century while he was on the hunt for authentic 19th century cowboy songs. Like many songs of this era, it refers to General Taylor by his nickname, "Old Rough and Ready." It sounds very much like a sea shanty that was converted into a rallying cry for the Mexican War effort. Shanties were songs sung by seafaring men to a slow tempo as they performed such tasks as raising anchor. The song makes racist references to Mexicans as "greasers" and includes a promise to "hang old Santa Anna soon."

Old Rough and Ready,
  he's a trump,
Yeo-ho, yeo-ho!
He'll wipe old Santa Anna out
And put the greasers all to rout,
Way down in Mexico.

We'll hang old Santa Anna soon,
Yo-ho, yo ho!
And all the greaser soldiers, too,
To the chune of "Yankee
  Doodle Doo,"
Way down in Mexico.

"Santy Anna," sometimes titled "Santy Anno," one of the most popular and frequently recorded songs about the Mexican leader, originated as a sea shanty around 1848 and refers to the dictator's defeat in the Mexican War by U.S. generals Taylor and Winfield Scott. As with many of these early songs, there are several alternative versions, including one referring to Emperor Maximilian. The song appears in contrasting forms that originated with British and U.S. sailors respectively. The British were not much more fond of the Americans than the Mexicans were. Thus, British sailors created fictional lyrics that had Santa Anna winning the day, rather than Taylor and Scott. John and Alan Lomax found that British and American sailors quarreled and fought over the song. A typical U.S. version is:

When Zacharias Taylor gained the day,
Heave away, Santy Anno;
He made poor Santy run away,
All on the plains of Mexico.

General Scott and Taylor, too,
Heave away, Santy Anno;
Made poor Santy meet his Waterloo
All on the plains of Mexico.

Santy Anno was a good old man,
Heave away, Santy Anno;
Till he got into war with your Uncle Sam,
All on the plains of Mexico.

An alternative British version features a victorious Santa Anna and a retreating Taylor. It is thought to have been made up by British seamen, reflecting Britain's opposition to the U.S. war in Mexico. Although historically inaccurate, it was apparently sung for many years by British sailors. In retrospect, it almost reads like an early-day attempt to construct a Santa Anna parody of the 20th century "Ballad of Davy Crockett."

O Santy Anna gained the day
Hooray, Santy Anna!
He lost it once but gained it twice,
All on the plains of Mexico

And Gen'ral Taylor ran away,
He ran away at Monterey.
Oh, Santy Anna fought for fame,
And there's where Santy gained his name.

Oh, Santy Anna fought for gold,
And the deeds he done have oft been told.

And Santy Anna fought for his life,
But he gained his way in the terrible strife.

Oh, Santy Anna's day is o'er,
And Santy Anna will fight no more.

I thought I heard the Old Man say
He'd give us grog this very day.

The following version was reportedly sung by African-American longshoremen at Southern ports during the Mexican War:

O have you heard the latest news?
Heave away Santy Anna!
The Yankees they took Vera Cruz,
All on the plains of Mexico!

O Santy Anna fought for fame,
Heave away Santy Anna!
He fought for fame and gained his name,
All on the plains of Mexico!

Old Santy Anna had a wooden leg,
Heave away, Santy Anna!
He used it for a wooden peg,
All on the plains of Mexico!

Brave General Taylor gained the day,
Heave away, Santy Anna!
And Santy Anna run away,
All on the plains of Mexico!

Ah, then we smashed them up and down;
Heave away, Santy Anna!
We captured all of that Mexican ground,
All on the plains of Mexico!

The ladies that I do adore,
Heave away, Santy Anna!

I always want to be ashore,
All on the plains of Mexico!

You've loved me dear and you've taught me well,
Heave away, Santy Anna!
I'd rather be here than frying in Hell,
All on the plains of Mexico!

Hermes Nye recorded a version in 1954 that included mention of Santa Anna losing his leg and released it on his album *Ballads of the Civil War*, which also included a fairly complete version of "Pompey Smash" (aka "Davy Crockett").

In 1961, Jimmie Driftwood composed, and later recorded, his own version under the title "Santy Anny O," which includes a unique stanza that mentions the Alamo. Another verse mentions Ulysses S. Grant and Robert E. Lee, both U.S. Army officers who served in the Mexican War.

In 1963, Alice Parker and Robert Shaw published their own arrangement of the song under the title "Santy Anna" (classified as an "American Sea Shanty"), for four-part chorus of men's voices a cappella. This version features highly imaginative lyrics that have the Mexican dictator fighting Prussians and the British, and even being executed, while Taylor is again portrayed as running away. This is clearly one of the most confused and confusing of Alamo-related songs.[3]

OTHER SONGS OF THE PERIOD

"Zachary Taylor," clearly an ode to the U.S. general, is another song that was most likely made up by soldiers in the field. It summarizes and glorifies the general's campaign against Mexico and twice mentions Santa Anna in an unusually flattering light and the 1847 battle of Buena Vista. The *Rough and Ready Songster* suggests it be played to the tune of "Billy Taylor."

Until he heard that valiant Santa Anna
To that place he had a mind to come
Twelve miles old 'Rough and Ready' traveled out to
    meet him
At Buena Vista Pass they had a bloody fight,
Santa Anna and his army had a touch of Yankee mettle,
That showed them 'the Elephant' just about right.

Like many Mexican War songs, "The Texas War-Cry" was sung to the tune of "The Star-Spangled Banner," considered a fairly difficult tune to play. The song expresses strong passion on the part of Texans in the war with Mexico and makes one of the few mentions of Sam Houston found in songs of the period:

Rush forth to the lines, then, these hirelings to meet;
Our lives and our homes we will yield unto no man.
Death! death, on our free soil we'll willingly meet,
Ere our free temple's soiled by the feet of the foeman;
Grasp rifle and blade,
With hearts undismayed,
And swear by the temple brave Houston has made,
That the bright star of Texas shall never be dim,
While her soil boasts a son to raise rifle or limb.

"Wave, Wave, the Banner High," played to the tune of "March to the Battle Field," also makes it clear that for many Americans, and particularly Texans, the Mexican War represented unfinished business. Because Mexico had never recognized Texas independence, and its borders had never been firmly established, Texans were understandably uneasy about their former masters to the south. Like many other war songs, it again conjures images from the Texan Revolution, including Crockett and Houston by name, leaving no doubt who had fought and bled for Texas, adding to the case for American possession of the territory. A belief that Texas had been won with the blood of Americans, combined with a strong faith in the righteousness of Manifest Destiny, underlies the song, as it did the war itself.

Wave, wave the banner high,
and onward to the field, boys,
by its true blue of the sky,
We ne'er will Texas yield, boys;
Each plain and wood,
Stained by the blood,
Of freedom's pilgrim sons, boys;
There Houston led,
And Crockett bled,
And brav'd the tyrants guns, boys,

Then wave, wave, etc.

All Europe's haughty powers, Have owned her a nation,
And we have made her ours by the Annexation.
A land so fair,
Shall foemen dare,
To crush or to enslave, boys,
No, by our veins,
We'll free her plains,
And dig each tyrants grave, boys.

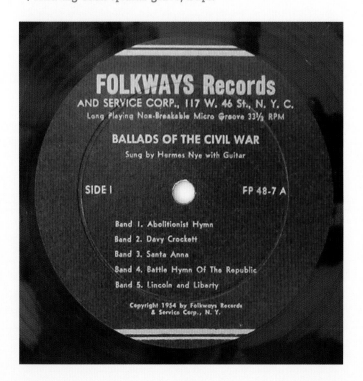

"Liberty and Texas," played to the tune of "The Satty Fair," presented yet another rallying cry for Americans to take up arms against Mexico. Americans are cast as the rescuers of a small, free republic that is being again threatened by freedom-hating Mexicans. The song's closing line even compares the situation to the Texan Revolution of 1836. In the following excerpts, Santa Anna and his hordes are predictably compared to Satan himself:

Rush into the noble strife,
For Freedom's infant land boys.
Strike in gallant Houston's van,
'Ere oppression ties him,
We'll show old sa-t-an Santa Anna,
That we can exorcise (exercise) him.

We'll unto the rescue go,
Or give our mite with free hand.
Then raise the gleaming Texas star,
'Gainst Mexico's old Nick boys,
Our rifle's fire shalt light him home,
As they did in '36 boys.

"Freedom and Texas" offers a clearer reference to the Texas republic representing an extension of the United States ("That caught its fires from our land"). The song, played to the tune of "Banks of Aberfeldy," inevitably takes yet another swipe at Santa Anna as the symbol of all that is evil:

Gallant patriots arm and out,
Raise banner and the battle shout,
The proud oppressor's force to rout,
For Freedom and for Texas,

Let not her freedom star so grand,
That caught its fires from our land,
Be pluck'd by the vile tyrant's band,
But arm and strike for Texas.

Come e'er the despot Santa Anna,
Man's on her soil fair freedom's plan,

Up and drive his murderous clan,
Far from the shores of Texas.

"Look Up on That Banner," written in 1849 by R. Horace Pratt, Esq., with music adapted and arranged by J. H. Hewitt, was dedicated to U.S. Lieutenant Colonel Dixon S. Miles and subtitled "Song of the patriot mother to her son." The published sheet music includes this extract from a letter from Mrs. Porter to her son, who had communicated to her the death of his brother in Mexico. "Come not to me! Go to Mexico — Revenge your brother's death, and sustain your country's honor." Although this song has nothing to do with the Alamo, it is typical of the feelings generated by the Mexican War among many Americans toward Mexico.

In some ways, the Mexican War was a continuation of the Texas War for Independence. Despite its nominal status as an independent republic, Mexico had never formally recognized Texas as a sovereign nation. Many in Mexico and the United States regarded the agreements signed by Santa Anna at San Jacinto as non-binding since he was a prisoner at the time, and Mexico never ratified them. Moreover, the boundary separating Texas from Mexico was never clearly established and many (including Abraham Lincoln) found no reason to recognize the Rio Grande as that boundary. Nonetheless, the United States annexed Texas in 1845, bringing on the war, which was ignited by a Mexican attack on American troops along the Rio Grande on April 25, 1846, and ended when U.S. General Winfield Scott occupied Mexico City on Sept. 14, 1847. The 15-month struggle officially ended with the Treaty of Guadalupe Hidalgo which added more than 525,000 square miles of territory to the United States, including all of the future states of California, Nevada and Utah, and parts of Arizona, New Mexico, Colorado and Wyoming.[4]

Many Americans regarded the Mexican War as little more than the confiscation of a weaker country's territory by conquest, and many historians have agreed with them. But the music of the period almost uniformly glorified the war and its American proponents and made simplistic villains of the Mexicans, who surely thought they were merely defending their homeland from a foreign invader. Some of that music resurrected images of Mexican brutality at the Alamo and Goliad a decade earlier, suggesting that those events earned Mexico similar treatment at American hands. If we were to rely only on the music that first stirred passions against Mexico and later celebrated the U.S. victory, shorn of all the legalities and history regarding that war, we might well reach the same conclusion.

[1] The song appeared in *Rough and Ready Songster* and with a musical arrangement by Philip Egner in Edward Arthur Dolph, *Sound Off!*, illustrated by Lawrence Schick. (Cosmopolitan Book Corporation, New York, 1929). The book includes an entire section with songs from the Texas and Mexican War periods, including "Remember the Alamo," "Death of Davy Crockett," "The Texas War Cry," "The Song of Texas (I Fear No Haughty Nation.)" Transcriptions are found in *Mel Bay Presents the American History Songbook* by Jerry Silverman (Mel Bay Publications, 1992, p. 36) and in Carl Peterson's *Now's the Day and Now's the Hour*, p. 83.

[2] From the *Fiddler's Companion* Website: http://www.ceolas.org/cgi_bin/ ht2/ht2_fc2/file=/tunes/fc2/fc.html&style=&refer=&abstract=&ftpstyle= &grab=&linemode=&max=250?davy+crockett]. Richard Carlin's instrumental /concertina medley "Santa Anna's Retreat"/"Greasy Coat" appears on the 1976 Folkways Records CD *The English Concertina*.

[3] The song's exact date is uncertain, but it probably originated after the Mexican War; Joanna C. Colcord dates it from that time (*Songs of American Sailormen*; Oak Publications, New York, 1938). John Lomax dates it from 1920 (in *Sea Songs and Shanties* by W. B. Whall; Glasgow: J. Brown & Son, 1920). The use of the phrase "Uncle Sam" does not necessarily date it from the 20th century, although World War I posters of the Uncle Sam caricature are sometimes thought to have marked the origination of the phrase. The letters "U.S." printed on government wagons and other items may have given rise to the name. According to the Americanabooks.net website (http://www.americanabooks.net/UncleSam.htm) the earliest surviving use of the term is from the September 3, 1813 edition of the *Troy Post*, a New York newspaper:

'Loss upon loss,' and 'no luck stirring but what lights upon Uncle Sam's shoulders,' exclaim the Government editors, in every part of the Country ... This cant name for our government has become almost as current as 'John Bull.'

[4] The Treaty of Guadalupe Hidalgo was signed on Feb. 2, 1848. It was subsequently ratified by the United States Senate and the Mexico government, and officially proclaimed on July 4, 1848.

Despite the album's title, this collection includes songs about Crockett and Santa Anna that date from their lifetimes.

VOL. X.—NO. 204.   NEW-YORK, SATURDAY, DECEMBER 29, 1860.

BALLADS OF THE CIVIL WAR

Sung by Hermes Nye with Guitar

1831—1865

John Brown

The Abolitionist Hymn
Davy Crockett
Santa Anna
Battle Hymn of the Republic
Lincoln and Liberty
Bonnie Blue Flag
Lorena
When this Cruel War is Over
Farewell Mother
There was an Old Soldier
General Patterson
The Cumberland's Crew
Cumberland Gap
When Johnny Comes Marching Home
In Charleston Jail
All Quiet Along The Potomac
Longstreet's Rangers
Goober Peas
Roll, Alabama, Roll
Abe Lincoln
Old Rebel

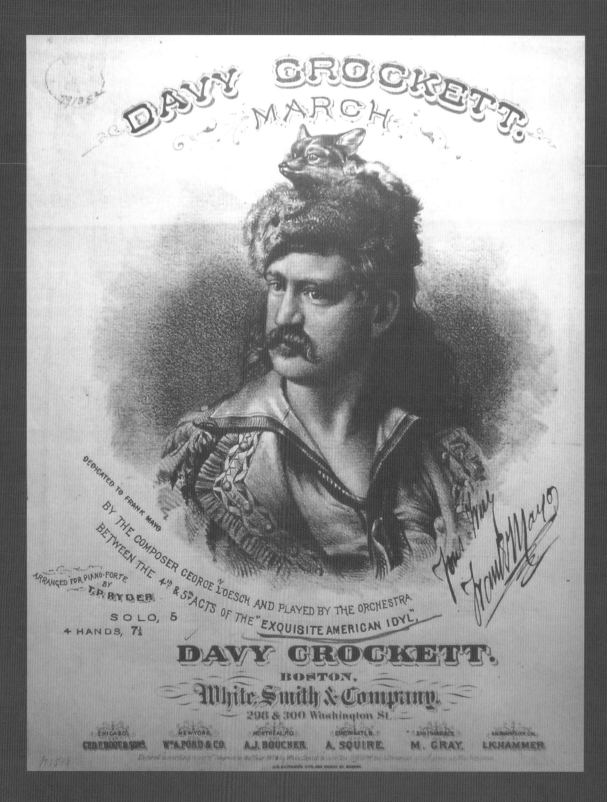

THE SECOND HALF
OF THE 19TH CENTURY

Then strike the harp for those who fought
For freedom long ago,
At San Jacinto and the Mier
And blood-stained Alamo.

"The Texian Heroes Song"

AFTER THE MEXICAN WAR, memories of the Alamo, its heroes and other symbols of the war and the Texas Revolution faded as new national issues arose. New songs about events of the 1830s and 1840s were few, although many of the old songs were still heard. The issue of slavery continued to be the major topic of national politics in the 1850s. Westward expansion under the Polk administration prompted a national debate about slavery's fate in the new territories. The Compromise of 1850, a series of measures signed by President Millard Fillmore, seemed to halt the debate as the Presidential election of 1852 approached. Both major political parties took dozens of ballots to nominate their respective candidates: the Democrats selected Franklin Pierce; the Whigs chose General Winfield Scott, a hero of the Mexican War. But Sam Houston also had been considered a candidate. Newspapers in several states endorsed Houston, who had, of course, already been the President of the Republic of Texas. One Texas newspaper, the San Augustine *Redland Herald*, provided musical support when it printed

lyrics to "Old Sam Houston," a political ditty penned by G. W. Pearce. Sung to the tune of "Oh, Susannah!," the song includes references to the Battle of San Jacinto, Santa Anna and Andrew Jackson, President of the United States during the Texas Revolution:

Come, all ye good Republicans
Come join the song with me,
Who want a man for President
To rule the brave and free.

Chorus:
Old Sam Houston, he's the boy for me,
He lives away in Texas, and a good old man is he.
Old Sam Houston, he's the boy for me,
He lives away in Texas, and a good old man is he.

He's of the Andrew Jackson school,
As true and tried as steel,
And loves the land of Freedom well,
Its glory and its weal.

[chorus]

Just listen to his sturdy voice,
Within the Nation's hall,
Proclaiming proudly to the world
The Union shall not fall.

[chorus]

At San Jacinto's bloody field,
Our Hero met the foe,
And Santa Anna there was fixed
For traveling very slow.

[chorus]

A statesman true and hero bold,
In him are both combined;
And with him we can whip the world,
'And the rest of (Whig) mankind.'

[chorus]

We'll bring him out in fifty-two
And on our banners high,
His name shall float for President,
So, Whiggies, don't you cry.

[chorus]

And when we've placed him in the chair,
Where brave Old Hick-ry sat,
We'll say good-bye, old Uncle Sam,
Hang up that broad-rim'd hat!

Old Sam Houston, he's the boy for me,
He does not live in Texas, for the President is he,
Old Sam Houston, a good old man is he;
The White House is his residence, Whiggies call and see.[1]

Although the Texas Democratic Convention nominated Houston to be the party's standard-bearer in the 1852 election, he fell far behind the pack of over a dozen national Democratic candidates. But his candidacy probably had the catchiest tune of the entire campaign, which was eventually won by Pierce. In any event, the nation drifted into civil war within a decade of Houston's failed Presidential campaign, and "Oh, Susannah!" retained its original regional flavor.

The Civil War gave rise to its own music, which did not conjure images of the earlier wars. Northerners were not anxious to glorify Southern heroes, and the South was more focused on the Northern enemy than older battles involving Mexico. When the North-South conflict ended in 1865, war fervor cooled and by the late 1800s the country found itself in a welcome era of peace.

Songs about the Civil War remained popular for years after the national struggle ended. Tunes like "Dixie's Land," "The Bonnie Blue Flag," "The Battle Hymn of the Republic," "The Battle Cry of Freedom" and "Marching Through Georgia" still stirred passions on both sides of the Mason-Dixon Line.

Many of the popular battle-inspired songs of the Texas and Mexican wars were no longer necessary or popular, but a few new Alamo-related songs were written. Some of them were simple marches, perhaps adaptations of older ones with new titles paying tribute to the battle's heroes. Again, Crockett dominated these songs and remained a pop culture perennial who transcended actual events.

Demographically, the late 19th century was marked by a wave of European immigration. These new Americans would soon hear songs about the exploits that had taken place decades earlier in places like San Antonio, Goliad and San Jacinto. Some were already familiar with Crockett.

"The Leaving of Liverpool" is an anonymous folk song that refers to a ship that had been named for Crockett. The David Crockett (referred to as the "Davy Crockett" in the song), a 220-foot, 1,679-ton ship, boasting a freshly-carved figurehead of the Alamo hero with his rifle, was launched on October 18, 1853. The song probably dates from after 1860 but before 1875 because it mentions Captain John A. Burgess, who became captain of the clipper ship in 1860 and died when he was washed overboard in June 1874.[2]

Crockett was again the subject of a highly successful stage play, *Davy Crockett; Or, Be Sure You're Right, Then Go Ahead*, written by Frank Murdock in 1872 and starring Frank Mayo as Crockett. The play was so successful that it would run continually in America and England for 24 years, with the same star, ending only when Mayo died in 1896. In 1874 the "Davy Crockett March," an instrumental composed by

George Loesch, played during the show's intermission, was published. The following year an even more ambitious songwriting effort by Sam Booth and Charles Schultz would produce "Davy Crocket's (sic) Motto 'Be sure you're right, then go ahead,'" an infectious period pop song that was "respectfully dedicated to Mr. Frank Mayo." The song is heavy on morality and "doing the right thing." It would have fit into the 1950s Walt Disney "Davy Crockett" television series and must have appealed to its 19th century audience.[3]

The world is full of crooked ways
And alleys dark and blind
And those that lead to happiness
Seem very hard to find
And as you choose your path in life.
Whatever may be said,

[chorus]

Be sure you're right, be sure you're right,
And then go ahead
And as you choose your path in life.
Whatever may be said,
Be sure you're right, be sure you're right,
And then go ahead

If fortune be your fame in life
The way seems hard and long
And often will the tempter try
To lead you in the wrong
But whether you can get wealth, or but
Enough for daily bread,

[chorus]

If fame be your ambition, though
The path be rough and high,
She gives her favors only to
The bold who bravely try.
And as you climb the rugged steep
Where glorious feet have led

[chorus]

Then keep a loyal heart while you
Your destiny fulfill
And let the craven words "I would,"
Still wait upon "I will."
Take Davy Crockett's quaint advice,
When in these words he said

[chorus]

Three years later the show was still going strongly enough to inspire yet another song — "Davy Crockett Polka" by Mrs. T. A. Wilson. The sheet music cover featured a rare postcard-size daguerreotype of Frank Mayo in formal dress rather than his Crockett costume, and bore the dedication "To Frank Mayo."

A few years later "The Alamo March" by Francis Muench was published. Other marches included "San Jacinto Memorial March" by William Amende, "Respectfully dedicated to the surviving heroes who shed their blood for the independence of Texas, Especially at the battle of San Jacinto," and "Alamo Grand March" by Gabriel Katzenberger, oddly dedicated to "the Executive Board of the 2nd San Antonio Volksfest."

"The Fall of the Alamo" is the first known attempt to dramatize the Alamo story for the stage or to put it in the form of a musical. Written in 1879 by Professor Francis Nona, this four-act musical in verse features all of the major Alamo characters, including Santa Anna and Sam Houston, and ends with an epilogue at the San Jacinto River on April 21, 1836. The songs include "Hymn of Texan Liberty," "Col. Crockett's Song," "Hymn of the Lone Star Flag," "Prayer Before Battle," "Anthem of the Alamo," "Mexican Battle March" and "Hymn of Victory."

"Col. Crockett's Song" is of particular interest as it anticipated the 20th century Disney hit "The Ballad of Davy Crockett." It included verses on the location of his birth, his hunting prowess, service in the Creek War, political career and finally his journey to the Alamo.

Born in the wilds of Tennessee
With Indians round about,
This child was reared, and grew to be
A daring hunter scout.

He fought the brined catamount
And dragged the panther from his haunt;
And grappled with the lynx and bear,
And scaled the eagles' cliff-built lair

And thus it came that with his name
Was blent a daring hunter's fame;
And thus it came that with his name
Was blent a daring hunter's fame.

The song then shifts to the first person, as Crockett relates his further adventures in the Creek War, his years in Congress and his final days in Texas.

And when about the neighborhood
The Creeks spread death and fear,
I shouldered for my country's good
My gun as volunteer.
I served Old Jackson as a guide,
Fought many battles at his side,
And often saved by timely aid
My comrades from an ambuscade.
And so it came that with my name
Was blent a gallant, Soldier's fame.
For Congress then a nominee
I took the stump and ran,
And was elected handsomely
O'er every other man.
In Congress, then, at Washington,

I sat as silent as a nun;
Yet though I spake but "Ay" and "Nay,"
My vote was honest any way.
And so I gained a world-wide fame,
As Congressman without a blame.

Now after a ten months' sojourn
'Mong my Comanche friends,
I have resolved my steps to turn
Where my life's journey ends.
My brethren in the Alamo
I come to join against the foe;
They will succumb before his might,
Yet it will be a glorious fight;
So will forever with my name
Be blent a *Martyr's* noble fame.

"The Texian Heroes' Song," written in 1884 by Mary Hunt McCaleb and G. P. Warner, was, according to 1885 sheet music, "first performed at a Soiree Musicale, given for the benefit of the Invalid Texian Heroes' Home, at Millett's Opera House, January 26th 1884." Like many songs of the period, it was sung to "Auld Lang Syne," and Carl Peterson recorded it to that tune for his 2001 CD *Scotland Remembers the Alamo* under the title "Texas Heroes." It goes beyond most Alamo songs by mentioning those killed at Goliad, San Jacinto and the ill-fated Mier Expedition as well as the Alamo:

Then strike the harp for those who fought
For freedom long ago,
At San Jacinto and the Mier
And blood-stained Alamo.

In 1895, Jennie Myers and Ella Rodeffer composed "The Alamo — In Memory of the Fallen Heroes of Texas — Patriotic Song and Chorus." It is a six-verse salute to the Alamo defenders in glorifying language, typical of the time and of many songs written about the Alamo. The legends are commemorated, including Travis drawing the line, the blar-

ing of the *degüello* and the flying of Santa Anna's "no mercy" red flag over San Fernando Church in San Antonio. The song contains some gruesome elements, such as the defenders sliding on the slippery, blood-soaked floors, sacrificing themselves on the altar of Texas liberty, while the Mexicans are cast as a "blood-thirsting" and "treacherous foe." Its graphic descriptions mark this as one of the more realistic musical accounts of the Alamo's fall. The chorus demands that Texans build a monument "over their tomb," which they eventually would in the form of the Alamo Cenotaph.[4]

A grim scarred spectre she seems as she stands,
Backward she's pointing with blood staind hands,
Back to the sepulchral black veil'd age,
Whose record burns as with fire the page,
As she pencils the deeds of the martyrs brave,
Who died the freedom of Texas to save
Whil'st surged the Mexicans to and fro,
Our brave sons guarded the Alamo.

On Sunday morn March the sixth, at three,
The "Deguello" sounded the death decree;
The blood-thirsting host sprang quick to arms,
Shrilly the bugle pealed loud alarms.
Nerved for fierce conflict our heroes stood
United by bonds of fond brotherhood.
Mad waved the flag on San Fernando,
Madder they fought at the Alamo.

The guns, peal on peal, boomed loud in the fight,
The smoke, cleaved by lightning, made blind the sight;
The earth-floor streamed with the welt'ring blood,
Dying they fell in the slippery flood.
Travis, Crockett and Bonham, and heroes all
Gave up their lives 'neath that dark reeking pall.
Burned they the dead on that day of woe,
Burned they the brave of the Alamo.

Respectfully Dedicated to MR. FRANK MAYO.

DAVY CROCKET'S MOTTO.

"Be sure you're right, then go ahead."

WORDS COMPOSED BY

SAM. BOOTH.

MUSIC BY

CHAS. SCHULTZ.

Published by **SHERMAN & HYDE,** 189 Kearny St.

(CORNER OF SUTTER,)

SAN FRANCISCO.

Chorus:
Arouse, loyal Texans! a monument build,
To tow'r above heroes who battling were kill'd;
Struggled they bravely in darkness and gloom,
Erect a monument over their tomb.

The closing of the frontier in the late 19th century and the corresponding growth of American industrialism generated a nostalgic interest in the West, or what the public thought the West was or had been. William F. Cody kept the spirit of the region alive with his "Buffalo Bill's Wild West" show and his 1888 book *Story of the Wild West*, which featured Crockett and other notable pioneers and scouts of the 19th century. And despite the development of more sophisticated musical expressions—particularly Henry Lee Higginson's establishment of the Boston Symphony Orchestra in 1881—the general public was still fascinated by those who died at the Alamo in 1836.

"The Texas Cowboy and the Mexican," an anonymous 19th century song, is among the most unusual with Alamo references. It is critical of anti-Mexican sentiments and relates the tale of a lone cowboy who is brave enough to stand up to a mob that is about to lynch a wounded Mexican. The lyrics make reference to the "powerful feelin' of hatred ag'in the whole Mexican race/That murdered bold Crockett and Bowie..."[5]

"The Texas Song" is a late-century, anonymous cowboy trail song that makes a passing reference to the Alamo, and which was later recorded by Gordon Bok. It also appeared under the title "Leavin' Ole Texas Now." The song was a harbinger of things to come in the early 20th century, which would see the Alamo used as a mere backdrop for songs that have nothing to do with the battle.

I'll take my horse, I'll take my rope,
And hit the trail upon a lope,
Say "Adios" to the Alamo,
And turn my head to Mexico.[6]

Another version offers these alternate lyrics:

I'm goin' to leave — ole Texas now
They've got no use — for the longhorn cow

They've plowed and fenced — my cattle range
And the people there are all so strange

I'll bid adios to the Alamo
And turn my face toward Mexico[7]

The explosion of the *U.S.S. Maine* on February 15, 1898, in Havana harbor triggered the Spanish-American War, and the spirit of the Alamo was resurrected by yet another generation of Americans at war.[8] The slogan "Remember the Maine" echoed "Remember the Alamo." Tunes like "Before the Maine Went Down," "We Have Remembered the Maine" and "Remember the Maine: Song and Chorus" competed with the popular marches of John Philip Sousa and the ragtime compositions of Scott Joplin as the century came to a close. However, the anti-Spanish sentiments in the songs that commemorated the loss of the *Maine* reinforced similar anti-Spanish, anti-Mexican feelings that had been established over the years in a number of Alamo-related songs, with the exception of "The Texas Cowboy and the Mexican."

Much of this vitriol would disappear from songs about the Alamo in the coming century. The once-bloody battlefield, a scene of unspeakable carnage on March 6, 1836, would find itself the instrument of romanticists, Tin Pan Alley tunesmiths, and Hollywood's dream factory.

[1] Mike Cox, "Old Sam Houston Song," *Texas Tales*, July 27, 2006; TexasEscapes.com website (http://www.texasescapes.com/ MikeCoxTexasTales/Old-Sam-Houston-Song.htm). Cox notes that the song was reprinted in a 1928 issue of *Bunker's Monthly* magazine.

[2] William R. Chemerka, "'David Crockett' Bicentennial," *The Crockett Chronicle* 2, November 2003, 4-5. "The Leaving of Liverpool" is performed periodically by the band Off Kilter at the Canadian pavilion in EPCOT at Walt Disney World. The band also recorded the song and it appears on its *Kick It* LP (2005).

[3] In 1955 a song of the same title, "Davy Crockett's Motto — Be Sure You're Right (Then Go Ahead)," emerged from another Crockett dramatic production — Walt Disney's "Davy Crockett" television series. The two stars of that series, Fess Parker and Buddy Ebsen, would outdo Frank Mayo by writing and recording the song themselves.

[4] Courtesy of the Daughters of the Republic of Texas Library at the Alamo. The Alamo Cenotaph was erected in 1939 on Alamo Plaza by the Texas Centennial Commission. Created by Pompeo Coppini, the theme of the cenotaph is "Spirit of Sacrifice" and features full-size sculpted images of such Alamo defenders as David Crockett, William B. Travis, James Bowie and James B. Bonham, among others. According to *The Alamo Almanac and Book of Lists* (Eakin Press, Austin, TX, 1997), "the monument's Georgia gray marble shaft reaches sixty feet from its pink Texas granite base." Street musicians in modern-day San Antonio sometimes perform at the Alamo Cenotaph.

[5] A transcription of the song appears in *Songs of the Cattle Trail and Cow Camp*, a collection of authentic 19th century cowboy songs collected by John A. Lomax, (New York: The Macmillan company, 1919). Also referred to as "The Texas Cowboy and the Mexican Greaser."

[6] John A. and Alan Lomax, *Cowboy Songs and Other Frontier Ballads* (MacMillan Co., New York, 1938).; Gordon Bok, *Time and the Flying Snow — Songs of Gordon Bok* (Folk-Legacy Records, Inc.; Sharon, Connecticut, 1977).

[7] Found in a small booklet called *Texas Songs* (typewritten with no date or authorship noted; appears to be self-printed; Library of Congress)

[8] Surprisingly, on March 6, 1898, the 62nd anniversary of the Battle of the Alamo, Spain requested the recall of the U.S. Cuban Consul, Fitzhugh Lee.

THE ALAMO

In Memory of the Fallen Heroes of Texas.

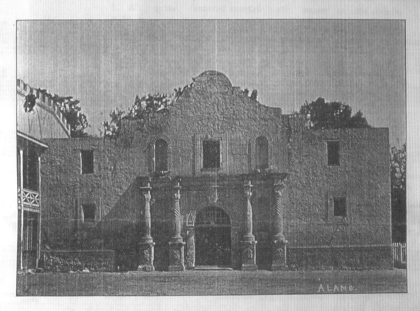

Words by

Mrs. Jennie Myers.

PATRIOTIC SONG
and
CHORUS.

4

Music by

Miss Ella Rodeffer.

PUBLISHED BY

J. MYERS and E. RODEFFER,

SAN ANTONIO, TEXAS.

Northrop, Nagel & Jesse, Print., San Antonio, Texas.

MUSIC OF THE ALAMO

THE EARLY 20TH CENTURY

Meet me in the mellow glow

Of the Alamo moon,

By the dreamy Alamo

We can cuddle and spoon

While moonbeams softly gleam
upon the silvr'y stream,

With you by my side what a dream it will seem

When we meet tonight in the glow
of the Alamo moon.

George L. Cobb & Jack Yellen
"In the Glow of the Alamo Moon" © 1918

AT THE START of the new century, America found itself in the midst of a welcomed, prolonged period of peace. With the exception of the brief Spanish-American War in 1898, the country was free of military conflict for some fifty years between the Civil War and World War I. Although songs about the Alamo, or those which at least invoked its familiar name, were written during this peaceful hiatus, many had nothing whatever to do with the famous battle or its legendary participants. Others, however, did follow more traditional lines and heaped the same kind of praise upon those heroes as songwriters had done in the 1800s. This era also saw the first classical compositions about the Alamo.

Crockett's image comes to mind in "Be Sure You're Right," a 1900 "Serio Comic Song" written by Captain P. Kelly and F. Younker. Although this title echoes the frontiersman's familiar motto, the song actually has nothing to do with him. It is, instead, a pep talk for those facing life's challenges and even tacks on the second part of that motto, "then go ahead." Similar instrumental titles from the period include "The Go Ahead Polka" and "The Go Ahead Gallop."

In 1903, "Flag Song of Texas," a rousing ode to the Lone Star State, praised Crockett, Travis, Bowie and other heroes of the Texas war, including Ben Milam who died during the Battle of Bexar in 1835, and James Fannin, who was killed in the Goliad Massacre of 1836. And, to be sure, the song includes the important battle cry "Remember the Alamo!"

And when on San Jacinto's plain,
The Texians heard the cry,
"Remember, men, the Alamo!"
They swore to win or die;

By deeds of arms our land was won,
And priceless the reward!
Brave Milam died and Fannin fell
Its sacred rights to guard;
Our patriot force with mighty will
Triumphant set it free,
And Travis, Bowie, Crockett gave their lives for Liberty!

Written by Lee C. Hardy and Aldridge B. Kidd, the song was the prizewinner in a contest sponsored by the Daughters of the Republic of Texas (DRT), custodians of the Alamo, to find "the best original song on the subject of the Texas Flag, suit-

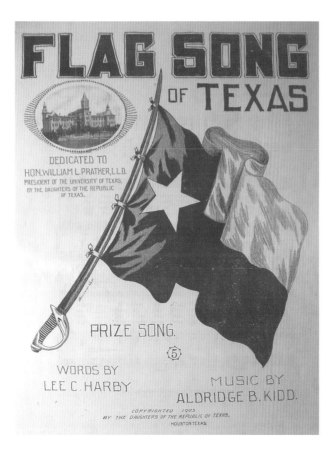

I met my love in the Alamo
When the moon was on the rise,
Her presence quite bedimm'd its light
So radiant were her eyes!
No star in Heaven's firmament
Can her bright smile out shine,
There's no one like that Alamo love of mine!

"The Alamo March," a 1904 instrumental, was a more tradi-tional Alamo number, "Dedicated to Miss Clara Driscoll," the celebrated "savior of the Alamo" and a member of the DRT. Driscoll, a descendant of San Jacinto veterans, con-tributed thousands of dollars to buy the Alamo's Long Barrack building, which had played an important role in the

able to be sung by the pupils of the public schools and the students of The University of Texas, especially on March 2nd, 'Texas Independence Day.'" The composers also received a one-hundred-dollar prize.[1]

The same year "Texas — A Patrioic Song," by C. Appleyard and Edmund Ludwig, mentioned the Texan victory at San Jacinto, but forgot the Alamo.

More typical of the time was "My Alamo Love," from the musical play *The Tenderfoot*, which featured lyrics by Richard Carle and music by H. L. (Harry Lawson) Heartz. The play was produced at Chicago's Dearborn Theatre in 1903. With increasing frequency, the Alamo would find itself an unlikely backdrop for romantic ballads, with such unmili-tary lyrics as these from "My Alamo Love":

battle. The sheet music even featured Jean Louis Theodore Gentilz's 1885 painting *Fall of the Alamo* on the cover. The song was recorded by The Paradise Entertainers in 1936.

"Alamo," by Edward Madden and Dorothy Jarden, was another "love song" of sorts. Here, a cowboy sings as he rides the range with his sweetheart, whose name is "Alamo," trying to lure her to his home in Oklahoma. When she turns him down, he takes the desperate measure of lassoing the reluctant lass and hauling her off, an image far removed from modern attitudes regarding gender.

"Crockett's Honeymoon" or "Honeymoon Reel" is an anonymous fiddle tune from around 1907 that has nothing to do with the Tennessean. Alternative titles include "Girl from the Country," "Ha'penny Reel," "Rooney's Reel," and "Maid Who Left the Mountains." It was recorded by the Clayfoot Strutters as part of "Three Reels" for the 1996 album *American Fogies Vol. 1*; as "Crockett's Honeymoon," part of a medley with "Yellow Rose of Texas," used as backing for a square dance caller recorded by Yankee Ingenuity for their 1989 album *Heatin' up the Hall*; and as "Crockett's Honeymoon" on Scott Nygaard's 1996 CD *Dreamer's Waltz*.[2]

Adina de Zavala, another Alamo "savior" and DRT member, was the subject of "Remember the Alamo," written in 1908 by Jessie Beattie Thomas, which commemorates the so-called "second battle of the Alamo" as well as the 1836 conflict. Although it summarizes the Alamo and San Jacinto battles, its real purpose was to honor Zavala for her efforts to save the convent section, or Long Barrack, of the original Alamo compound, where many Alamo defenders met their deaths. Zavala and her supporters were at odds with Clara Driscoll and others who wanted to focus on preserving the now-familiar Alamo church, although little actual fighting had taken place within its walls. The convent building had been operated as a wholesale grocery by the Hugo and Schmeltzer Company since 1886, and the Driscoll faction sought to demolish it since it obscured part of the view of the Alamo church from the street. Driscoll and her supporters also may have believed that little, if any, of the original Long Barrack building had survived its years of reconfiguration for commer-

cial use. However, while some of the original structure had been destroyed, part of it had survived. Zavala sought to preserve what remained of the Long Barrack and found herself at odds with Driscoll. Zavala's efforts were instrumental in saving part of the original convent building when in February 1908 she barricaded herself inside of it for three days to draw public attention to the debate. Time eventually vindicated her. Although its second story, which may have housed the Alamo hospital where the sick and wounded were slaughtered, is gone, the Long Barrack's first floor survived and is now a museum that includes a small movie theater, ironically named the Clara Driscoll Theater.

Sheet music for the song was sold to raise funds for the Alamo's preservation. It featured a portrait of Zavala, "The Heroine of the Alamo," and was "Respectfully Commended to the Daughters of the Republic of Texas, for the Preservation of the Alamo in the Glory of the State." The song's message is summarized in its third verse:

Let commerce not sway sentiment
Nor trade e'er change the spot
That's hallow'd as a monument
For freedom dearly bought.
A daughter of the Alamo
Within the walls today
Stands guard to save its over throw
And all true Texans say:
Hurrah for the maid of the Alamo,
Of Texas the fair lone star

© 1908, Thomas & Davis, St. Louis, Mo.[3]

"My Dream of the USA," by Leonard Chick, Charles Roth, and Ted Snyder, was published the same year. Its lyrics paid tribute to several American heroes, including George Washington, Andrew Jackson and Davy Crockett.[4]

More typical of the time was "Alamo Rag," a ditty penned by Ben Deely and Percy Wenrich and recorded by Dolly Connolly, a successful vaudeville performer who was married to Wenrich. The song has nothing to do with the fortress, but mentions that the Alamo is, indeed, in San Antonio, where the Alamo Rag (according to the song's lyrics) is all the rage. Wenrich wrote many songs, but his rags were his most successful and included "Peaches and Cream," "Red Rose Rag," and "The Smiler."[5]

"Heroes of the Alamo," a rousing tribute to the Texan garrison, written by Chris and James C. Quinn, was published in 1914. This World War I-era ode is replete with typically over-the-top images of the Alamo defenders, who die happily smiling, and mentions several of the better-known heroes, including two non-documented named Leeds and Roe, along with the "game rank and file."

I am standing tonight,
In the soft waning light,
'Neath the shade of the Alamo,
And my thoughts slowly turn,
To the mem'ries that burn,
Of those heroes of long, long ago.

And I call each great name,
That is linked with fame,

Bowie, Crockett Travis, Leeds and Roe.
And the game rank and file,
Who met death with a smile,
Those heroes of the Alamo.

Chorus
Old Alamo, Old Alamo,
Where those brave heroes bled and died,
Your fame lives in song and in story,
The tales of brave deeds and of glory,
Old Alamo, Old Alamo,
Your defenders were staunch and true,
And they fought man to man,
As Americans can,
Heroes of the Alamo.

When the moon swings low,
O'er the old Alamo,
Down in quaint dreamy San Antone,
And the stars in the skies,
Peep with bright twinkling eyes,
As I stand here in tho't all alone –
Then in fancy I hear,
Whisp'ring voices near;

With a message from the long ago –
When the words that I hear,
Come to me strong and clear,
Remember the Alamo.

Nineteen-fourteen also marked the debut of one of the more notable romantic ballads set beside the Alamo. "When It's Moonlight on the Alamo," by Alfred Bryan and Fred Fisher, became the first known commercially recorded song about the Alamo when Albert H. Campbell and Irving Gillette (aka Henry Burr) released their version on a wax cylinder by the Edison company, a format that preceded the modern record. The song was recorded again in 1917 by Frederick Wheeler and Reed Miller. Bryan and Fisher also created "Peg O' My Heart" and "I'm on My Way to Mandalay."[6]

Alamo-based romantic music reached a peak in 1922 with "On the Alamo," written by Gilbert Keyes and Joe Lyons, with music by Isham Jones. The song sets a romantic rendezvous in moonlight that shines on the Alamo. Countless recordings of the song have been released, perhaps the first in 1922 on wax cylinder by Harry Raderman's Jazz Orchestra, which listed Jones and Raderman as the co-composers, although it was also released the same year on a 78 rpm single by Nathan Glantz's Orchestra.[7]

Although many songs have been written about the Alamo and its courageous defenders, Davy Crockett continued to enjoy greater notoriety and affection than any of them in the 20th century. He is almost always mentioned in Alamo songs and even in some that are not specifically about the battle. The other defenders, even the well-known Bowie and Travis, barely get a musical mention. Even Houston, who led the Texans to victory at San Jacinto, takes a distant backseat to Crockett in the musical tributes to those who fought in the Texas war. This is doubtless due to the celebrity that Crockett had already achieved during his lifetime and his popularity among Americans, who felt a special sadness at the loss of the Tennessean at the hands of Mexico on the eve of the Manifest Destiny era.

No Crockett song has survived as long as the early 19th century minstrel tune "Pompey Smash." It had appeared in sheet music and songsters during that period and was frequently performed onstage. In the 20th century many versions of the song were collected or recorded by musicologists throughout the United States.

For example, "Pom Smash" was a Civil-War-era version that included all of the original verses about Crockett. It was located by Mr. Warren Wilhite of Sherwood, Arkansas, who said that his father, Farmer Wilhite, had written it down in 1950.

Farmer was a singer and poet who had picked up many songs from his uncle, John Goodner, who lived in Oden, Arkansas.[8]

Another version, found in 1900 in Knott County, Kentucky, by Josiah E. Combs, but not published until 1925, reflects changes in the song's lyrics and attitude. The language and vernacular are changed; the grinning of bark off of a tree is missing, but the climactic fight between Davy and Pompey is preserved.[9]

In 1906 the first published version under the title "Davy Crockett" appeared, which consisted of one verse and provides a clear example of how much the tone and colloquial speech had changed by that time.

> Don't you want to hear about Davy Crockett,
> Half horse, half man, and half sky rocket?
> He went out one night when the folks were all asleep.
> The stars were lying on the ground about knee-deep.[10]

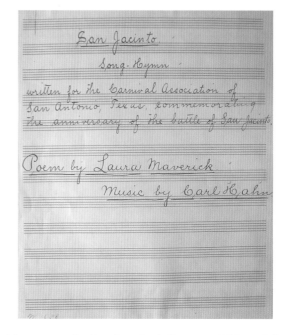

A more complete version, titled "Davy Crockett," with 13 verses was discovered in 1917 by John Harrington Cox in Harrison County, West Virginia, and published in 1925. It does not use Crockett's last name and he is only referred to somewhat obliquely as "Davy" or "Uncle Davy." The Negro vernacular is largely toned down or completely gone. However, the essential elements of the Pompey-Davy encounter are there.[11]

A 1927 version collected by Julia Beazley and titled "The Ballad of Davy Crockett," is said to be the most widely printed version of the song. It reduced the Negro vernacular and "improved" the grammar, but remained generally faithful to the original. Beazley said she'd heard some sailors singing it around the turn of the century. However, the version that she published in 1927 came from someone known only as "Mrs. Melton" of Houston, Texas, who later made a recording of the song and has slightly different lyrics from the version Beazley had heard the sailors singing.[12]

A version titled "Davy Crockett" was collected in 1930 by F. M. Goodhue of Mena, Arkansas, which he'd gotten from

an "old woman who lived in the hills west of Mena." As with most of the other "Davy Crockett" iterations, this is viewed as only a fragment of the original "Pompey Smash" and somewhat "corrupted" in its alteration of words and vernacular. The story is changed, too, in that neither is fooled by the pine knot and they seem to fight over nothing. Also, they pin their own ears back, rather than each other's. A 1931 version, performed by Mrs. Samuel Leake, included only three stanzas.[13]

Another variation appeared in 1938 that gave both characters equal billing under the title "Pompey Smash and Davy Crockett," published in *Texas Folk Songs* by William A. Owens. Owens says that this version was sung to him by Lemuel Jeffus of Lovelady, Texas, in 1938 near the Davy Crockett Memorial in Crockett, Texas. The song not only mentions Zip Coon, Pompey Smash and Davy Crockett, but also Jim Crow, another stock character from minstrel shows. Again, the lyrics and vernacular have been altered to eliminate the racial stereotypes of the original.[14]

The following year another version of "Davy Crockett" was found in *America Sings* by Carl Carmer. This revision of

THE EARLY 20TH CENTURY

"Pompey Smash" anticipated the more sanitized version of the legendary Crockett that Disney would cultivate 15 years later. The song is preceded by Carmer's rendition of Crockett tall stories, including his grinning the bark off a tree, but the original Negro vernacular is now completely gone.

Many unreleased field recordings of the song were made in the early 20th century, but the first commercial recording of the song was "Davey Crockett," performed by Chubby Parker. Parker was a well-known singer who was heard on Chicago radio station WLS's "National Barn Dance," an early country and western program that later helped to make a national star of Gene Autry. Parker recorded his version of the song on October 15, 1931, in New York, and the record was released the following spring on the Conqueror label, which sold its records exclusively through the Sears catalog. Parker's uptempo rendition is one of the most authentic and pleasing adaptations of this Crockett perennial.

Other adaptations were recorded by Sarah Ogan Gunning and Hermes Nye. Gunning's a cappella rendition features only verses that include Crockett, some of them with revised

lyrics. Nye, a Dallas attorney, added a few Crockett bragging stories midway through the song. His album also includes the 19th century sea song "Santa Anna." Most recorded versions include *only* the Crockett verses and omit all of Pompey's other adventures, indicating the increased prominence that Crockett's image had achieved and suggesting that his appearance in the song is the primary reason for its long-term success.

The song was still being recorded later in the century. A 1978 field recording of "Davy Crockett" by Dee Hicks of Fentress County, Tennessee, recorded by Bobby Fulchjer, is the only version known to have been collected in Crockett's native Tennessee; it was released on the LP *Tennessee: The Folk Heritage, Vol. 2: The Mountains*.

Hobert Stollard recorded an a cappella rendering that includes several verses that don't involve Crockett, and one that places Crockett where Zip Coon, a rival of Pompey's, appears in the early versions of the song. Other verses refer to education at colleges, boys who served as drummers or fifers, and other non-Crockett lyrics, along with a few Crockett verses, such as his fight with Pompey Smash. Stollard's recording was released in 1996 on the CD *Land of Yahoe — Children's Entertainments from the Days Before Television*.

New songs about the Texas War also emerged during the period, including Laura Maverick's 1914 poem, "San Jacinto — Song Hymn," set to music by Carl Hahn. The composers noted that the song was "Written for the Carnival Association of San Antonio, Texas, commemorating the anniversary of the Battle of San Jacinto," but it also remembers the Alamo:

> The Alamo remember, its portals decorate.
> Let all true Texans garlands bring,
> All hail to the Lone Star State!

©1914 Laura Maverick & Carl Hahn; Jerome H. Remick & Co.

"Somewhere in Mexico (Remember the Alamo)," written in 1916 by Francis J. Lowe, may be the only song written in support of the 1916 U.S. invasion of Mexico in pursuit of Pancho Villa. The composer, an Iowan, dedicated the piece to an Iowa National Guard unit that was deployed during the war. The song employs the Alamo as a device to rally support for the war and resurrects the anti-Mexican racism of the previous century:

> Somewhere in Mexico,
> Remember the Alamo.
> Our Boys so brave and true,
> Are hiking two by two,
> The Army and Navy forever,
> Three cheers for the Red, White and Blue.
> You bet your life, they'll set things right,
> And show some Greasers how to fight,
> Down in Mexico.

© 1916 Francis J. Lowe

Romance returned to the Alamo in 1918 with "In the Glow of the Alamo Moon," a ragtime ditty written by George L. Cobb with lyrics by Jack Yellen, that finds two lovers in the moonlight beside the old fortress. Obviously, this rendezvous did not take place in early March, 1836:

> Meet me in the mellow glow
> Of the Alamo moon,
> By the dreamy Alamo
> We can cuddle and spoon
> While moonbeams softly gleam upon the silvr'y stream,
> With you by my side what a dream it will seem,
> When we meet tonight in the glow of the Alamo moon.

© 1918 George L. Cobb & Jack Yellen

Texas general and first president Sam Houston had the attention of songwriters like Victor Alessandro, who penned the "Sam Houston March" in 1925. His sheet music boasted that he was also "Introducing 'Come to the Bow'r' — The Song used by the soldiers of Sam Houston as they marched to the 'Battle of San Jacinto.'"

"Texas Our Texas," a 1929 composition by Gladys Yoakum Wright and William J. Marsh, was so inspiring that the Texas legislature adopted it as the official state song that year. It is a rousing salute to the Lone Star State and notes the glory of the Alamo and San Jacinto.

"Beautiful Texas," written by W. Lee O'Daniel in 1933, is an equally laudatory Texas tribute that native Texan Willie Nelson recorded for his 1967 album *Texas in My Soul*. O'Daniel and his Light Crust Doughboys also recorded the anonymous "Alamo Waltz" in 1934, the same year that the anonymous "Alamo Schottische," originally titled "Nightingale Clog," appeared; it was later recorded by Adoph Hofner.[15]

SAN ANTONIO
(The City Of So Many Charms)

Words and Music by
WALTER JURMANN
A.S.C.A.P.

Price 75¢
in U.S.A.

MIRADOR MUSIC PUBLISHER
Sole Selling Agent
Southern Music Company
1100 Broadway, San Antonio, Texas 78201

At least two songs titled "San Antonio" paid tribute to the Alamo city. The first, "San Antonio" by Mattie Craig Carnathan and A. R. Walton was written in 1924. The second, also titled "San Antonio," was written by J. Frank Davis, Alva R. Willgus and Mrs. Willgus. It is a musical tribute by Davis, a newspaperman and author, who moved to San Antonio in 1910, to his adopted city. His sheet music bears a sketch of the Alamo. The famous church would later grace the 1966 sheet music "San Antonio" (pictured at left).

The Alamo again made it to the legitimate stage in 1935 with *Tejas*, a historical opera with libretto by May Abney Mayes and Willie Megee, and music by Theophilus Fitz. A preview of the vocal numbers from the piece was presented by the Texas Centennial Opera Company on November 25, 1935, at the St. Anthony Hotel in San Antonio. The characters in the opera include Sam Houston, William B. Travis, Mrs. Dickinson and Santa Anna. However, in this piece, Crockett is a rare musical no-show.

In 1936, Texas celebrated the Centennial of the Alamo's 13 days of glory. To mark the occasion, the Republic of Texas Centennial Commission authorized the construction of the Alamo Cenotaph on Alamo Plaza and work began on the Alamo's museum and gift shop building.

The battle's 100th anniversary also was marked by Cal Cohen's "The Spirit of the Alamo." Although the song refers to San Jacinto and the Civil War, it says virtually nothing about the Alamo, making only brief mention of the spirit of the hallowed shrine. Cohen claimed to be the first Jewish child born in Houston, Texas, and was an old vaudeville song-and-dance man who often performed in blackface. A year later, a story in the *San Antonio Express* illustrated how such emotional odes were received at that time, the degree of hyperbole that public responses to them reached, and featured perhaps a record-setting run-on sentence:

"Today, just 101 years ago, was the saddest event in the history of Texas. It was on that day when the smoke from the funeral pyre of the heroes of the Alamo ascended heavenward following the bloody massacre in this holy shrine after a siege which began on February 23, 1836, and ended on March 6, to mark the most heroic defense of a noble cause in American history. So on this day we bow our heads in sorrow as we honor the memory of Crockett, Bowie and Travis among others who gave their lives in the struggle to make this a land of freedom."[16]

The Texas centennial inspired several new songs. "The San Jacinto Tango," by S. S. Gay and Harve' Le Roy, provided some dance music for the state's 100th birthday. "Dear Texas," by Fern Jay Smith and Alta Lee Smith, mentions both the Alamo and San Jacinto, while "The Texas Centennial Waltz," by Basil Bell, refers rather clumsily to the Alamo and Goliad.

The centennial may have inspired more serious composers to take on the Alamo, beginning with Kurt Weill, who teamed with lyricist H. R. Hays to compose *Davy Crockett*, a collection of songs that wove a narrative of the frontiersman's life. The work was never completed or performed publicly, although the songs, described as "musical fragments," were recorded by soprano Joy Bogen and released in 2000. Those "fragments" include "Song of the Trees," "Hillbilly Narrative — Davy and Sarah's Marriage," "The Hand is Quicker than the Eye," "The Death of Josh Hawkins," and "Time Is Standing Still." The project began with the Columbia University Players and was to have starred Henry Fonda, but Weill's music is far from his best, with only "Time Is Standing Still" viewed as an exception. The 2000 CD liner notes by Patrick O'Connor note that the production was to have been titled *One Man from Tennessee* and would cover Crockett's life from age 14 to his death at the Alamo. However, Weill dropped the project when he became distracted by a new one, *Knickerbocker Holiday*, which was produced in 1938 and included "September Song," one of Weill's most memorable compositions.[17]

More "Alamo romances" appeared too, such as "Alamo Serenade" by Eileen Pike. This 1938 love song makes a passing reference to the shrine as a place where one can find serenity, hardly the case for the Alamo defenders.

The first sound motion picture about the Alamo, *Heroes of the Alamo*, debuted in 1937. Although the low-budget offering lacks an original musical score, the defenders join in singing "The Yellow Rose of Texas" shortly before the battle. It did not trouble producer Anthony J. Xydias or director Henry Fraser that the song wasn't written until after the Texas Revolution; they had the Alamo defenders sing it anyway.[18]

In 1938, Bob Wills, the legendary western swing innovator who was born on the 69th anniversary of the Battle of the Alamo, recorded "San Antonio Rose" as an instrumental, which was released by Vocalion and later by Columbia. Irving Berlin then asked Wills to put words to the song and in 1940 he did (including a reference to the Alamo), recorded it, and released it on the Columbia label as "New San Antonio Rose." What distinguishes Wills' song from most

Words by DAVID STEVENS

Music by OSCAR J. FOX

C. C. Birchard & Company, Boston, Massachusetts

other Alamo-related love ballads which have nothing to do with the battle is that it became one of the biggest hits of its time and is still performed and recorded today.[19]

The Texas Sesquicentennial had generated widespread public consciousness about the Texas Revolution and its heroes. Juan Seguin, the famous Tejano Alamo courier and hero of San Jacinto, received the honor of having a town named after him in 1839. That municipal name was changed from Walnut Branch to Seguin and acknowledged in song a century later with "Seguin: A Centennial Song, 1838-1938," written by Jennie Hollamon and Rev. L. J. FitzSimon. But the song really addressed the town rather than its namesake. Unfortunately, Juan Seguin and the other Tejano heroes would languish in musical obscurity for much of the remaining 20th century.

In 1941, Roy Rogers, Hollywood's "King of the Cowboys," waxed the excellent western swing number "Down by the Old Alamo," written by Lew Potter and Johnny Lange. The movie hero left his six-shooters at home, however, as this is another romantic tune with no relevance to the battle.

World War II gave rise to a few new Alamo songs, including "The Alamo" by J. Meredith Tatton and arranged by David Stevens, published in 1942. Written for children, it encouraged American youngsters to not only remember the Alamo martyrs, but to shed tears for them as well.

Stevens collaborated with Oscar J. Fox in 1946 to produce "Sam Houston," one of several musical tributes to the Texas general, which, like many Alamo songs, suggests that these were flawless men, worthy of nothing less than complete respect. The Stevens-Fox sheet music assures listeners that "The swing of this easily learned song should help fix in the memory the name and some of the characteristics of a prominent son of Texas," and so it does, with over-the-top references to a larger-than-life Sam Houston.

Two years later Fox teamed with Evantha Caldwell to write "The Alamo," which appeared in a 1948 folio titled *Southern Secular Choral Music* and offered a familiar dose of hushed respect for Alamo martyrs. Fox, a native Texan who studied music in Switzerland, New York and Texas, is said to have never written lyrics, but composed musical arrangements for new works and many traditional cowboy poems, including "The Old Chisholm Trail," "Oh Bury Me Not on the Lone Prairie," and "The Cowboy's Lament." He served for ten years as choirmaster of the First Presbyterian Church in San Antonio, which may account for his Alamo inspiration.[20]

James N. Cooper and J. Schatenstein collaborated on a different song called "The Alamo" that same year, with lyrics that were virtually interchangeable with the Fox-Caldwell composition.

On the other hand, "Fightin' Flo from the Alamo" is surely one of the more bizarre Alamo songs. Written in 1944 by Lou Breese and the Baers, it was introduced in the Baers' vintage comic strip "The Toodle Family." It relates the adventures of a wolf-like woman who meets Dangerous Dave, but only one of its four stanzas refers to any fighting at the Alamo, and then only obliquely:

> The battle lights were all aglow
> The fight was on for the Alamo
> The night was dark, the sky aflame
> When up popped Dave with his fightin' dame.

"Fightin' Flo from the Alamo"
by Lou Breese and the Baers
Copyright 1944 Songs of Universal, Inc. (BMI)
Copyright renewed.
Used By Permission. All Rights Reserved.[21]

Popular songs continued to surround the Alamo, including two 1946 ditties, both bearing the title "Rose of the Alamo." The

first, written by George Lomas and Sophie & Julie Murray and recorded by Dick Thomas with Sante Fe Rangers, has nothing to do with Moses Rose, the man who allegedly left the Alamo prior to the battle, or anything else about the famous last stand.

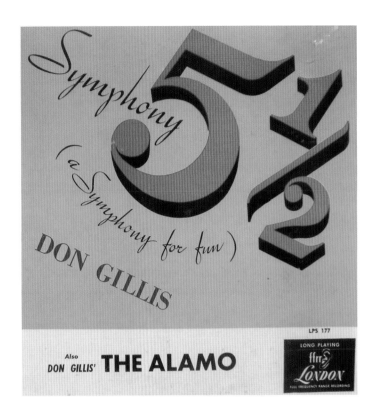

The second, a more uptempo number written by Billy Hughes, was recorded by several artists, including Chet Atkins with the Carter Sisters and Mother Maybelle, Rosalie Allen, Tex Williams & His Western Caravan, and Wesley Tuttle. Like its namesake, it says nothing about the battle.

Nor did "Across the Alley from the Alamo," penned by Joe Greene in 1947, which became as popular with big bands and vocalists as "On the Alamo." A classic example of swing era music, it was recorded by countless artists, notably the Mills Brothers, Woody Herman, Stan Kenton, country and western star Hank Thompson, and western swing maestro Bob Wills.

Don Gillis composed a tone poem titled *The Alamo* in 1947 as part of a trilogy that included *Portrait of a Frontier Town* and *Saga of a Prairie School (Symphony No. 7)*. Gillis dedicated *The Alamo* to "the people of the state of Texas" and described his composition as "an attempt to portray musically the deep feelings of emotion that arise in the contemplation of the heroism and courage expressed by the defenders of the Alamo as they gave their lives in their defense of freedom." The 13-minute piece lives up to that billing: it begins quietly, but builds in tension as it leads to the climactic battle. The music suggests both the open country that inspired the defenders, and the desperate claustrophobia of the siege. The piece underwent substantial revision before reaching its final form and premiered on March 6, 1949, performed by the San Antonio Symphony Orchestra conducted by Dr. Max Reiter. Gillis's recording of *The Alamo* with the New Symphony Orchestra was released in 1950 on a 10-inch LP that also included his *Symphony 5 1/2*. That recording, with the full trilogy, was released on CD by Vocalion; a stereo recording of the piece by Sinfonia Varsovia, conducted by Ian Hobson, was released on CD by Albany Records. An early version of the work was performed in 1942 by the Baylor University Band of Waco, Texas, led by Gid Waldrop. An unreleased 1961 recording of the piece by Dr. Joseph E. Maddy and the National High School Symphony Orchestra of Interlochen is housed at the North Texas State University library.[22]

Nineteen forty-seven saw the debut of "Santa Ana — Canción Rítmica," ("Santa Ana — Rhythmic Song") by Ricardo Fábrega, which had nothing to do with the Mexican tyrant, but was a Spanish-language ode to the composer's home town, Santiago de Veraguas, Panama.[23]

Pee Wee King's "Waltz of the Alamo," written in 1949, was in the same vein as "Across the Alley from the Alamo," although less successful. King recorded it with his Golden West Cowboys and it was waxed the same year by Ray Smith. "Beside the Alamo," written the same year by Charles Leont, is a western swing ballad about a romance in the shadow of the fortress; it was recorded by the 101 Ranch Boys and later by Jimmy Collett.

The 1950s would usher in the era of big Alamo movies and television programs, but the decade's second half began with a more modest effort called *The Fall of the Alamo*, written in 1951 by Samuel E. Asbury, who planned it as a stage musical. He published sheet music for three songs, each billed as part

of the larger work comprising a fictional *Song Book of Davy Crockett and His Minstrels*. However, "Gentlemen of Virginia," "The Valley of Humiliation" and "James Butler Bonham's Carolina Carol" have nothing to do with the Alamo, but are merely sung by Crockett and other Alamo defenders ("His Minstrels"), presumably during the siege. For example, "The Valley of Humiliation" is described by Asbury as "not an Alamo 'comeback' song, but a straight 'knock' by 'Davy Crockett and His Minstrels' at three states, Virginia, North Carolina and South Carolina." The work was never finished, although Asbury listed several more songs "in preparation" ("Ballad of the Honorable Williamses of Coneticute (sic)," "O Albert Martin, Albert Martin of Rhode Island," "The Honorable John Adams Defends His Friend, the Honorable Thomas Jefferson," "High Peaks of Glory," "For the Honor of Virginia" and "others"). However, Asbury added the disclaimer that "nothing is ever perfected; nothing is ever completed; so I have had photo-printed a hundred copies of this version of 'The Valley of Humiliation' to send free of charge to my friends for criticism, suggestions and comments." Apparently, response to the completed songs was not promising, or Asbury abandoned the project for other reasons.[24]

By mid-century, the Alamo had been used (and, perhaps abused) by composers of every sort. The old fortress had found itself the subject of historical tributes and martial salutes, but also as a most unlikely backdrop to romantic encounters and paeans to the city of San Antonio, as well as inspiration to classical composers and librettists. It also had seen service among country and western artists, and jazz and pop musicians of every persuasion. These years may have seemed a highpoint in the nation's continuing musical celebration of the Alamo, but it was all relatively minor compared to the future impact the Shrine of Texas Liberty would have on the national psyche — and on its music.

[1] Courtesy of DRT Library.

[2] From *The Folk Music Index* website:http://www.ibiblio.org/keefer/index.htm and: http://www.ibiblio.org/keefer/d03.htm#Davcr

[3] John F. Rios, (compiler and editor). *Readings on the Alamo* (New York/Washington/Atlanta Los Angeles/Chicago; Vantage Press, 1987), courtesy of the DRT Library; Texas Handbook Online: http://www.tshaonline.org/handbook/online/articles/ZZ/fzafg.html]

[4] From Lester S. Levy Collection of Sheet Music; http://levysheetmusic.mse.jhu.edu/otcgi/llscgi60.

[5] Summarized from Percy Wenrich — "The Joplin Kid"; http://parlorsongs.com/bios/pwenrich/pwenrich.asp.

[6] From *The Edison Phonograph Monthly*, v. 12 (1914); from the Todd Collection. One edition of 1914 sheet music features the names Clifton Lyons and Gertrude Selby, possibly singers who also recorded the song.

[7] "On the Alamo" was recorded by many artists, including Guy Lombardo, the Dave Brubeck Quartet, the Norman Petty Trio, The Al Cohn-Zoot Sims Quintet, the BBC Band, Benny Goodman, Betty Carter, Clark Terry, Dizzy Gillespie, Eddie Heywood, Frank Tate, George Masso & Ken Peplowski, Jerry Murad's Harmonicats, Tommy Dorsey, Jimmy Dorsey, Johnny Gimble, Les Brown and His Band of Renown, Louis Armstrong, Noel Boggs, Stan Getz, Wild Bill Davison, Eddie Getz, and Henry Busse. See R. Dethlefson, *Edison Blue Amberol Recordings*, v. 2 (1981). Artists often copyright their own arrangements to previously published songs, which can create confusion regarding original authorship. Various arrangements were made of "On the Alamo" by many artists. Examples are located in Special Collections, Performing Arts — Cylinder 6082 in the Donald C. Davidson Library at the University of California, Santa Barbara, as part of the Cylinder Digitization and Preservation Project Website (cylinders.library.ucsb.edu), which includes information about "On the Alamo" and "When It's Moonlight on the Alamo."

[8] "A Mixture of Yarns about Davy Crockett" (no author) *The Ozarks Mountaineer* (Vo. 40, Nos. 6&7; July/Aug 1992; Kirbyville, Mo.; 52-53).

[9] *Folk-songs du midi des Etats-Unis*; Paris: 1925; translation reprinted as *Folk-Songs of the Southern United States*, ed. D. K. Wilgus. Austin: Univ. of Texas Press/American Folklore Society, 1967, 182-83.

[10] It appeared in a Missouri collection compiled by Henry M. Belden in 1910, *Song-Ballads and Other Popular Poetry*, but had been collected in 1906 from C. H. Williams, who said he'd first heard it several years earlier.

[11] See Wolfe "Davy Crockett Songs," 168-169 for full text; also John Harrington Cox, *Folk-songs of the South* (Collected under the auspices of the West Virginia Folk-Lore Society; Dover Publications, Inc., N 1967; original ed. 1925). No. 177 is a version of "Davy Crockett"/"Pompey Smash," 494-500.

[12] Beazley also credited Mrs. Tom C. Rowe, also of Houston, who transcribed the music for the song, as sung by Mrs. Melton. Beazley's version was published in the *Texas Folk-Lore Society Publications* 6, (1927), 205-6, reprinted in Alan and John Lomax, eds., *American Ballads and Folk Songs* (New York: McMillan, 1934), 251-53; in B. A. Botkin, ed., *A Treasury of American Folklore* (New York: Crown, 1944), 15-16, and (New York: Bantam, 1980); in B.A. Botkin, ed., *The American People* (London: Pilot Press, 1946), 33; and in William Owens, *Texas Folk Songs* (Austin: Texas Folklore Society, 1950).

[13] V. Randolph; *Songs of the Ozarks*, 1982; Arthur Kyle Davis, Jr. *Folk-Songs of Virginia* (1949). Virginia Folklore Society Collection, Univ. of Virginia., Charlottesville.

[14] William A. Owens; musical transcriptions by Jessie Ann Owens; *Texas Folk Songs* (SMU Press, Dallas, 1950; second edition 1976). Also, William A. Owens, *Texas Folk Songs; Musical Arrangements by Willa Mae Kelly Koehn* (Austin; Texas Folklore Society, University Press in Dallas; 1950). Other texts appear in Randolph Vance's *Ozark Mountain Folks* (New York: Vanguard , 1932), 138-39, and his *Ozark Folk Songs Vol. 3* (Columbia: University of Missouri Press, 1949), 165-67.

[15] Booth Tucker, *One Hundred Favorite Songs of the Salvation Army* (1893).

[16] "Old Performer Sends Greetings to the Alamo, Set to Music," *San Antonio Express* (March 6, 1937), 16 (Courtesy DRT Library).

[17] From Classics Today.com http://www.classicstoday.com/review.asp?ReviewNum=1548; The Kurt Weill website, (http://www.kwf.org/pages/kw/kwchron5.html); The Papers of Kurt Weill and Lotte Lenya in the Irving S. Gilmore Music Library of Yale University and website http://webtext.library.yale.edu/xml2html/Music/kw_nd.htm; the Library of Congress holds "Davy Crockett" — Kurt Weill; sketches; "Letter to Davy Crockett" sheet music for *Davy Crockett*; a projected folk opera; photo copy of holograph. This is draft sheet music dated "[1939?]" in pencil. There are a few penciled words in various places on the sheet music, which are very difficult to read. One appears to say "I'll cook the taters."

[18] The first copyrighted edition of "The Yellow Rose of Texas" was published in New York in 1858. The sheet music cover notes that the tune was "Composed and Arranged Expressly for Charles H. Brown by J.K." *Heroes of the Alamo* credits: Mary Daggett Lake and William J. Marsh of Fort Worth, Texas; copyright owners who gave the production company special permission to use the song.

[19] Bob Wills website: www.bobwills.com

[20] *Handbook Of Texas Online* (http://www.tshaonline.org/handbook/online/articles/FF/ffo26.html); *Daily Texan*, October 18, 1925. *Dallas Morning News*, July 30, 1961. *San Antonio Express*, December 8, 1931. Lota M. Spell, *Music in Texas* (Austin, 1936; rpt., New York: AMS, 1973); Armitage, et al, *Our Land of Song*.

[21] Sheet music courtesy of the Cunningham Memorial Library; Indiana State University Library Services.

[22] See the University of North Texas Libraries website: http://www.library.unt.edu/music/special_collections/don_gillis/tape_transcripts#23_symphonic_poem_the; and the Audiofile Audition website: http://www.audaud.com/article.php?ArticleID=1474

[23] Translation courtesy of Tom Kailbourn; also see website: http://mensual.prensa.com/mensual/contenido/2003/02/09/hoy/revista/871841.html

[24] Sheet music and notes courtesy of the DRT Library.

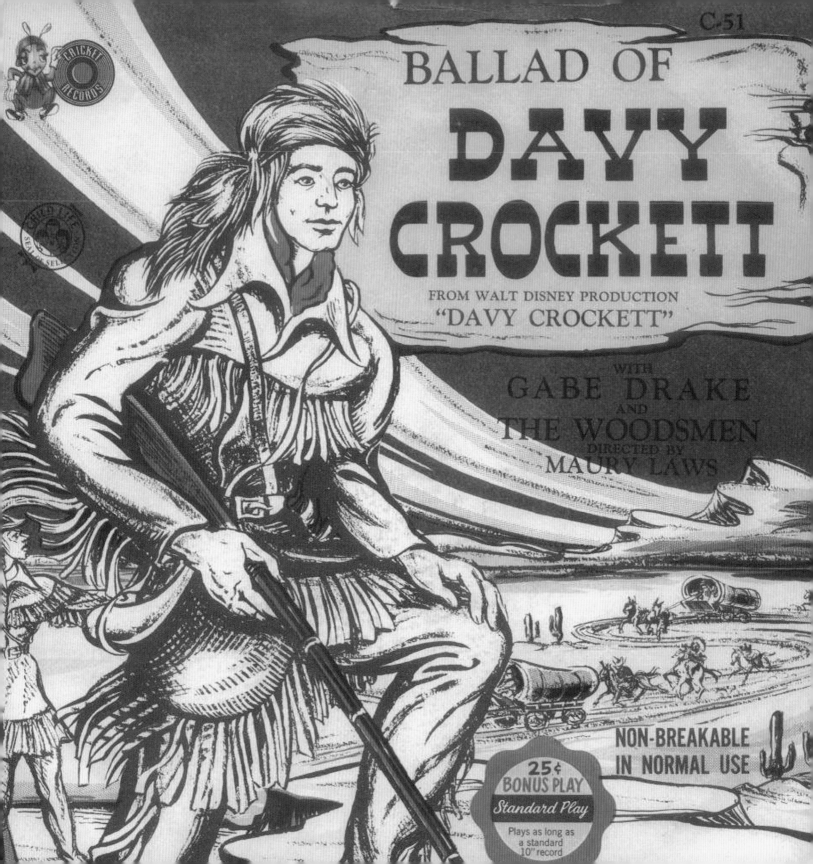

"THE BALLAD OF DAVY CROCKETT"

He heard of Houston and Austin an' so
To the Texas plains he jest had to go.
Where Freedom was fightin' another foe,
An' they needed him at the Alamo
Davy, Davy Crockett, the man
who don't know fear

The Ballad of Davy Crockett
from Walt Disney's DAVY CROCKETT
Words by Tom Blackburn
Music by George Bruns
©1954 Wonderland Music Co., Inc.
Copyright Renewed
All Rights Reserved Used by permission

ON FEBRUARY 23, 1955, the 119th anniversary of the Battle of the Alamo, yet another generation of Americans was introduced to the Shrine of Texas Liberty thanks to "Davy Crockett at the Alamo," the third episode in Walt Disney's enormously popular "Davy Crockett" series on the *Disneyland* television show.

The three-part trilogy, TV's first mini-series — "Davy Crockett, Indian Fighter;" "Davy Crockett Goes to Congress;" and "Davy Crockett at the Alamo" — starred Fess Parker as Davy Crockett and Buddy Ebsen as his guitar-playing sidekick, Georgie Russel.

The most pervasive characteristic of the entire series was "The Ballad of Davy Crockett," a tune that was sung from coast to coast — and eventually around the world — by every kid wearing a coonskin cap and toting a plastic flintlock rifle. When the series became the surprise hit of the decade, followed by an unprecedented merchandising bonanza, the song became its most familiar and ubiquitous byproduct. It was a biographical tale of Crockett that traced his life in 20 easy-on-the-ears verses. Surprisingly, the song wasn't originally planned for the production, but Disney believed that some sort of musical transitional pieces were needed to connect the diverse action scenes.

"When the first rushes started coming back from the Creek Indian War episode, we noticed that the transition between scenes wasn't as smooth as we had liked," said screenwriter Tom Blackburn. "So something had to be done, something like a narration bridge — but set to music. I started writing lyrics to what was to become 'The Ballad of Davy Crockett' by looking at the daily footage. I made up the first few verses right away and took them over to George Bruns, who came up with the melody."[1]

Blackburn brought a copy of the song home for his wife and daughter to hear. "When I first played a tape of the song to my family, they laughed," said Blackburn. "But when they each got a brand new car from that song a few months later, they didn't laugh anymore."[2]

After Fess Parker was signed by Disney to portray Crockett he was quickly sent to the recording studio. "When the sheet music was first presented to me to take a look at, I noticed that my name was spelled F-E-Z at the top of the page," said

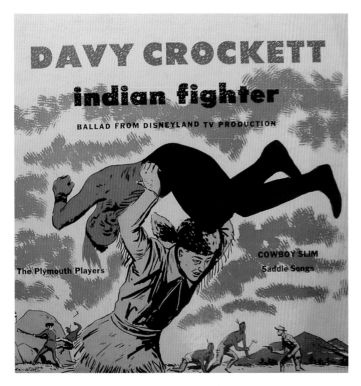

Many story records relating Crockett's adventures were released in the wake of the Disney "Crockett Craze," including a series by the Plymouth Players.

Parker, who still has the misspelled sheet music. "Obviously, I wasn't exactly a household word at that time."[3]

Parker's original recording of the song, on which he was backed by the Gus Norman Singers, was never released commercially, but was issued as a promotional single distributed to radio stations. The flip side was "Lonely," a song written by Parker which also remains unreleased. The TV series' success, and Parker's sudden stardom, brought him back into the studio to record a new version of the Crockett ballad, which was released.

To some observers the Crockett series and "The Ballad of Davy Crockett" reflected Cold War sentiments. The song contains strong patriotic references such as answering "his country's call" and "freedom...fightin' another foe."

"It was just the opposite," said Blackburn. "For me, the country was basically unchanged, despite efforts by the likes of the House [of Representatives] Committee on Un-American Activities. I merely attempted to take one part of American history and make it into a story."[4]

The song was first performed by Fess Parker on the debut broadcast of the new *Disneyland* TV program on October 27, 1954. Introduced by Walt Disney, the show featured a segment in which Parker, costumed as Davy Crockett, delivered the catchy tune while playing a guitar at a studio-created frontier log cabin. Parker was accompanied by three other pioneer-looking backup musician-vocalists.

The actual title of the song, as printed on the sheet music cover in 1954, was "The Ballad of Davy Crockett: His Early Life, Hunting Adventures, Services Under General Jackson In The Creek War, Electioneering Speeches, Career In Congress, Triumphal Tour In The Northern States, And Services In The Texan War." Obviously, there was only so much space on a 45 rpm single's label so the lengthy title was logically shortened to "The Ballad of Davy Crockett." And since the song's original 20 verses would never fit on a 45 rpm or a 78 rpm single, most artists selected a few key verses when they recorded it. Fred Waring and the Pennsylvanians, however, did record all 20 verses on a British single, also released on the U.S. LP *A Visit to Disneyland.*

All the recorded versions included the memorable first verse: "Born on a mountain top in Tennessee/Greenest state in the

The first of several LP editions of audio recordings of the original Disney Crockett television adventures, with Fess Parker and Buddy Ebsen reprising their roles.

CL 666

Columbia

LP

WALT DISNEY'S DAVY CROCKETT
KING OF THE WILD FRONTIER!

Featuring
FESS PARKER and BUDDY EBSEN

From the soundtrack of Walt Disney's
Technicolor motion picture,
"DAVY CROCKETT
King of the Wild Frontier"

The
ORIGINAL STORIES
from Television and
Motion Picture!

Land of the Free/Raised in the woods so's he knew ev'ry tree/ kilt him a b'ar when he was only three." But it was the hook-laden chorus — "Davy, Davy Crockett, King of the wild frontier" — that captured the musical imagination of every young listener.

The Ballad of Davy Crockett

from Walt Disney's DAVY CROCKETT

Words by Tom Blackburn

Music by George Bruns

©1954 Wonderland Music Co., Inc.

Copyright Renewed

All Rights Reserved Used by permission

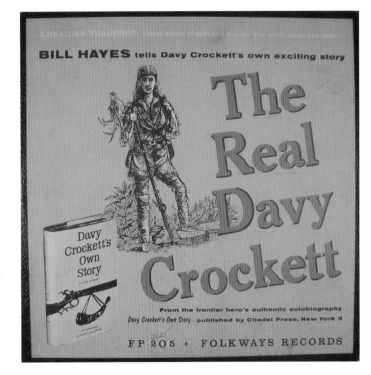

At first, Disney didn't realize the hit potential of the song. But other music entrepreneurs did.

"Archie Bleyer of Cadence Records asked Disney if he could lease the song for his label's release," said Parker. "He did, of course, and he had a very big hit with it."[5] Bleyer signed Bill Hayes to record the song, and it became the most popular version. The flip side of the record was "Farewell," a poignant ballad supposedly based upon a poem written by Davy Crockett and featured in "Davy Crockett at the Alamo." Once again, composer George Bruns added the music.

Within weeks of its release in early 1955, sales of the song started to register on the popular music charts of the day. *Billboard* magazine did not publish its "Top 100 Record Sides" until November of 1955. Prior to that, the weekly music publication printed shorter rosters of recordings that included "Best Sellers in Stores," "Most Played in Jukeboxes" and "Most Played by Jockeys."

"The Ballad of Davy Crockett" by Bill Hayes broke onto the "Best Sellers in Stores" roster of 30 singles at the number 16 position on February 26, making it the highest debuting song of the survey week which actually ended on February 16. A week earlier *Billboard* proclaimed: "Not since Joan Weber's 'Let Me Go, Lover' has a record taken off with the excitement sparked by this disk since being introduced on

a recent TV show."[6] The next week, his recording reached number nine, edging out "Earth Angel" by the Penguins on the top ten list.

Hayes, like most of the artists who covered the song, was restricted by the time available on a 45 rpm record and only recorded selected verses of the Blackburn-Bruns composition. He competently delivered five verses of the song and, in its third week on the charts, his rendition climbed to number six. That same week Parker's recording debuted, backed with "I Gave My Love," on Columbia Records in the number 16 slot. A promotional record of Parker's recording also was issued, b/w "Farewell" on the Buena Vista label. Later, Columbia Records issued Parker's version of "Farewell" backed with "I'm Lonely My Darlin' (Green Grow the Lilacs)." Parker said that the scene from "Davy Crockett at the Alamo" in which he sang "Farewell" was his favorite part of the episode. "The singing of 'Farewell' by Crockett and the men of the Alamo on the night before the final battle is a

Farewell to the mountains whose mazes to me
Were more beautiful far than Eden could be;
No fruit was forbidden, but Nature had spread
Her bountiful board, and her children were fed.
The bills were our garners — our herds wildly grew,
And Nature was shepherd and husbandman too.
I felt like a monarch, yet thought like a man,
As I thank'd the Great Giver, and worshipp'd his plan.

The home I forsake where my offspring arose:
The graves I forsake where my children repose.
The home I redeem'd from the savage and wild;
The home I have loved as a father his child;
The corn that I planted, the fields that I clear'd,
The flocks that I raised, and the cabin I rear'd;
The wife of my bosom — Farewell to ye all!
In the land of the stranger I rise — or I fall.

Farewell to my country! — I fought for thee well.
When the Savage rush'd forth like the demons from hell.
In peace or in war I have stood by thy side —
My country, for thee I have lived — would have died!
But I am cast off — my career now is run,
And I wander abroad like the prodigal son —
Where the wild savage roves, and the broad prairies spread,
The fallen — despised — will again go ahead!

scene that immediately comes to mind," said Parker. "It was a poignant moment for those men who were about to die. I think the scene was well done."[7]

Parker, on guitar, begins the song and is then joined by Ebsen and some of the other defenders. It is a pensive scene, delicately directed by Norman Foster. The music was written by George Bruns and the lyrics were credited to Crockett, but the words were actually written by 19th century playwright and author Richard Penn Smith: "Farewell to the mountains whose mazes to me/more beautiful far than Eden could be/The home I redeemed from the savage and wild/The home I have loved as a father his child/The wife of my bosom/Farewell to ye all/In the land of the stranger I rise or I fall."

The original poem appeared in *Col. Crockett's Exploits and Adventures in Texas*, which purported to be Crockett's own account of his Texas adventures, but actually was ghost written by Smith. It is both longer and more melancholy than the film adaptation:

On March 5, *Billboard* reported: "Despite the fact that Bill Hayes' version of this tune got off to an early lead, the demand for the 'original' (Parker's record) has continued to be so strong that it seems likely to follow the Cadence disk on the charts."[8]

DAVY CROCKETT

Autobiography read by Bill Hayes

Folkways Records FC 7125

Besides its climb on the "Best Sellers in Stores" chart, Hayes' "The Ballad of Davy Crockett" also made its mark for the first time on the "Most Played in Juke Boxes" roster and the "Most Played by Jockeys" list on March 12. The next week, Hayes reached number three, Parker climbed to number 11 and Tennessee Ernie Ford entered the charts with his version of the song on Capitol Records.

Five weeks after its release, Bill Hayes' recording topped the *Billboard* charts on March 26; the Fess Parker version rose to number seven and the Tennessee Ernie Ford cover climbed to number 17.

For the next four weeks, Bill Hayes topped the "Best Sellers in Stores" charts; in fact, his version topped all three *Billboard* charts on April 23. All of the versions received a promotional boost when Walt Disney rebroadcast the episodes on April 13, April 27, and May 11.

Fess Parker's version peaked at number five and Ford's recording climbed as high as number seven. Even Walter

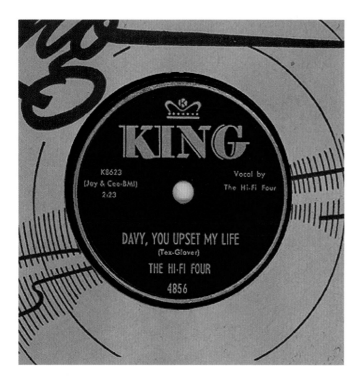

Schumann's rendition on RCA Victor broke into the charts at number 29 and managed to climb to number 14 on *Billboard's* "Most Played by Jockeys" roster.

The practice of covering other artists' songs was popular in the 1950s. As long as the authors of the song were credited on the record label, artists could record their own version of another performer's song. On some occasions, the cover version managed to out perform the original recording. For example, Pat Boone's cover of Fats Domino's "Ain't That a Shame" and the Crew-Cuts' version of the Chords' "Sh-Boom" both topped the charts. Only several songs in the 1950s managed to spawn as many as four or five different versions that charted in the same year. In 1955, only "The Ballad of Davy Crockett" and Les Baxter's "Unchained Melody" managed to top the record charts and also generate three additional top 40 versions.[9]

Other artists joined "The Ballad of Davy Crockett" bandwagon en masse. Subsequent cover versions were recorded by the likes of Gabe Drake and the Woodsman, The Sandpipers, the Sons of the Pioneers, Bill Hart with the Mountaineer Boys and Orchestra, Tommy Scott, Steve Allen, Burl Ives, Rusty Draper, James Brown and the Trailwinders, Mac Wiseman, Jack Richards with the Corwin Group, Jack Andrews, the Rhythmaires, Vincent Lopez and the Forty-Niners among many others. Derby Foods' Peter Pan Peanut Butter offered a Sandpipers' version of "The Ballad of Davy Crockett" for 25 cents and "any part of a Peter Pan Peanut Butter label" to kids who wanted background dining music.

Across the Atlantic, the song was recorded by Gary Miller with Tony Osborne and his orchestra and the Beryl Stott Chorus on Great Britain's Pye records label. Jacques Helian (Trianon) and Serge Singer (RCA) later added their French-language versions to the growing stack of vinyl releases.

The popularity of the Davy Crockett series was so enormous that some singers who covered "The Ballad of Davy Crockett" became even more famous simply by recording the song. Bill Hayes and Burl Ives, for example, made successful promotional tours around the United States. [10]

Even novelty versions of the song were recorded, like Mickey Katz' "Duvid Crockett," Homer and Jethro's "The Ballad of Davy Crew-Cut," Bob Campbell's "Dizzy Crockett," and the Irving Fields Trio's "Davy Crockett Mambo." The most successful offbeat version was Lalo Guerrero's "Pancho Lopez."

Other curious recordings followed including "The Ballad of Davy Crockett" by Pinky and Perky, identified on the record sleeve as a pair of friendly toy pigs, and "Davy Crockett," performed by a no-frills hand-puppet called Seymour!

Additional Davy Crockett music fed public demand with the release of "Be Sure You're Right (Then Go Ahead)" backed with "Old Betsy." "Be Sure You're Right," a musical moral about Crockett's famous motto, was written by Fess Parker and Buddy Ebsen. The flip side, "Old Betsy," written by Gil George (George was actually Hazel Gilman George, a Disney Studio nurse and songwriter.) and George Bruns, was a safety-first testament to Crockett's most famous rifle. Besides the Fess Parker and Buddy Ebsen Columbia Records release, Jimmie Dodd and the Frontier Men recorded the songs for Golden Records.

Added to the musical mix was a three-record, boxed set (in both 45 and 78 rpm editions) offered by Columbia Records featuring studio dramatizations of the three episodes: "Davy Crockett, Indian Fighter," "Davy Crockett Goes to Congress" and "Davy Crockett at the Alamo," with Parker and Ebsen recreating their roles.

The release of *Davy Crockett, King of the Wild Frontier* in theaters in May of 1955 gave legs to all the recordings. The three most popular cover versions remained together on the charts until July 2. Bill Hayes and Tennessee Ernie Ford's versions stayed on the "Best Sellers in Stores" charts until July 9 when "Rock Around the Clock" by Bill Haley and His Comets topped the charts and unofficially launched the rock and roll era. Yet, the Tennessee Ernie Ford rendition of the Blackburn-Bruns composition remained on the "Most Played in Juke Boxes" chart until July 23.

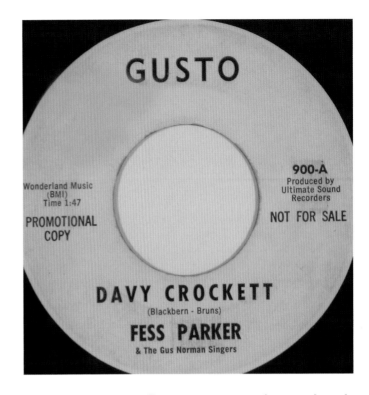

Rare promotional record with Fess Parker's first, unreleased version of "The Ballad of Davy Crockett," which he would record three more times.

Incredibly, "The Ballad of Davy Crockett" entered the national record charts on February 26, 1955, three days after "Davy Crockett at the Alamo" aired on TV, and remained on the vinyl roster in one version or another for over five months! The song's lengthy track record on the charts created quite a challenge for the musical cast of *Your Hit Parade*, a weekly TV program that featured performances of the nation's top hits. Week after week, regulars like Snooky Lanson and Russell Arms wore coonskin caps and sang the popular song. Over and over. The program used traditional frontier and western backdrop scenarios so frequently for its singers that it resorted to all kinds of substitute sets as the song continued to maintain its strong chart position. For example, on May 7, 1955 program regular Giselle MacKenzie sang the song as she acted as a kind of elementary school art teacher. A young boy dressed as Davy Crockett stood by as his four classmates drew his picture.

The rarest Davy Crockett recording was a 1955 U.S. Treasury Department radio transcription disc that promoted U.S. Savings Bonds via the federal government's 15-minute *Guest Star* program. Hosted by Del Sharbutt, program #433 starred Fess Parker and featured the George Bruns Orchestra.

This special program featured a recording of Parker's October 27, 1954 *Disneyland* TV show performance of "The Ballad of Davy Crockett" and three other recordings, "Farewell," "I Gave My Love (The Riddle Song)" and "I'm Lonely My Darlin' (Green Grow the Lilacs)." In between the songs, Parker endorses the purchasing of bonds: "Believe me, there's no surer way to make your dreams come true than to plan for them with savings bonds." The program ends with an abbreviated chorus of the previously-played "Ballad of Davy Crockett."

The Recording Industry Association of America (RIAA) only began its certification of "gold" records in 1958. At the time, a "gold" single represented sales of one million or more units. Technically, none of the versions of "The Ballad of Davy Crockett" qualified for precious metal status, although the Bill Hayes and Fess Parker versions each sold millions. A year later, Parker recorded another version of the song and included it on his Disneyland LP *Yarns and Songs*. And in 1964, Parker recorded yet another rendition of the tune — a lively, uptempo interpretation featuring spirited fiddle work — for the RCA LP *Great American Heroes*.

Additional lyrics appear in the televised production but not in the published sheet music. For example, in the final moments of "Davy Crockett at the Alamo," viewers hear the lyrics tell that the Alamo defenders were "all cut low" but their spirits will live on as long as the Alamo is remembered. "I never wrote that verse," said Blackburn. "That was added by some others on the Disney team to end the film."[11] In actuality, nine lyrical

passages were added to complete the production's musical track.[12]

By the end of the decade, American advisers would be stationed in South Vietnam — a place where the Eisenhower Administration believed "freedom was fightin' another foe." Ironically, as the war escalated in the 1960s, many of the coonskin-cap wearing youngsters who fought invisible Creek warriors and Mexican soldados in their backyards found themselves in the jungles of Southeast Asia. "They needed" Davy Crockett. And he came. Fess Parker, then starring as TV's *Daniel Boone*, made a number of visits to American troops and was warmly welcomed.[13]

Parker went on to make more records for Disney, including "Wringle Wrangle," a song written by Stan Jones for the 1956 motion picture *Westward Ho, The Wagons*, which starred Parker. The flip side, "The Ballad of John Colter," was another Blackburn-Bruns collaboration. Parker's recording reached number 12 on February 23, 1957, two years after "Davy Crockett at the Alamo" aired on national TV. And Parker finally topped Bill Hayes, whose cover of "Wringle Wrangle" peaked at only number 33 on the charts.

In 1968, jazz great Louis Armstrong contributed a delightful version of "The Ballad of Davy Crockett" on his *Disney Songs the Satchmo Way* LP. A year later, while Fess Parker was portraying Daniel Boone on NBC TV, Disneyland Records reminded listeners that he was still Davy Crockett courtesy of the LP *Cowboy and Indian Songs*. The album featured one of Parker's renditions of "The Ballad of Davy Crockett."

Since 1955, musical performers from all over the world have recorded versions of "The Ballad of Davy Crockett," some in foreign languages. Such diverse artists as Dean Shostak, Moose and the Pelicans, the Kentucky Headhunters, Riders in the Sky, Douchka, Arne Bendiksen, Asleep at the Wheel and many more have added their names to the scores of performers who previously recorded the song.

One of the most captivating and sincere versions of the song recorded since the mid-50s Crockett Craze is a 1985 rendi-

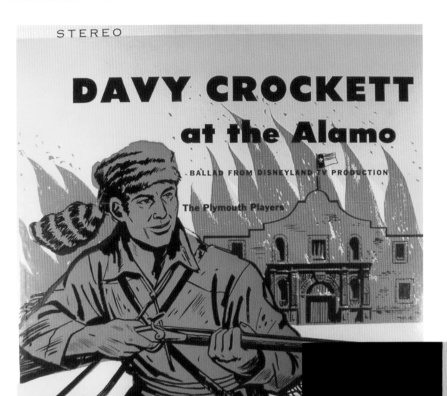

STEREO

DAVY CROCKETT
at the Alamo

BALLAD FROM DISNEYLAND TV PRODUCTION

The Plymouth Players

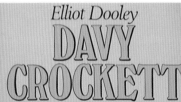

ILLUSTRATED CLASSICS
33⅓ RPM

C8R 207   SIDE 2

DAVY CROCKETT

MADE IN U.S.A.
ILLUSTRATED CLASSICS
P.O. BOX 5096, NEWARK, N.J.

Elliot Dooley

DAVY CROCKETT

King Classics

tion on the *Taste of the Phabulous Pheromones* LP. The band's Jim Luft introduces the song with a narrated passage that decries "political graft and corruption" and "nuclear warfare."[14] The group's restrained dirge-like folk version of the song is preceded with a wishful thought from Luft: "what we need is a hero who we can all look up to."[15]

As recently as 2007, "The Ballad of Davy Crockett" appeared on *American Music Legends Presents Walt Disney*, an exclusive 10-track collection produced and manufactured for the Cracker Barrel Old Country Store chain. The Mellomen version from 1954 is included on the CD, although the vocal group, which performed the song in the original TV series, is uncredited.

"The Ballad of Davy Crockett" remains the most popular song ever associated with the Alamo or any of its participants. And it remains one of the all-time popular recordings with estimated sales at over ten million. It's an iconic tune that not only recalls the 1950s, but represents a time when an historical hero was enthusiastically embraced by the young.

"King of the Wild Frontier," indeed.

[1] Bill Chemerka, "The Fess Parker Interview (Part One)," *The Alamo Journal* 57 (Sept. 1987), 5.

[2] Ibid.

[3] Ibid.

[4] Bill Chemerka, "The Fess Parker Interview (Part Two)," *The Alamo Journal* 58 (Nov. 1987), 6.

[5] Ibid., 4

[6] Joel Whitburn, *Joel Whitburn Presents The Billboard Pop Charts: 1955-1959* (Menomonee, WI, 1992), Feb. 19, 1955, 42.

[7] William R. Chemerka, *The Davy Crockett Almanac and Book of Lists* (Austin, TX, 2000), 170.

[8] Whitburn, March 5, 1955, 26.

[9] Joel Whitburn, *The Billboard Book of Top 40 Hits: 1955 to present*, (New York, 1983), 307. Other songs from the 1950s to chart at least four versions within the same year include "Banana Boat Song," "It's Almost Tomorrow," "Mack the Knife," theme from "Man With the Golden Arm," "Melody of Love" and "Nuttin' for Christmas."

[10] "U.S. Again Is Subdued By Davy," *Life* magazine, April 25, 1955, 30-31.

[11] *Alamo Journal* 58 (Nov. 1987), 4.

[12] Peder Gustawson, "The (Complete!) Ballad of Davy Crockett," *The Alamo Journal* 76 (April, 1991), 15-17.

[13] "Talkin With Fess," *The Crockett Chronicle* 19 (Feb. 2008), 9. A letter from a Vietnam vet to Fess Parker stated: "You have my enduring gratitude for bringing smiles and a little bit of home to all of us. Your selflessness and caring are still remembered to this day."

[14] Ironically, Davy Crockett became part of the American nuclear arsenal in 1956. The U.S. government manufactured the *Davy Crockett*, a relatively light-weight, surface-to-surface nuclear missile between 1956 and 1963. See William R. Chemerka, *The Davy Crockett Almanac and Book of Lists* (Austin, TX, 2000), 95-96.

[15] The Phabulous Pheromones were Mat Kastner (guitar and vocals), Jim Luft (violin and vocals), Cliff Furnald (guitar, mandolin and vocals) and Bobo Lavorgna (bass). Kastner currently plays in The Bluelights. In a previous incarnation, the band was described by Alamo artist and songwriter ("The Alamo") Eric von Schmidt as "the best since Kweskin's Jug Band in the sixties."

THE MOVIE & TV SOUNDTRACK ERA

In the southern part of Texas
near the town of San Antone,
Stands a fortress all in ruins
that the weeds have overgrown
You may look in vain for crosses
and you'll never see a one,
But sometimes between the setting
and the rising of the sun,
You can hear a ghostly bugle
as the men go marching by
You can hear them as they answer
To that roll call in the sky.

"The Ballad of the Alamo"
by Dimitri Tiomkin and Paul Webster
© 1960 Volta Music Corp./Webster Music Co.
Copyright renewed.
All rights for Volta Music Corp. administered
by Universal Music Corp. (ASCAP)
Used By Permission. All Rights Reserved.

WALT DISNEY'S "DAVY CROCKETT" CRAZE swept the nation in 1955. The "Ballad of Davy Crockett" stayed on the record charts for nearly half a year, — from February 26 until July 9 — but there was still more Alamo music to come. Before the year was out, another Alamo movie hit the big screen when *The Last Command* was released in theaters on August 3, 1955.

The Last Command was a "B" movie that had an "A" movie soundtrack. The Republic film, directed by Frank Lloyd and starring Sterling Hayden as Jim Bowie, featured a score composed and conducted by legendary Hollywood music man Max Steiner of *King Kong, Gone with the Wind* and *Casablanca* fame. Steiner had some previous experience writing original music for Alamo heroes. He created the original score for *The Iron Mistress*, the 1952 film about Jim Bowie.

The film begins with a title song, "(What a Man was Six-Foot-Six) Jim Bowie," performed off-screen by Gordon MacRae. The tune, written by Steiner, with lyrics penned by Sidney Clare and Sheila MacRae, reflects the fact that the production is essentially a Jim Bowie movie; Arthur Hunnicutt's Davy Crockett and Richard Carlson's William Travis are supporting players. MacRae's bold vocal delivery is punctuated with martial-like brass licks that properly introduce Bowie's bold image. The lyrics, which clearly suggest that Bowie was not someone to be challenged and was a man who was willing to make the ultimate sacrifice, were seen by some as a reflection of the posture of the United States during the first full decade of the Cold War.

What a man was six-foot-six Jim Bowie
Not a man would face the Bowie Knife
As a man he never wanted praise nor glory
But to stand and take the Last Command

JIM BOWIE (from "The Last Command")
Words and Music by SHEILA MACRAE, SIDNEY CLARE
    and MAX STEINER
© 1983 (renewed) CHAPPEL & Co., INC.
All rights reserved. Used by permission of ALFRED PUBLISHING CO., INC.

Steiner's music is such a strong component of *The Last Command*, particularly the pulsating passages that underscore the final attack on the Alamo, that it sometimes rivals the performances of the cast. For example, the composer's interpretation of the *degüello*, the Mexican bugle call for no quarter, is so eerily delivered in layers of trumpet lines that the Alamo defenders seem to react more to the music than to the armed Mexicans outside as they accept the inevitability of the final assault. "It gives me the shivers," says Hunnicutt to Hayden.

But *The Last Command* was not a rousing success at the box office. Its lively soundtrack was soon forgotten by many and it would not be released on record until 1980, although MacRae's recording of the theme was issued as a single in 1955. Simply put, *The Last Command*'s fate was the same as that of other "B" movies of the 1950s, which were losing audiences to the rapid growth of television.

Meanwhile, over at Disney Studios, "Davy Crockett at the Alamo" may have seemed like the end of Fess Parker's coonskin-cap wearing hero, but the performer returned to TV and the big screen courtesy of "Davy Crockett's Keelboat Race" and "Davy Crockett and the River Pirates." TV's first prequels were subsequently edited into the 1956 big-screen release *Davy Crockett and The River Pirates*. Coinciding with the picture's release was Parker's Columbia Records single with two new songs from these adventures, "King of the River" b/w "Yaller Yaller Gold." However, the disc failed to chart, although the songs were recorded by other artists as well.

Disney was not finished with Crockett either and released the LP *Davy Crockett de Walt Disney* in France in 1956, a French-language adaptation of the Disney series read by Francois Perier with Serge Reggiani in the role of Davy Crockett, Jacques Provins as Georgie Russel, Michel Mery as Norton and Christian Gentil as Jackson. The music was composed by Maurice Jarre, the composer of such film scores as *Lawrence of Arabia*, *Doctor Zhivago* and *The Longest Day*. It is interesting to hear the story read in French, with a French-speaking Davy, and a French rendition of "The Ballad of Davy Crockett," sung by Olivier Jeanes. The LP was released in Canada in 1967.

Alamo music got a small screen boost thanks to the TV series *The Adventures of Jim Bowie*, which debuted on Sept. 7, 1956. Ironically, the TV series' title tune, "Jim Bowie," was written by big-screen composer-conductor Ken Darby who had won Oscars® for *The King and I*, *Porgy and Bess*, and *Camelot*. Unfortunately, Darby's male vocal group arrangements, performed by the King's Men, frequently interrupt the action of star Scott Forbes and his fellow performers with ungainly harmonic chants that underscore many scenes. Still, "Jim Bowie" is superior to the version used in the series' pilot episode, "Natural Man, Jim Bowie," in which the famous knife fighter's last name is mispronounced as "*bow*-ee" (as in pop

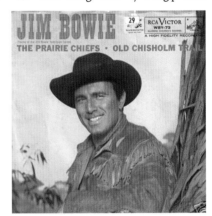

singer David Bowie), rather than the proper "*boo*-ee." Recordings by the Prairie Chiefs and Mitch Miller with the Sandpipers did nothing to enhance the song's appeal and, if anything, were worse than the TV version. In any event, *The Adventures of Jim Bowie* kept this song about one of the most famous Alamo defenders playing until May 23, 1958, when the series ended.

Another Alamo hero, William Barret Travis, received a musical acknowledgement in 1956 thanks to Robert L. (Bob) Travis, who wrote an unpublished and unrecorded tune about his namesake. However, Travis' biographical salute to the Alamo commander is undermined by a few errors, including the incorrect spelling of the famous officer's middle name: "Col. William *Barrat* Travis."

One of the most familiar original songs about the Alamo battle and mythology was penned in 1955 by Jane Bowers (nee Jane Gardner Riley). Bowers' song captures most of the legendary set pieces of the Alamo story, including its major figures, the garrison's grim determination, and the line that Travis is said to have drawn before his men, offering them the choice of fighting to the death or attempting escape.

> A hundred and eighty were challenged by Travis to die
> By the line that he drew with his sword when
>   the battle was nigh.
> "The man who will fight to the death, cross over;
>   but him who would live better fly."
> And over the line went a hundred and seventy nine.
>
> Though Bowie lay dyin', his powder was ready and dry.
> From flat on his back, Bowie killed him a few in reply.
> And brave Davy Crockett was singin' and laughin',
> With gallantry fierce in his eye,
> For God and for freedom, a man more than willin' to die.

They sent a young scout thru the battlements
    bloody and loud
With words of farewell from a garrison valiant and proud.
"Grieve not, little darlin', my dyin';
    if Texas is sov'reign and free,
We'll never surrender and ever with liberty be.

Chorus
Ae-ee, Santa Anna
We're killing your soldiers below
That men wherever they go
Will remember the Alamo

Bowers had registered a copyright for an earlier version of this song under the title "Legend of the Alamo" on March 21, 1955. The title was changed to "Remember the Alamo" and the lyrics revised a few months later when the song was published by Vidor Publications, a music publishing company established by Tex Ritter and Johnny Bond that year. It is, thus, not surprising that Ritter was the first to record the song, or that his version is closest to Bowers' original lyrics. Ironically, Vidor's copyright changed Bowers' original line "*young* Davy Crockett" to "*brave* Davy Crockett," but Ritter used the original line on his recording anyway, although Crockett was nearly 50 when he died at the Alamo. The original version also added a "Prelude: Alamo, and the stubborn band that stood in the path of invasion," which was omitted from all recordings. Although Bowers is still listed as the song's composer, it is likely that Ritter and/or Bond suggested the new lyrics for the recording and that Bowers accepted them. The label from Ritter's original Capitol Records single notes that the song is "From the Warner Brothers Production *Down Freedom Road*," although the film, released in 1956, starring Ritter and Angie Dickinson, was actually titled *Down Liberty Road*, and also appeared under the title *Freedom Highway*.

Development of Jane Bowers' "Remember The Alamo"

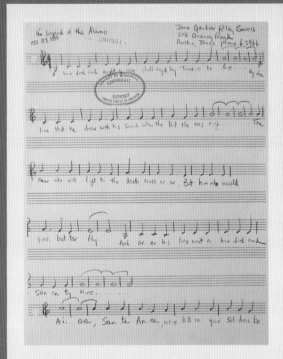

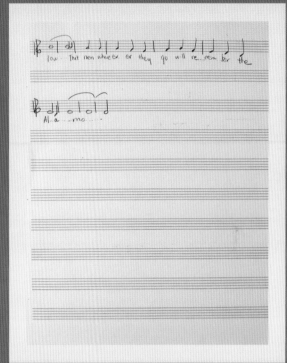

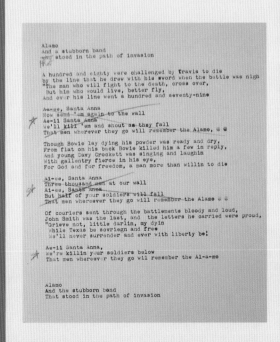

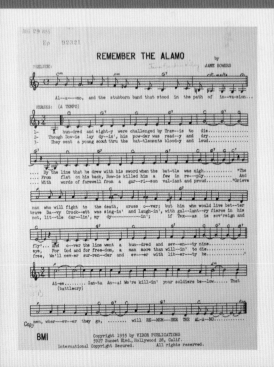

Bowers' original lyrics included different choruses, such as:

Ae-ee, Santa Anna
Now send 'em again to the wall
Ae-ii Santa Anna
We'll kill 'em and shout as they fall
That men wherever they go will remember the Alamo

Original lyrics that mentioned Alamo courier John W. Smith also were dropped from the published version:

Of couriers sent through the battlements bloody and loud,
John Smith was the last, and the letters he carried
    were proud,
"Grieve not, little darlin, my dyin'
While Texas be sovriegn (sic) and free
We'll never surrender and ever with liberty be!

Arguably, the most convincing version of Bowers' "Remember the Alamo" was featured on *Ring of Fire: The Best of Johnny Cash*. Released during the summer of 1963, the album topped the country charts and managed to reach the number 26 position on the pop album charts. Cash's unique vocal delivery gave the song a rough and ready roadhouse feel that generated sincerity and believability. At times, Cash sounds as if he's with the men of the Alamo, preparing to meet the ultimate challenge on that long-ago March 6 morning with gritty determination. Cash would go on to record two more versions of the song.

In 1968, Willie Nelson — a clean shaven and short haired Willie Nelson — released *Texas in My Soul*, an appropriately titled collection which not only featured a version of Bowers' "Remember the Alamo" but a reading of Alamo commander William B. Travis' famous February 24, 1836 letter addressed to "The People of Texas and all Americans in the world." Eighteen years later, Willie Nelson — the one with the beard

and long hair — performed at the Sesquicentennial of the Battle of San Jacinto event near Baytown, Texas, proving he still had Texas in his soul.

"Remember the Alamo" is one of the most familiar and frequently recorded songs about the battle. Ritter's partner, Johnny Bond, also recorded it and Ritter cut a second version, released on several LPs. One of the most important recordings of the song was the Kingston Trio's rendition, which appeared on the Capitol LP *The Kingston Trio at Large*, released June 1, 1959. The album became a best-seller that gave the song broad exposure. The folk trio also recorded a live version in 1959, but it was not released until 1994 on the CD *Live in Newport*. Gil Prather released it under the odd title "Santa Anna" and other artists have tinkered with the lyrics. Alan Leatherwood recorded two versions for his 2004 CD *Rock, Bop, Folk and Pop Vol. 1*. Leatherwood corrected the reference to Crockett's age by altering that line to "Old Davy Crockett," not as a commentary on the Tennessean's years, but as a reference to the Crockett character as an "old friend" personified by Fess Parker's 1950s television portrayal of the frontiersman. Leatherwood's "Tribute Version" refers to the September 11, 2001 attack on the World Trade Center and Pentagon by replacing Santa Anna's name with a reference to Osama bin Laden. Once again, the Alamo was invoked as inspiration in time of war.

Coincidentally, *The Kingston Trio at Large* climbed towards the top of the album charts in the summer of 1959, when the biggest Alamo project of all time was already underway: John Wayne's big-screen epic, *The Alamo*.

John Wayne began directing *The Alamo* in Brackettville, Texas on September 9, 1959. The big-budget film starred Wayne as Crockett, Richard Widmark as Bowie, Laurence Harvey as Travis, and Richard Boone as Sam Houston. Supporting players included Frankie Avalon, Chill Wills, Linda Cristal, Patrick Wayne, Ken Curtis, Joan O'Brien and thousands of extras. The cast performed before the cameras until mid-December when principal photography ended and post-production began. The most critical creative element that still needed to be added to the film was its musical score. Wayne hired Dimitri Tiomkin to complete that task.

Tiomkin was a highly respected and accomplished film composer who had created the soundtracks to such films as *Lost Horizon, It's a Wonderful Life, The Thing (from Another World), High Noon,* and *The High and the Mighty,* which starred John Wayne. The Russian-born composer also created the soundtrack to another Wayne film, *Rio Bravo,* which was released in early 1959. In that Howard Hawks-directed film, Tiomkin created a simple but effective piece titled "De Guello," based on the Mexican bugle call *degüello.* Tiomkin later rescored it and used it in *The Alamo.*

The Wayne-Tiomkin partnership could have been awkward from a political point of view. Wayne was a celebrated Hollywood anti-Communist and Tiomkin had helped create the "The Storming of the Winter Palace" in 1920 in St. Petersburg, Russia, a massive spectacle that celebrated the Bolshevik takeover of the provisional revolutionary government in 1917. But Tiomkin's participation in the event, decades earlier, was motivated more by creativity than politics and it never became an issue between Wayne and the composer.

For *The Alamo* project, Tiomkin teamed with lyricist Paul Francis Webster, the prolific tunesmith who had won Best Song Oscars® for "Secret Love" (1953) and "Love Is a Many-Splendored Thing" (1955). Tiomkin and Webster combined to create a sweeping orchestral tapestry that remains highly regarded today. And the music and lyrics for *The Alamo* reflected Wayne's patriotic fervor, his passion for freedom and his genuine interest and respect for those who took part in the battle of the Alamo.

Tiomkin and his orchestra entered Radio Recorders studio in Hollywood, California on September 10, 1960 to begin work on several tracks. The session continued the next day and resumed for a final day of recording on September 15. Columbia records released the "original soundtrack recording" of *The Alamo* on October 17, 1960, one week before the film's debut. The LP was a 14-track collection of both film music and additional commercial performances.

"Mr. Tiomkin was faced with the assignment of creating a background in sound for a story of rough, warring frontiersmen going down magnificently to defeat at the hands of a Mexican foe in the Texas of 1836," wrote Patterson Greene in the LP's liner notes. "Obviously, he could not write erudite music, complex in structure, elusive in themes. It must have the aspect of rustic simplicity and crude vigor."

To be sure, songs like the restrained "Tennessee Babe," the rowdy "Here's to the Ladies" and the traditional Western-like "David Crockett Arrives" accurately reflect Greene's observations. But Tiomkin did, indeed, create some songs that were wonderfully complex in structure. And memorable.

The "Overture" is a grand introductory theme, which builds in emotional intensity but is embellished with thoughtful and beautiful orchestral phrasing. And its final measures create a touching and reflective mood that underscores the inevitable fate of the Alamo defenders.

The most beautiful and important composition on the soundtrack is "The Green Leaves of Summer." The song is mournfully reflective and shares a spiritual affinity with the Biblical "times" mentioned in *Ecclesiastes 3:1-8.* In the film, the defenders sense their impending doom on the eve of battle and they reflect on life while sitting around a campfire. An exquisite a cappella choral rendition of "The Green Leaves of Summer" provides the ideal backdrop to this wonderfully subdued scene.

A time to be reapin,'a time to be sowin.'
The green leaves of summer are callin' me home.
It was good to be young then, in the season of plenty,
When the catfish were jumpin' as high as the sky.

"The Green Leaves of Summer"
by Dimitri Tiomkin and Paul Webster
© 1960 Volta Music Corp. / Webster Music Co. Copyright renewed.
All rights for Volta Music Corp. administered
by Universal Music Corp. (ASCAP)
Used By Permission. All Rights Reserved.

The theme is heard in several emotional scenes including one in which Wayne bids a painful farewell to his on-screen love (Linda Cristal's Flaca) and another where Mexican women tend to their wounded and dead husbands following the first attack. "Now, what has begun as a theme shared by an Anglo American and the Mexican woman he loves ripens into a musical device which binds the two opposing sides together in the common ground of their shared suffering," wrote Ken Sutak, author of *The Great Motion Picture Soundtrack Robbery*, in *The Alamo Journal*.[1]

"The Green Leaves of Summer" remains the film's most pervasive musical theme, one that essentially connects every important event in a reserved but passionate way. And it represents Tiomkin at his very best. No wonder Tiomkin's biographer Christopher Palmer called *The Alamo* the composer's "last great Western score and an apotheosis of his achievements in the genre."[2]

But an earlier composition may have inspired Tiomkin to create the song. According to researcher Jerry Laing, Antonio Salieri's *Variations on Folia di Espagne* (*Variations of the Leaves of Spain*), which was created around 1815, is surprisingly similar to "The Green Leaves of Summer." "The basic theme dates back to a Portuguese folk song similarly titled," wrote Laing. "It is quite possible that Tiomkin was already familiar with one or several of these works, and therefore, based both theme and title for 'The Green Leaves of Summer' on 'La Folia.'"[3]

A version of "The Green Leaves of Summer" performed by the Brothers Four was added to the soundtrack album. The vocal group released it as a single (it reached number 65 on the pop music charts) and later performed the song at the 1961 Oscar® ceremonies. The song was also performed by arranger Nick Perito on the United Artists' LP, *Original Sound Tracks and Hit Music from Great Motion Picture Themes*. Perito also released the song as a single, as did Kenny Ball and his Jazzmen. Numerous recordings of the song followed.

Another track on the album that was not used in the movie was

"Ballad of the Alamo" by Marty Robbins, who had nine Top 40 hits to his credit. One of those was the chart-topping "El Paso," which told the sad tale of a cowboy who loses his life over his sweetheart. Ironically "El Paso" bumped *Alamo* star Frankie Avalon's "Why" from its number one chart position during the first week of January in 1960. Robbins was the perfect vocalist to sing the Tiomkin-Webster composition. Like "El Paso," the "Ballad of the Alamo" is performed in a kind of gentle speak-sing delivery that emphasizes the story over the song.

The lyrics describe a cowboy's view of the Alamo years after the battle: "There's a fortress all in ruins that the weeds have overgrown." But the song quickly reminds listeners what the Alamo was all about:

> **Back in eighteen thirty-six — Houston said to Travis**
> **"Get some volunteers and go — fortify the Alamo"**
> **Well, the men came from Texas and from old Tennessee**
> **And they joined up with Travis —**
> **just to fight for the right to be free**
>
> **"The Ballad of the Alamo"**
> by Dimitri Tiomkin and Paul Webster
> © 1960 Volta Music Corp. / Webster Music Co. Copyright renewed.
> All rights for Volta Music Corp. administered
> by Universal Music Corp. (ASCAP)
> Used By Permission. All Rights Reserved.

Robbins' recording of "Ballad of The Alamo" entered the *Billboard* charts during the week of *The Alamo's* premier and eventually climbed to the number 34 position.

The talented folk guitar duo, Bud and Travis, also recorded "Ballad of the Alamo" for Liberty Records. Their version, which featured "The Green Leaves of Summer" on the flip side of the single, peaked at number 64. Michael Stewart and The Sons of Texas contributed a version of the song on Golden Records, a label that promoted music for children.

Frankie Avalon released a four-song EP of film compositions — "Ballad of the Alamo," "Tennessee Babe (Oh, Lisa!)," "The Green Leaves of Summer" and "Here's to the Ladies" — on the Chancellor label. Two of the songs, "The Green Leaves of

RCA CAMDEN
A PRODUCT OF RADIO CORPORATION OF AMERICA

MUSIC FROM THE FILM

THE ALAMO

AS PLAYED BY
TEX BENEKE AND HIS ORCHESTRA

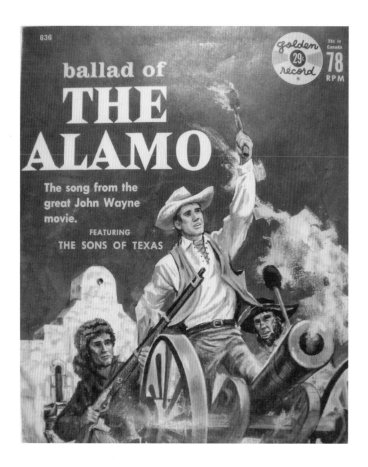

The original soundtrack album from *The Alamo* remained on the best-selling LP charts for 47 weeks, peaking at the number seven position. It later appeared in two CD editions, the second an expanded version that added voice tracks and other music from the soundtrack.

Tiomkin received a Golden Globe Award in 1961 for "Best Original Score," and he earned two Academy Award® nominations — one for "Best Music, Original Song" ("The Green Leaves of Summer") and another for "Best Music, Scoring for a Dramatic or Comedy Picture."

The music of the Alamo and the spoken word have been combined on a number of recordings. The first to capitalize on the release of *The Alamo* was *Remember the Alamo*, a 1960 Noble Records documentary LP that features the music of Tony Mottola and the narration of actor Claude Rains. Another interesting spoken word release was *The Alamo*, a history tour narrated by Rex Allen, the singing movie and TV cowboy star.

On the popular front, jazz vocalist Betty Carter performed an upbeat version of "On the Alamo," the Isham Jones-Gus Kahn composition," on *The Modern Sound of Betty Carter* in 1960. Carter sang the song's traditional Alamo lines before delivering some rhythmic scatting in an extended solo.

A year later, Marty Robbins wrote and recorded "Jimmy Martinez," a song about a Mexican soldier who leaves his sweetheart to fight at the Alamo. The tune, which appeared later on the artist's 1966 *Saddle Tramp* LP, provides listeners with a reminder that many of Santa Anna's soldiers also died fighting at the Alamo. In fact, Robbins' song is the first recording to seriously acknowledge the sacrifice of a specific Mexican soldier — although a fictional one — who fought and died during the Texas Revolution's most memorable conflict.

The Kingston Trio again managed to give kudos to Davy Crockett and his fellow Alamo defenders in the lyrics to "Coming from the Mountains," a song written by John Stewart for the group's 1961 LP, *Close Up*.

Summer" and "Here's to the Ladies," were released as a single. The vinyl releases weren't hits but they remain the only musical recordings that feature songs from the movie performed by a member of *The Alamo* cast. Ironically, the version of "Tennessee Babe" sung in the film by Ken Curtis and Joan O'Brien has never been released.

The Tiomkin-Webster tunes even got recognition from *Hit Parader*, the monthly magazine that printed hit song lyrics and published stories about the top rock 'n' roll idols of the day. The January 1961 issue, which featured cover photos of Paul Anka, Annette Funicello and Bobby Rydell, included the lyrics to "Here's to the Ladies," "The Green Leaves of Summer" and "Tennessee Babe (Oh, Lisa!)."[4]

President Lyndon Johnson's January 15, 1965 inauguration featured "Remember the Alamo," a tone poem by Julia Smith in collaboration with Cecile Vashaw and performed by the U.S. Navy Band at the Departmental Auditorium in Washington, D.C. The performance began with a reading of Travis' famous letter of February 24, 1836 and the piece weaves together "[Will You] Come to the Bower," "Bury Me Not....," "Deguello" and concludes with a chorus singing "Texas Hymn." Johnson, a native Texan, expressed his appreciation for the performance in a letter to the band.

There were other songs written about the Alamo and Davy Crockett that had nothing to do with Hollywood, but in the wake of the Beatles-led British Invasion in 1964 they had little chance of climbing very high on the charts. Nonetheless, artists on both sides of the Atlantic continued to record songs about the Shrine of Texas Liberty and its most famous defender. To be sure, the times were "a-changin,'" but British folkie Donovan still placed Jane Bowers' "Remember the Alamo" on his 1965 *Catch the Wind* Album, and it stayed on the U.S. charts for nearly six months.

Diana Ross and the Supremes recorded a version of "The Ballad of Davy Crockett" in 1967, but it wasn't released until 20 years later on the extremely rare *The Never Before Released Masters* LP. The Blackburn-Bruns original composition was reworked Motown style with some additional lyrics including a line about Crockett's beard.

In the 1968 film *Speedway*, Elvis Presley delivered one of the most off-beat lyrical lines about the Alamo when he and Bill Bixby performed the somewhat goofy "He's Your Uncle, Not Your Dad." After singing about Pearl Harbor, Presley chanted "The Alamos and nothing could be worse." What did Elvis say? The song can be found on the soundtrack CD as well as the *Elvis Double Features* CD, *Easy Come Easy Go/Speedway*.

The next original soundtrack album about the Alamo appeared in 1969 with *Viva Max!*, a big-screen comedy about a modern Mexican Army general, played by Peter Ustinov, who attempts to take back the famous Texas land-mark from the likes of Jonathan Winters. The movie was a so-so comedic effort but the *Viva Max!* soundtrack LP, composed by Hugo Montenegro, Ralph Dino and John Sembello, was quite good. Trumpeter Al Hirt demonstrated his usual powerful delivery on a number of tracks especially the "Viva Max March." The LP features such diverse selections as "The Viva Max Hat Dance," an uptempo arrangement of the familiar "Jarabe Tapatío" or "Mexican Hat Dance," and the comical "Sentries Charge." Yet, "Paula's Theme," named after the character played by Pamela Tiffin, is as relaxing and pleasant a song as any that graced a soundtrack album in the 1960s.

The 1970s was marked by Watergate, Kent State, the end of the Vietnam War, stagflation, the Iranian Hostage Crisis, and, of course, the U.S. Bicentennial, which included Alamo tributes. Some of the musical compilations were traditional and patriotic salutes to America's special birthday, like Johnny Cash's 1972 LP *America: A 200-Year Salute in Story and Song*, which included a new recording of "Remember the Alamo." Julian Lee Rayford's 1975 LP *A Bicentennial Collection of American Folklore* featured musical acknowledgements to Davy Crockett and Sam Houston, among others.

In 1971, Dick Campbell and Key Pashine wrote "Alamo Cowboy," a song that begins as a familiar lament of a cowboy pining away for his lost love. But this cowboy has left her to join the Alamo garrison, where he is personally welcomed by Crockett only moments before the final Mexican assault on the fort:

The British band, Babe Ruth performed a song titled "The Mexican" on its 1973 debut LP, *First Base*. The rocking arrangement focused on Chico Fernandez, a soldier in Santa Anna's army, and the girl he left behind. In the song, he's warned that he may end up as the first Mexican casualty at the Battle of the Alamo.

Some other recordings from the '70s seem to have been Alamo-related, but a closer look shows that they were not.

Alamo, an Atlantic Records rock quartet, released its self-titled LP in 1971, but other than a sketch of the famous Texas shrine on the cover, the album had nothing to do with the historical Alamo. Likewise, a 1973 Rolling Stones bootleg LP titled *The Boys at the Alamo*, featured a cover shot of the band standing in front of the Alamo, but the 2-LP package was nothing more than a Danish concert mix of Rolling Stones standards. The Stones did, however, redeem themselves two decades later when they mentioned Crockett's stand at the Alamo on "Mean Disposition," a song from their 1994 *Voodoo Lounge* album.

The Nation's Bicentennial was acknowledged with an interesting spoken word LP: *The American Spirit 1776-1976*. Famous American heroes, like Alamo commander William B. Travis, played by Forrest Tucker, were featured on the 1975 recording. But, coincidentally, some of the other historical personalities on the album were portrayed by individuals who had previously appeared in various Alamo films: Thomas Jefferson by Richard Carlson (*The Last Command*); Andrew Jackson by Jonathan Winters (*Viva Max!*); Harry Truman by Ernest Borgnine (*The Last Command*); Lyndon Johnson by Hugh O'Brian (*Man From the Alamo*); and both William Lloyd Garrison and Chester A. Arthur by William Bakewell (Disney's "Davy Crockett" TV series).

ZZ Top, the Texas-based hard rock 'n' blues trio, recorded *Deguello*, a 1979 LP that acknowledged Santa Anna's fateful Alamo bugle call. But the album was devoid of any Santa Anna or other Alamo-related song selections. Still, the band had a sense of Texas heritage. In an interview, the band's Billy Gibbons said he was saddened by the Alamo's modern-day appearance. "It's a kind of shame how it looks today," said the guitarist-vocalist. "But it's got its history."[5]

Southern rocker Danny Joe Brown, the former vocalist with the group Molly Hatchet, contributed "The Alamo" on his self-titled LP in 1981. Brown's lyrics may have included an undersized garrison of 180 Alamo defenders and a 12-day siege, but his tune was replete with such patriotic ingredients as strength and bravery.

Not to be left out, ex-Beatle Paul McCartney reminisced about the era of Disney's Crockett Craze in the song "Ballroom Dancing" on his 1982 album *Tug of War*.

The top grossing film of 1985, *Back to the Future*, featured a scene with star Michael J. Fox in which the Fess Parker version of "The Ballad of Davy Crockett" is heard playing on a jukebox. The scene takes place on November 5, 1955, four months after any version of the popular tune remained on the charts. Unfortunately, the song was not included on the film's soundtrack release.

The nation's Bicentennial was one thing, but the Texas Sesquicentennial in 1986 was something else again. Texas celebrated the 150th anniversary of the battle and many musical artists responded.

That year, Donnie McCormick, Tommy Carlisle and Larry Bowie, recorded their *Remember the Alamo* LP, which featured such tracks as "Men of the Alamo," "Santa Anna's Coming" and "No Dictators in Texas." (See below)

THE SKIES OF TEXAS
A SESQUICENTENNIAL SALUTE

Col. Benny L. Knudsen
Commander/Conductor

The United States Air Force Band of the West, under the baton of conductor Col. Benny L. Knudsen, recorded the LP *The Skies of Texas: A Sesquicentennial Salute* in 1986. The recording, which featured narration by Gordon Jump, included such appropriate tracks as "The Ballad of the Alamo," "The Green Leaves of Summer," and "Across the Alley from the Alamo," which punctuate "The Skies of Texas," a compact history lesson of the Lone Star State. But the album was not made for the commercial market; it was a promotional LP that was distributed only to radio stations selected by the U.S. Department of Defense, making it a true Alamo music rarity.

On March 6, 1986 ceremonies were held in front of the Alamo. The 5th Army Band played patriotic songs and later in the day country music star Charlie Daniels played fiddle, while Pipe Major Gavin Stoddart, a Scottish piper with the British infantry, played bagpipes, recalling the similar musical duels between Crockett and John McGregor during the 1836 siege.

Two days later, at a battle reenactment held at Alamo Village in Brackettville, Texas, the site of John Wayne's *The Alamo*, singer-songwriter-painter Eric Von Schmidt performed his original song, "The Alamo." The composition, described by von Schmidt as "a song to honor the sesquicentennial of the battle," coincided with the artist's creation of *The Storming of the Alamo*, a large canvas depicting the final phase of the 1836 conflict.[6] Von Schmidt, an important member of the East Coast folk revival of the late 1950s and early 60s, weaved lyrical passages about Bowie, Moses Rose, Santa Anna and Crockett before providing his tune with a gritty, sing-a-long conclusion and chorus:

> They charged 'em once,
> & they charged them twice,
> at a fearful loss of men.
> Their cannon ball had breached the wall,
> and then they charged again.
> As the bloody tide,
> it swept inside,

> it was fighting hand to hand,
> Bayonet with Bowie-knife met,
> as each man made his stand.
>
> And as they died, they cursed & they cried;
> the terrible dawn it rose —
> They'd come from all over Ameri-cay,
> they'd come from Mexico.
> And when the fighting was over &
> the funeral pyre did glow, —
> Well, there's no one here,
> & there's no one there,
> who'll forget the Alamo.
>
> Take off your buckskin jackets,
> & give your bones a rest. —
> And we'll all remember the Alamo,
> & the boys who stood the test.

The small screen benefited from Dennis McCarthy's score for *Houston: The Legend of Texas*. The 1986 TV movie (later titled *Gone to Texas*) included the obligatory musical crescendos, which concluded each segment and signaled upcoming commercial breaks, but a number of other excellent passages enhanced several scenes. The Battle of the Alamo aftermath sequence features a trumpet solo that clearly recalls Tiomkin's "Main Title: DeGeulla" theme from John Wayne's *The Alamo*. And McCarthy's dramatically subdued measures that underscore the scene in which the bodies of Travis, Crockett and Bowie are identified are eloquently powerful.

In 1987, Peter Bernstein created a satisfactory score for the TV movie *The Alamo: 13 Days to Glory*. But the composer's music was overshadowed by the much-maligned production, which relied on stock footage from *The Last Command* to enhance its final battle scenes. The film was shot at Alamo Village in Brackettville, Texas, on the set used for John Wayne's epic film, and starred Brian Keith as Davy Crockett, James Arness as Jim Bowie, and Alec Baldwin as William Travis. It generated low ratings and poor reviews, but Bernstein's music was workman-like and efficient.

A year later, another Alamo film reached the big screen — make that the giant screen of IMAX® — with *Alamo...The Price of Freedom*. Directed by Kieth Merrill, the film featured a relatively unknown cast — Casey Biggs starred as Travis and Merrill Connally played Crockett — but a first rate soundtrack recording was subsequently released on cassette and CD. Merrill Jenson's riveting score is replete with powerful anthems ("Main Theme"), melancholy compositions ("The Ring"), and arresting, martial-like mini-symphonies ("Cavalry Attack"). Jenson is superb in his creation of a kind of Biblical motif in the music that shrouded Biggs' reading of Travis' famous letter ("To The People of Texas"), and the composer embellished the film's emotional final track ("No Small Affair/Finale") with a choir that blended religious poignancy with Old West sensibilities. The soundtrack album also added the original song "Price of Freedom," written by Clint McAlister and performed by Sergio Salinas.

Ray Herbeck, Jr., the Associate Producer of *Alamo...The Price of Freedom*, also produced an historical album on cassette in 1989 titled *Remember the Alamo! — Mexican & Texian Music of 1836*. Herbeck, who played rhythm guitar on the

collection, recruited musicians who specialized in period music. Using such instruments as the fife, recorder, mandolin, fiddle, bagpipes and wooden flute, Herbeck and his musical comrades carefully replicated such historical compositions as "The Girl I Left Behind," "Old Rosin the Bow," and "De Guello."

On the pop scene, singer-songwriter Billy Joel recorded his post-World War II history lesson, "We Didn't Start the Fire," which included a quick reference to Walt Disney's "Davy Crockett." Joel, who had aspired to become a history teacher as a young man, took the song to the top of the charts in December 1989.

Two years later, the Kentucky Headhunters released a rollicking version of "The Ballad of Davy Crockett" off their LP *Electric Barnyard*. Drummer Fred Young told *The Alamo Journal*: "We needed to come out with 'Davy Crockett,' make it fast, make it rock."[7] The song reached the number 47 position on the country charts.

Moses Rose, the Alamo defender who, according to legend, left the mission-fortress when given the opportunity by William Travis, was acknowledged in a 1995 song: "Moses Rose of Texas." Written by Stephen L. Suffet and sung to the tune "Yellow Rose of Texas," Rose gets a celebratory boost of sorts because of his survivor status:

> When gallant Colonel Travis,
> Drew a line down in the sand,
> Everyone stepped over,
> But one solitary man.
> They called him Rose the Coward,
> And they called him Yellow Rose,
> But it takes bravery to stand alone,
> As God Almighty knows.
>
> He said, "I'm not a coward,
> I just think it isn't right,
> For me to throw my life away,
> In someone else's fight.
> I have no quarrel with Mexicans,
> Nor with the Texans, too,"
> So Moses Rose of Texas,
> He bid the men adieu.
>
> Whenever you are up against it,
> Pressure from your peers,
> Or a challenge to your manhood,
> Or frightened by the jeers,

Remember that discretion,
Is valor's better part,
And let the life of Moses Rose,
Put courage in your heart.

So shed a tear for Travis,
And Davy Crockett, too,
And cry for old Jim Bowie,
They saw the battle through.
But when you're finished weeping,
And you're finished with your wail,
Then give a grin for Moses Rose,
Who lived to tell the tale!

By Stephen L. Suffet ©1995. Used by permission.

The 1990s was also a particularly fruitful decade for recordings of older songs about Davy Crockett. The famous Alamo defender appeared on vinyl, cassette and CD releases by such artists as Clyde Case, Fess Parker, Hobert Stollard, Punch Miller and Louis Gallard, the Rolling Stones and the English Chamber Orchestra. Crockett was even embraced by fusionist Col. Bruce Hampton and the Aquarium Rescue Unit. The band delivered an original, off-the-wall version of "The Ballad of Davy Crockett" on its self-titled 1992 "live" LP with such break-neck speed and rhythmic intensity that few listeners associated it with the Blackburn-Bruns original.

Nineteen ninety-two also saw the release of one of the more unorthodox Alamo songs, "Davey Crockett," which appeared on a single by the British group Thee Headcoatees. This punk rock ditty, derived from an earlier tune titled "Farmer John," paid tribute to Crockett and the 1950s Disney series, the Alamo and Jim Bowie's legendary knife, as well as making quirky references to Crockett's clothing.

Coinciding with the opening of *The Texas Adventure*, a new attraction in San Antonio's Alamo Plaza in 1994, was the release of the CD *Songs for the Alamo*, produced by Bob Flick.[8] The collection is a rewarding assortment of diverse instrumental and vocal performances. "Crockett's Dance" is a

lively country jig, "Dawn at the Alamo" is a reflective instrumental, and the Belltown Chorus' "Never, Never Forget" is a powerful chant-like remember-the-Alamo reminder. Also noteworthy is Edo Guidotti's "Theme from the 'Texas Adventure'" and the lovely "Sweet Texas Rain," sung by Julie Hoy and Terry Lauber, a heart-wrenching lament for the fallen Alamo defenders. The Brothers Four contributed a new, more reflective version of "The Green Leaves of Summer."

"The Ballad of Davy Crockett" was revived once again in 1996 with a unique musical twist on *Bibbidi Bobbidi Bach*, a collection of Disney tunes played in the style of such great classical composers as Beethoven, Haydn, Debussy, Chopin, Bernstein and Pachelbel, among others. "The Ballad of Davy Crockett" emerges as the most "classical" of the album's 15 songs. Inspired by Aaron Copland's *Fanfare for the Common Man* and performed by the English Chamber Orchestra, "The Ballad of Davy Crockett" is a lofty and eloquent performance that is on a par with some of cinema's most impressive themes.

However, 1996 also marked the most eccentric interpretation of "The Ballad of Davy Crockett," courtesy of Tim Curry, who had gained international fame in 1975 as Dr. Frank-N-Furter in *The Rocky Horror Picture Show*. On this rhythmic, funky-soul version from the CD *Disney's Music From the Park*, Curry speaks more than he sings; in fact, he interjects a number of comedic adlibs about Crockett, campfires, and coonskin caps.

One of the most enjoyable musical efforts to celebrate the Alamo was *K. R. Wood's Fathers of Texas* CD, a 1997 assortment of poetry, classic Texas tunes and original compositions

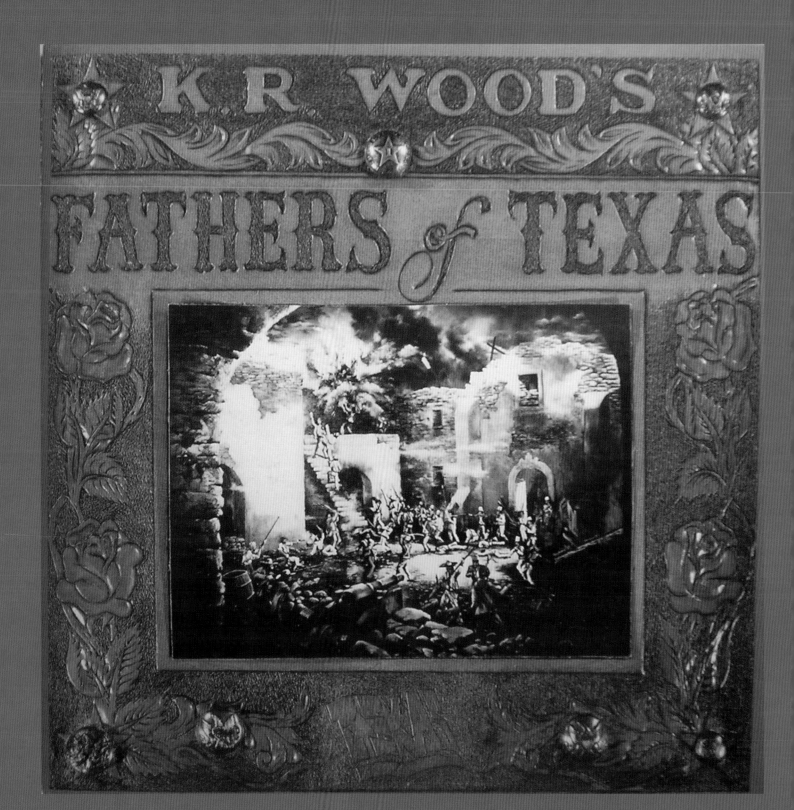

that were dedicated "to the loving memory of all the veterans of war from Texas and the United States, and our brothers who are with us in spirit." Wood and his fellow musicians and narrators created a captivating homespun atmosphere on the 25-track collection that is thoroughly informative and entertaining.

One of the songs, "Mother of the Alamo," features the vocals of Eliza Gilkyson. Her father, Terry Gilkyson, along with the Easy Riders, recorded the *Remember the Alamo* LP in 1960. This marks a unique Alamo music connection: Terry and Eliza Gilkyson are the only father-daughter team to record songs about the Alamo. Wood later reworked the song under the title "Women of the Alamo."

Additional tracks on *Fathers of Texas* like "Bonham's Last Ride," "Men of Goliad" and "General Sam Houston" seem to have been written expressly for the reassuring comforts of a late-night campfire.

The most ambitious Alamo musical project of the decade was *Liberty! The Siege of the Alamo*, Bernard J Taylor's staged musical. The Missy Miller-directed production had its initial limited opening at the Josephine Theatre in San Antonio November 11-14, 1999. The performance received a lukewarm review from the *San Antonio Express-News* and an unflattering assessment from film historian Frank Thompson.[9]

The 1999 "international studio cast recording" on a 24-track 2-CD release featured songs from all the familiar Alamo characters and such lesser known individuals as Alamo defenders Daniel Cloud and Micajah Autry, among others. All of the vocalists on the CD are quite competent, and the Capital City Men's Chorus is particularly impressive, but most of the songs lack the necessary hooks that are needed to retain audience enthusiasm. "Thinking of You," for example, performed by Warren Davis as Autry, is a heart-felt love song that never reaches its emotional potential due to an ineffective chorus. Furthermore, "Santa Anna's Revenge" is stereotypical, and "A Line in the Sand," Richard (Travis) Austin's signature song, is underpowered by electronic instrumentation, which, unfortunately substitutes for an orchestra.

Michael Berlet (Crockett), however, comes to the rescue with a fine performance of "The Legend and the Man," an arresting, introspective composition that describes the conflict between David Crockett the man and Davy Crockett the larger-than-life hero.

There's a great many stories they tell about me
I'm a frontiersman, sinner and saint
Everyone thinks they know me
From stories they've heard
And I have no real cause for complaint
But I'm no longer sure
What is true and is false
In the things they have said about me
I am trapped in the legend of who I've become
And what people want me to be
I'm just a man
Doing the best that he can
Trying to make some real sense of who I am
A legend or a man
I'm a man of the people;
That's what folks have said
And it's true I have acted the part
I have tried hard to be
What's expected of me
But there's times when it all falls apart
Once they sent me to Congress
And folks made a fuss
Of this plain-speaking Tennessee man
But then they decided my face didn't fit
And I found myself back on the land
I'm just a man
Doing the best that he can
Trying to make some real sense of who I am
A legend and a man
I did the best that I could
Leastwise I know that I tried
But when they no longer wanted me
Something inside of me died

I'm just a man
Doing the best that he can
Trying to make some real sense of who I am
A legend or a man

©1999 Bernard J Taylor, 1998-2008; www.bernardjtaylor.com.
Used by permission.

Taylor's production is an uneven but sincere effort. The composer's affection for the Shrine of Texas Liberty is unadulterated from the first track to the last, which is appropriately titled "Remember the Alamo."

The last non-theatrical, original recording of the 20th century dealing with the Alamo and its participants was Danny McBride's "Heroes (Davy Crockett)," a track from his 1999 CD *16 Tunes...and whaddaya get...A Songwriter's Portfolio*. McBride, a former member of the oldies revival band Sha Na Na, delivered a formula-style country performance of this original Crockett song. But, before the decade was over, "The Ballad of Davy Crockett" appeared yet again on the album *Mannheim Steamroller Meets the Mouse*, a 12-song assortment of classic Walt Disney songs.

From their first appearances on Edison wax cylinders, through the eras of 78 and 45 rpm singles, 33 1/3 LPs, cassettes and CDs, the 20th century featured hundreds of recordings about the Alamo and its most famous defender, Davy Crockett. The nation may have developed from a horse 'n buggy country to one that regularly sent space shuttles into Earth orbit, but its citizens still maintained their fascination for an abandoned 18th century mission and an uneducated backwoodsman who wore a coonskin cap.

[1] Ken Sutak, "Dimitri Tiomkin's Alamo Score," *The Alamo Journal* 68 (Oct. 1989), 3-9. See also Ken Sutak, "The Alamo on Compact Disc," *The Alamo Journal* 68 (Oct. 1989), 10-12, and "On Film: The Alamo Remembered," *Sound Collector's Newsletter* 8 (1976).

[2] Christopher Palmer, *Dimitri Tiomkin: A Portrait* (London, 1984), 91.

[3] Jerry A. Laing, "The Green Leaves of Summer," *The Alamo Journal* 63 (Oct. 1988), 11-12. Laing pointed out other similar versions of the melody including works by Arcangelo Corelli (*Violin Sonata in D Minor — "La Folia,"* and *La Folia Variations*, Op. 5, No. 12); Francesco Geminiani (*Concerto Grosso No. 12 in D Minor — La Folia*), and Mauro Giuliani (*Variations on Folies D'Espagne*, Op. 45), among others.

[4] *Hit Parader*, January 1961, 24, 26-27.

[5] William Chemerka, "ZZ Top: That Little 'Ol Band From The Lone Star State Shoots For Outer Space," *The Aquarian Weekly*, 329, August 27, 1980.

[6] See "The Alamo Remembered — From a Painter's Point of View," *Smithsonian* (March 1986), 54-67. Complete lyrics of "The Alamo" were included on prints of *The Storming of the Alamo*. A March 8, 1986 cassette tape recording of Von Schmidt is the only recording of the song. The painting was on display at the Witte Museum in 1986.

[7] William Chemerka, "The Kentucky Headhunters," *The Alamo Journal* 76, April, 1991, 3-4.

[8] *The Texas Adventure* was a 21,000 sq. ft. entertainment complex that featured a 200-seat special effects theater that reproduced the battle of the Alamo. The entrance way included a detailed diorama built by Tom Feely titled "Crockett's Last Stand," which depicted the Alamo church and court yard area. An accompanying music soundtrack for the diorama was created by Mike Boldt, who later created the CD *The Alamo: A Musical Tribute to John Wayne's Epic Film* (2004).

[9] Frank Thompson, *The Alamo: A Cultural History* (Dallas, 2001), 139-141.

Among the many audio dramatizations of the Alamo story, this one, narrated by Claude Rains, remains a standout

REMEMBER
THE ALAMO

Narrated by **CLAUDE RAINS**

Music composed by
TONY MOTTOLA

The Gates of Glory
Davy Crockett and His Long Gun
Jim Bowie, Big Knife of the Alamo
William Barrett Travis, Commandant of the Alamo
Long Guns to Glory—General Sam Houston to Victory

Country Music Series

Remember The Alamo

Ken & Billie Ford

DOLBY SYSTEM ®

STEREO

THE 21ST CENTURY

We rode down to Texas
From our homes out in Tennessee
Looking for a reason worth fighting for
Some people called it liberty
Never dreamed we'd be so outnumbered
I guess I'd have to do it again
Don't you worry about me sweet daughter
I am with my friends

"I Am With My Friends"
(Michael J. Martin)
K.R. Wood
K.R. Wood's The Crockett Chronicles
©2002 Texanna Records

THE NEW MILLENNIUM may have been intrinsically linked with the future but its first few years still featured musical artists who created vocal and instrumental works about the events of March 6, 1836. In fact, the first decade of the 21st century saw an explosion of Alamo music, especially produced by small independent labels. Perhaps these Baby Boomer music makers were celebrating their childhood as they drifted beyond middle age, or maybe they were longing for a yesteryear in which national and international problems seemed easier to address and solve. Or they simply may have longed for heroes — heroes like Davy Crockett.

The year 2001 began with *Scotland Remembers the Alamo*, an impressive collection of 19th century songs performed acoustically by Carl Peterson and a talented group of background musicians. The double-CD, which is a tribute of sorts to Alamo defender John MacGregor of Scotland, includes such representative selections as "Remember the Alamo," "Death of Crockett" and "San Jacinto." Peterson even published a companion book, *Now's the Day and Now's the Hour*, to accompany the 30-track production. The CD and the book reaffirm Peterson's acknowledgement of the Ulster Scots' contributions to American cultural history.[1]

The next year, Dean Shostak released *Davy Crockett's Fiddle*, a wonderful collection of primarily 19th century tunes. Shostak

DEAN SHOSTAK

Davy Crockett's Fiddle

Featuring
the fiddle that
is believed to have
belonged to
**Davy
Crockett**
(1786–1836)

visited the Witte Museum in San Antonio and borrowed the fiddle that is believed to have once belonged to Crockett.[2] Shostak restored the instrument and then assembled other highly-accomplished acoustic musicians to create a pristine tapestry of America's musical past on the 21-track collection.

Shostak's "Old Zip Coon," "The Girl I Left Behind Me" and an interpretation of the 1817 version of "Star Spangled Banner" are particularly noteworthy. The inclusion of "Hunters of Kentucky" is an appropriate addition to the CD, since the tune was featured in the 1837 edition of *Crockett's Free and Easy Songbook*. The most celebratory track is "The Legend of Davy Crockett," a medley that incorporates two 19th century songs, "Remember the Alamo" and "The Ballad of Davy Crockett" (aka "Pompey Smash") with passages from the best-selling Blackburn-Bruns 1954 composition, "The Ballad of Davy Crockett."

K. R. Wood, who recorded the impressive *Fathers of Texas* CD in 1997, returned in 2002 with *K.R. Wood's The Crockett Chronicles*, a joyously sentimental album of reworked traditional ballads and carefully-crafted originals. Supported by a small cadre of musicians and narrators, Wood elevates the life and legend of the famous Tennessean in unabashed passion. His most memorable track is "I'm With My Friends," a tune penned by Michael J. Martin. The song follows a reading of a letter that Crockett allegedly wrote from Texas on Jan. 9, 1836 to his daughter and son-in-law. "Don't you worry about me sweet daughter," sings Wood reassuringly. "I am with my friends."

Songs like "Across the Alley from the Alamo," "San Antonio Rose" and "Home in San Antone" appeared on the 2002 CD *Deep in the Heart of Texas: Favorite Songs of the Lone Star State*. The instrumental selections were more cowboy than Alamo, but the Craig Duncan-production made sure that listeners received a dose of latter day Lone Star State history.

Across the Atlantic, the *Country In This Country* CD (2002) featured Italian recording artists who specialized in, of all things, American bluegrass and country music. One of the

19 selections is "Jim Bonham's Last Ride," an original instrumental salute to Alamo defender James Butler Bonham. The tune, written by Fabio Ragghianti and performed by his band, the Low-Tech Boys, is a bouncy composition that recalls the Ramrods' 1961 hit version of "(Ghost) Riders in the Sky."

Several Alamo music productions were released in 2003, making it one of the most productive years ever for Alamo-related recordings. Part of the motivation was probably the news that a major motion picture titled *The Alamo* was soon to debut. Recordings associated with both Walt Disney's 1954-55 "Davy Crockett" TV series and John Wayne's *The Alamo* from 1960 had performed remarkably well decades earlier, and the new music makers were probably thinking along the same lines.

Brian Burns' *The Eagle and the Snake: Songs of the Texians* is an interesting assortment of songs that is arranged chronologically, from the so-called "1810" opening track (Marty

Robbins' 1963 chestnut, "Man Walks Among Us") to the "2144" closing tune ("The Last Living Cowboy"). There's even a song about a hitchhiking loner who departs California in 1976 because "the music died with Jimmy Hendrix."

Fortunately, though, there is the "1836" heart of this album, a four-song compilation about the Texas Revolution that includes the classic Tiomkin-Webster composition, "Ballad of the Alamo" and the subdued "Goliad." Burns also delivers a reading of "Travis' Letter," which adds to the historical flavor of the 15-track CD.

In the production's liner notes, written by J. R. Edmondson, author of *The Alamo Story*, Burns' vocal-instrumental offering is described as "a diverse and delectable platter of pure Tex-Mex." It is clearly that and then some.

Asleep at the Wheel Remembers the Alamo also concentrated on songs about the Texas Revolution and its most revered battle. The 2003 production covered all the expected musical bases in grand style, from "Green Leaves of Summer" and

BRIAN BURNS

THE EAGLE & THE SNAKE: SONGS OF THE TEXIANS

"Ballad of the Alamo" to "Across the Alley from the Alamo" and the "Ballad of Davy Crockett." The popular Western swing band also delivered a comedic musical warning to Ozzy Osbourne, the British hard rocker who was arrested for urinating on Alamo Plaza in 1982. The song title says it all: "Don't Go There." And the humorous warning is backed up with a quirky refrain from "The Eyes of Texas" that's interjected in the arrangement.

K. R. Wood released another impressive collection in 2003: *K. R. Wood's Los Tejanos*, a bilingual lineup of narration selections and original tunes about Tejano history. The 38-track CD provides both Spanish and English versions of such historical tidbits as "Early Texas," "Beginning of the Texas Revolution" and "Napoleon of the West." What is important about *Los Tejanos* is that it appropriately acknowledges and recognizes Tejano contributions during the Texas Revolution, particularly at the Alamo, something clearly missing from earlier Alamo music. The cultural face of Texas in general — and San Antonio in particular — has changed since the time of John Wayne's *The Alamo*, and *Los Tejanos* reflects those cultural changes. For example, Gregorio Esparza, the only Alamo defender to receive a burial after the battle, is properly saluted in "The Ballad of Gregorio Esparza."

As with his previous albums, Wood assembled a talented support group of musicians and vocalists, most notably Greg Lowery (accordion, Spanish guitar and mandolin) and Mary Welch, who elevates the CD's title track to more than just a catchy ethnic tune.

Country and western artists have long been drawn to the Alamo for inspiration. Bobby Boyd's "Ghost of the Alamo" in 2003 is a sincere ode to the Alamo defenders and a superior example of the way the genre has handled the subject. Others have taken on a highly nationalistic flavor that attempts to put the Alamo myth in the context of modern events. Those songs often are appeals to patriotism that typically use the Alamo as an analogy for contemporary war. Many resurrect the mythical line that Travis supposedly drew in the dirt as if it were being metaphorically drawn before us today, simplistically

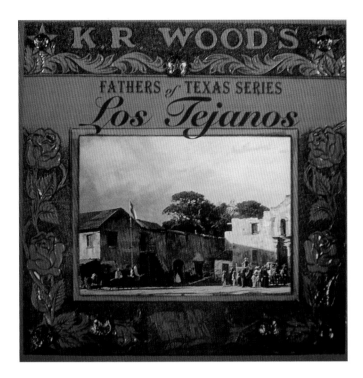

suggesting that all conflicts represent the same conditions faced by the Alamo garrison. Boyd's song departs from that pattern and focuses instead on the personal sacrifices of those who perished that day. His lyrics are so subtle that it is impossible to identify who these ghosts are and not to think of *all* of the Alamo dead — Anglos, Tejanos, and the Mexican *soldados* — all brave, all ghosts who haunt us still.

The grandest Alamo music project of 2003 was *Gone to Texas: The Musical*, an original cast recording of the production which debuted a year earlier at The Josephine Theatre in San Antonio, Texas.

Gone to Texas: the Musical, with a book by Steve Warren, lyrics by June Rachel-Ospa, and music by Tom Masinter, traces the story of the Texas Revolution through the eyes of its participants, from the famous to the lesser known. The songs, like "Gone To Texas," "Davy and Me," "Brand New Day," and "Remember These Men" are Broadway-aimed but Texas-inspired.

An original cast recording was made during a live perform-

ance in 2003 at The Josephine Theatre but never released. The 19-tracks include an "Overture" performed by the Agarita Cantina Orchestra and several ensemble numbers.

Central to the staged performances and the unreleased recording is the song "We Draw the Line," which was performed by the Bowie, Travis and Crockett characters. But the composition does more than reflect the events of 1836; Rachelson-Ospa's lyrics seem to also foreshadow the Iraq War which began in March 2003.

We'll do what we have to do
It is a patriotic plan
We know it is our duty
To protect each and every man
Protect our wives and children
There is no other way
We're damned proud of our choice
Even with a price to pay

[chorus]
We draw the line
And it stops right here
We draw the line
And it's crystal clear
We stand tall for one and all
They'll see, we'll not decline
Today we draw the line

Bring on Santa Anna's troops
Let his cannons pierce the sky
We will charge ahead
We must do or die
You'll never see us falter
Not even at our last breath
We will fight for Texas
For liberty or death

[chorus]
We draw the line
And it stops right here

> We draw the line
> Though war is near
> We stand tall for one and all
> In battle we will shine
> Right now we draw the line

©2002 June Rachelson-Ospa

Surprisingly, Rachelson-Ospa is not a saber-rattling lyricist; on the contrary, she describes herself as a "60s lady" who "believes in peace." In fact, several of the songs are distinctly anti-war compositions.[3]

The costumed cast, accompanied by Masinter on keyboards, performed "Davy and Me" at the 2007 Alamo Society Symposium in San Antonio. A full production was staged at the Bob Bullock Texas State History Museum in Austin later that year.

One Alamo-related song that had nothing to do with Alamo movies past or planned was "Tear Me Down" by Meat Loaf, the singer who is best known for his outrageous performance on the incredibly successful *Bat Out of Hell* LP in 1977, as well as his brief appearance in the cult movie *The Rocky Horror Picture Show* two years earlier. But Meat Loaf is a native born Texan (birth name: Marvin Lee Aday) and he remembers the Alamo. The song appeared on his 2003 album, *Couldn't Have Said It Better*. Meat Loaf adapted his song from the original of the same name that was featured in the off-Broadway play and film, *Hedwig and the Angry Inch*. Instead of references to the once-divided German city, Berlin, Meat Loaf's song features a strategic narration by a Giselda Vachky who briefly talks about the Battle of the Alamo and the singer's life.[4]

Riders in the Sky, the good-natured cowboy quartet, released *Riders in the Sky Present Davy Crockett: King of the Wild Frontier* in 2004. The nine-track lineup was heavy on Disney tunes from 1954 and 1955, like "Old Betsy," "Be Sure You're Right, and Then Go Ahead," "Farewell" and, of course, "The Ballad of Davy Crockett." But there's also "Heading for

Texas," an original composition that recalls Crockett's fateful journey to revolutionary Tejas, and a traditional interpretation of Bowers' "Remember The Alamo."

Other songs on the CD were inspired by the "tall tales" Davy Crockett, the one popularized in the 1830s almanacs and ghost-written biographies. Tracks like "The Grinning Tale," a Jimmie Driftwood song that celebrates Crockett's ability to grin down animals instead of shooting them, and "Colonel Crockett's Speech to Congress" are straight-as-an-arrow fun, just as the Riders in the Sky intended.

British songster Terry Friend released "The Alamo" in 2004, a two-track CD single featuring the title track, a country tune with the vocals of Friend and Cheryl Murphy backed by Alter Ego, and "The Alamo Narrative," a descriptive piece that is embellished with subtle instrumentation. Two years later Friend released a new version of "The Alamo" on the CD *Strange Journey: The Anthology Part 2: The CD Years*. Finally, in 2007, he recorded a third, lengthier and definitive version with a new lineup of musicians, which was released on a CD single, again with "The Alamo Narrative." Coincidentally, this final version runs exactly 18:36. Both CD singles featured the same liner notes, which reflect Friend's admiration for the Alamo defenders who "made their stand against the tyrannical dictatorship of the ruler of Mexico, Santa Anna."

On April 9, 2004, *The Alamo* debuted in theaters nationwide. The film starred Dennis Quaid as Houston, Billy Bob Thornton as Crockett, Jason Patric as Jim Bowie, and Patrick Wilson as Travis. Directed by John Lee Hancock, the big-budget film, however, was a disappointment at the box office.

Hancock noted that one of his main purposes in shooting the picture was to humanize the real story behind the Alamo myth. He retained Carter Burwell to write a score in tune with his humanistic approach to the subject matter. Burwell's music for the film is restrained and rather subdued throughout, and it creates an appropriate atmosphere for the doom that awaits the Alamo defenders. The veteran composer — *Rob Roy, Fargo, No Country for Old Men* — executed his

THE ALAMO

TERRY FRIEND

vast musical landscape with pristine production techniques and the contributions of scores of competent musicians, especially such featured artists as violinists Craig Eastman and Laura Seaton-Finn, and flutist David Weiss.

While the 1960 Tiomkin score is quite melodic in nature, the Burwell score is a far more accurate representation of the type of music played during the 1830s. Burwell effectively utilized ethnic flutes, fiddles, bugles, fifes, mandolin, guitar-ron, folk viola, and an orchestra of 16 percussion players for his 26-track compilation.

For the most part, the soundtrack lacks the memorable selec-tions that Tiomkin created for John Wayne's film in 1960, and Burwell's score lacks any signature tunes, such as "The Green Leaves of Summer." Still, selections like "300 Miles of Snow," "Bonham's Ride," and "The Last Night" are worthy of attention. And the six-part "Battle of the Alamo" segments recall all of the on-screen action that Hancock choreo-graphed so vividly. Like the film's best scene, the album's best track is the emotionally captivating "Deguello de Crockett," a simple but effective juxtaposition of Mexican military music and Tennessee fiddling.[5]

Coincidentally, Tiomkin's soundtrack was resurrected and reinterpreted in 2004 on *The Alamo: A Musical Tribute to John Wayne's Epic Film* by Mike Boldt, a composer who was inspired by the 1960 production. On the 11-song collec-tion, Boldt provides a fascinating lineup of reworked Tiomkin classics and originals. His upbeat interpretation of Marty Robbins' "Ballad of the Alamo" is uniquely inventive, and his background music on three narration tracks devoted to Crockett ("I Am With My Friends"), Travis ("I Will Never Surrender or Retreat") and Susanna Dickinson ("A Parting Kiss") is appropriately understated.

Boldt appeared the following year as a performer with Tony Pasqua and Bill Chemerka on the CD *At the Alamo*. Three tracks on the disc were unique since they had been performed inside the Alamo church during ceremonies conducted by the Alamo Defenders Descendants Association. Ironically, the four-track CD has a running time of 18:36.

The first song, "We Remember the Alamo" recognizes the multi-cultural background of the Alamo defenders and the price they paid for Texas' freedom. But the tune also suggests that all citizens have obligations in the post-September 11, 2001 world.

> There is a shrine in Texas
> Was once a fort so long ago
> It stands for liberty and freedom
> Made by those who fell of this we know
>
> Yet some pass by and never notice
> The walls which once housed life
> But there are those who remember
> Their pain and hope and strife
>
> We remember the Alamo
> We remember through the years
> We remember the Alamo
> We remember through the years
>
> The roll call sounds and they step forward
> Travis, Bonham and Bowie
> Losoya and Esparza
> And Crockett from Tennessee
> Their sacrifice reminds us
> That liberty be sought
> With faith and hope and conviction
> Oppression must be fought

©2005 William Chemerka, BeeTee Music

Another song, "Memory of the Alamo, " written by William Pasqua, Tony Pasqua and Mike Boldt in 1985, displays the traditional story-telling aspect of so many songs about the Alamo's gallant garrison.

> They came to this big land to try and settle down
> They'd fight for the freedom,
>   to build their lives from the ground
> In a mission down in San Antone
> They would stand alone,
> They couldn't hide...they had their Texas pride

Soon the storm was comin,' all over the land
Santa Anna led his army, across the Rio Grande
They crossed the line that night
They chose to stay and fight
They wouldn't hide...they showed their Texas pride

I'm sure you know the story
They fought their way to glory
Against the odds they stood
They gave it all they could
All the names and faces
In history took their places
I can't let go...the memory of the Alamo

Broke the silence of that cold March morning
Like a raging storm it came without warning
They heard the bugles sound, the Texans
    stood their ground
Soon the widows cried...they showed their Texas pride
Just some stone walls, not much left of it
But standing tall is a never dying spirit
Heaven calls their name, they didn't die in vain
I can't let go...the memory of the Alamo

©1985 Pasqua, Boldt, Pasqua, Alamo Music

A flurry of Davy Crockett songs recorded by European artists were released in 2006 and 2007.

The Norwegian singer Ronald performed the Disney "Ballad of Davy Crockett" on his *Ronald 15* album in 2006.

Italian guitarist Riccardo Zara played the Disney best-seller in the twangy syle of Rock and Roll Hall of Famer Duane Eddy on the appropriately titled *Tribute to Duane Eddy* album in 2007.

That same year K.R. Wood released *Crockett's Fiddle Plays On, Live in the Alamo*. Wood and his fellow musicians and vocalists recorded 14 of the 17 tracks in the Alamo church, and six of those — "Bonnie Kate Reel," "Waltz of the Wind," "Plainsman," "Soldier Joy," "Midnight on the Wind —

Bonaparte's Retreat," and "Ashokan Farewell" — featured the Crockett fiddle.[6]

The CD was the latest in Wood's "Fathers of Texas" series and, like the previous releases, it is rich in traditional and original compositions that harken back to tunes of the 19th century. "Crockett Plays His Fiddle Tonight," the album's first track, is a lively Irish jig that captures the essence of Crockett's spirit, and "Mother of the Alamo," a remake of Wood's "Women of the Alamo" from his *Los Tejanos* CD, is a thoughtful reflection about the Alamo's surviving non-combatants.

One of the collection's most memorable compositions is "Listen to the Wind," a nocturnal reminder to those who visit the Alamo after dark:

Listen to the wind
Listen to the wind
Late at night at the Alamo
You can hear those songs again
Still old Crockett and MacGregor
A puttin' on a show
Music would fill the air
As the wind began to blow
Won't you listen to the wind

©2007 K.R. Wood, Texana Records

Visitors to the world's most frequented tourist destination, Walt Disney World, can still hear songs about the Alamo's most celebrated hero on a regular basis. But they have to listen carefully. Instrumental portions of "The Ballad of Davy Crockett" can be heard on the theme park's music track as one enters the Magic Kingdom, and the instrumental melody from "Old Betsy" plays on the music track at the entrance to Big Thunder Mountain Railroad in Frontierland. And Fess Parker's "The Ballad of Davy Crockett" is even in the musical mix when a caller is placed on hold at Walt Disney World Reservations. Similar music can also be heard at the Disneyland Resort.

And in 2008 Disney's transcendent "Ballad of Davy Crockett" got a 21st century overhaul in the hands of the group They Might Be Giants. In this updated rendition, released on the CD *Disney Music Block Party*, Davy is an astronaut finding new adventures in outer space.

A remarkable number of songs about the Alamo and its participants have been written since Susanna Dickinson recalled how "Colonel Crockett was a performer on the fiddle, and often during the battle took it up and played the favorite tunes" back in 1836. And they have appeared in every musical genre: Love ballads and military marches; sing-a-long chants and folk songs; movie soundtrack anthems and TV theme songs; country & western classics and rock 'n' roll-flavored compositions; orchestral performances and swing music numbers; novelty songs and speak-sing history lessons; minstrel show tunes and waltzes; sea shanties and big band arrangements; children's songs and jazz-fusion interpretations.

The story of the Alamo is one filled with the elements of determination, sacrifice, bravery and courage. These characteristics are not only universally admirable but they also are emotional — so basic to the human experience that they have been easily interpreted by artists in many fields over the centuries. Each of them has helped us remember the Alamo.

[1] Carl Peterson, *Now's the Day and Now's the Hour: Scotland Remembers the Alamo* (Mexico Beach, FL, 2004).

[2] An inscription is written inside the instrument that reads, "This fiddle is my property, Davy Crockett, Franklin County, Tenn. Feb. 14, 1819." The liner notes also trace the limited provenance of the instrument from 1859, when it was allegedly owned by one of Crockett's sons, to the 1930s when it was placed in the Witte Museum in San Antonio by Mayor Judge C. K. Quin. For discussion of Crockett's alleged fiddling see Charles K. Wofle, "Davy Crocktt's Dance and Old Hickory's Fandango" (*The Devil's Box*, 16; September 1982) and William Groneman III, "Fiddling with History" (*True West*, March 2007).

[3] June Rachelson-Ospa to William Chemerka, Feb. 24, 2008. "Quite a few of the lyrics I wrote for GTT are anti-war songs. 'We Draw The Line' is most certainly about protecting our country. I also wrote 'Everyday Man' about soldiers having to step up to the plate and join their 'everyday' brothers and fight together to protect young and old."

[4] Meat Loaf had used the same idea on his hit song "Paradise from the Dashboard Light," from the album *Bat Out of Hell*, which included a spoken segment about baseball, read by Hall of Famer Phil Rizzuto.

[5] The most important instrument in the film was a handmade, 150-year-old American violin. Veteran musician Craig Eastman played Crockett's fiddle parts in the film. Upon hearing the chilling battle call known as *degüello* played by Santa Anna's band, Crockett, who some sources say was a capable fiddler, accompanies the song for the Texian defenders, in effect doing musical battle with the Mexicans. "You would have to play a violin for ten years before you'd be able to play something like DeGuello," Eastman noted. In the CD liner notes Hancock says of the soundtrack, "Carter had reduced every emotion in the film, everything we'd been trying to say, into a lamentation that was beautiful, bittersweet and incredibly moving." Summarized from Jeff Hause, Comedy on Tap website: http://www.comedyontap.com/pantheon/crockett/crockettsongs.htm.

[6] This is the same instrument that Dean Shostak used on *Davy Crockett's Fiddle* CD (2002).

STEREO INTENDED FOR USE ON EITHER STEREO OR MONAURAL PHONOGRAPHS

CAEDMON TC 1319
VOLUME TWO

ADRIEN STOUTENBURG

AMERICAN TALL TALES
DAVY CROCKETT · PECOS BILL
READ BY ED BEGLEY

DAVY CROCKETT

ALAMO SONG TITLES AND DISCOGRAPHY

EARLY 19TH CENTURY

(c. 1818) "Will You Come to the Bower?" — An old Irish song that was played by Texian musicians during the battle of San Jacinto on April 21, 1836. The song was written by Thomas Moore (1779-1852); an adaptation of his original version by H. F. Estill was published in 1936 with music by Oscar J. Fox, written to commemorate the Texas Centennial. Recordings were made by Carl Peterson for his CD *Scotland Remembers the Alamo*; by Townes Van Zandt for K. R. Wood's CD *Fathers of Texas*; by Keith & Rusty McNeil for the CD *Moving West Songs*, and by various musicians arranged by Charles Davis on *Remember the Alamo! Mexican & Texian Music of 1836*.

(c. 1834) "Colonel Crockett's March" (H. Dielman). Composed and arranged for the piano forte. Published by John Cole and Son, Baltimore.

(1835) "'Go Ahead' — A March Dedicated to Colonel Crockett" (aka "The Crockett Victory March") — Sheet music published by Firth and Hall, New York, in 1835.

The above two titles, both instrumentals, are thought to be the first popular songs about David Crockett and were published during his lifetime.

ZIP COON

(c. 1815-30) "Zip Coon" or "Old Zip Coon" (Anonymous). The first known song to include lyrics about Crockett, this minstrel tune may date from as early as 1815, with lyrics about Crockett added in the early 1830s. Many versions and arrangements have appeared. A few examples include:

(1834) The Crow Quadrilles — Arranged for piano forte by John H. Hewitt, a folio that includes only instrumental music, without words, and instructions for dancers.

(c. 1835) "Zip Coon". As performed by George Washington Dixon. An undated version (date printed only as "18__") with a cover sheet that announces "Zip Coon — A Popular Negro Song as sung by Mr. Geo. W. Dixon with great applause" (New York, Published by Firth & Hall, No. 1. Franklin Sq.). Another copy was published in Baltimore by G. Willig. Both copyrights contain identical lyrics and music, but no author. Another Dixon version was published as "Zip Coon, A Favorite Comic Song" (Turkey in the Straw) Sung by Mr. G. W. Dixon (published by J. L. Hewitt & Co., N. Y., ca 1835).

(1839) *Crockett's Free-and-Easy Song Book*: includes a version of "Zip Coon," with two stanzas that mention Crockett.

(1840) George Frederick Bristow published his own instrumental arrangement of the song, without words, as "The Celebrated Air Zip Coon, with Brilliant Variations" — Composed for the piano forte by George F. Bristow (New York; Firth, Pond Co., Franklin Sq. — 1840), copyright entered by Firth & Hall, not Firth, Pond Co.

(1924) "Old Zip Coon" — Published version with four verses written by Larry E. Johnson, subtitled an "Old American Air;" copyright by T. S. Denison & company, Publishers, Chicago.

(1955) A traditional version titled "Old Zip Coon (Turkey in the Straw)," with the tune from "Turkey in the Straw," was included in a folio of Crockett song sheet music published by Disney during the Crockett craze that followed the Crockett television series. Ironically, the brief lyrics are from the traditional "Turkey in the Straw" and make no mention of Crockett.

(1960-1965) A 1965 copyright exists for "Old Zip Coon" (American traditional song; copyright Novello & Company Limited 1965; printed in England); music by Paul Paviour; words by D. (David) Stevens. The words for this version, credited to Stevens, also appear in *Singing Together* (Autumn 1960, BBC Publications), which used as its source *The Club Song Book for Boys*, (Boosey and Hawkes). It is possible that the music by Paul Paviour was not written until 1965 for the words Stevens had written several years earlier. The 1965 sheet music was part of a series, "Singing Class Music — Edward Arnold's Series, Edited by Herbert Howells; published by Novello & Co. Ltd., London, W.I."

The song is designated "For Newnham School Junior Choir, Bedord," so it is possible that this is merely a British copyright of a new arrangement by Paviour for the Stevens lyrics.

There also are a number of recorded versions of "Zip Coon," both with and without lyrics, some of which were issued as "Turkey in the Straw."

(1916) 78 rpm single "Old Zip Coon" (with intro from "Old Folks at Home")/"Arkansas Traveler" — Don Richardson (violin & piano); recorded May 6, 1916 (Columbia A2140).

(1919) 78 rpm single "Fiddler's Contest — Medley of Country Reels: Old Zip Coon" — Joseph Samuels (violin & piano) (Silvertone 2649; Emerson 10615; and Madison 8125).

(1919) 78 rpm single. "Devil's Dream Medley" — Joseph Samuels (Edison 50653); "Zip Coon" is the final tune in this medley.

(1921) "Old Zip Coon & Medley Reels" — Joseph Samuels (violin & piano) (Federal 5057 and Silvertone 2057).

(1926) 78 rpm single "Zip Coon" — Uncredited instrumental fiddle tune (Edison 51830).

(1928) 78 rpm single "Old Zip Coon and Medley Reels" — Fiddlin' Doc Roberts (violin & guitar); recorded May 15, 1928 in Richmond, Indiana (Gennett 6495 & Champion 15564, where he is billed as Fiddlin' Jim Burke).

(1929) 78 rpm single "Old Zip Coon" — Arkansas Charlie (pseud. for Charles Craver) (Vocalion 5384); recorded July 16, 1929 in Chicago.

(1939) "Old Zippy Coon" — Lafe Cogar (non-commercial recording made by Louis Watson Chappell in Calhoun County, W.V.; WVU Archives disc 222).

(1940) "Zip Coon" — Tom Whit (non-commercial recording made by Louis Watson Chappell in Mingo County, W.V.; WVU Archives disc 422). Although this song is titled "Zip

Coon," it bears a very close resemblance to "Pompey Smash," including the story of Crockett going coon hunting without a gun.

(1988) LP *Sackett's Harbor — Nineteenth Century Dance Music from Western New York State* - Jim Kimball, Betsy Gamble, Mitzie Collins, Eric Rounds, Glenn McClure, Karen Park. (Sampler Records S8809). Includes a version of "Zip Coon."

(2002) CD *Davy Crockett's Fiddle* — Dean Shostak (Coastline Music DS 0151). Includes "Turkey in the Straw or Old Zip Coon."

(1836) *Crockett's Free-and-Easy Song Book*. Earliest known edition of this music collection; there may have been an earlier edition since this one is billed as a "new edition," but none has yet been found. The 1836 edition contains 304 pages, but does not list a publisher and has no title page. There were reportedly at least five editions between 1836 and 1846. The 1839 edition announced a future volume titled *Colonel Crockett's Free-and-Easy Recitation Book*. The 1837 edition was titled *Crockett's Free-and-Easy Song Book: A New Collection of the Most Popular Stage Songs, as Given by the Best Vocalists of the Present Day: and also of Favorite Dinner and Parlour Songs* (Philadelphia and Pittsburgh: Kay and Company, 1837; 128 pages). At least some Alamo-related songs appeared in that edition, including "The Alamo, or the Death of Crockett" by Robert T. Conrad, and in the 1839 edition. The 1839 edition included 300 songs, without music, with suggested tunes or "airs" to which they could be played. It includes at least five songs about Crockett or which mention him, including "Go Ahead" and "The Yankee Volunteer," which probably pre-dates Crockett's death, but to which has been added references to Santa Anna, Sam Houston and, of course, Crockett. The 1839 edition added the notice "Since the appearance of the first edition of this very popular Manual for the Vocalist, the remarkable individual whose name introduced it to the notice of the public has paid the debt of nature" and mentions that Texian songs

have been added. Many of the songs in these songsters were erroneously attributed to Crockett. The title of the 1846 edition was even more long-winded: *Crockett's Free-and-Easy Song Book: Comic, Sentimental, Amatory, Sporting, African, Scotch, Irish, Western and Texian National, Military, Naval and Anacreonic: A New Collectin of the Most Popular State Songs, together with Glees, Duets, Recitations, and Medleys* (Philadelphia: Kay and Troutman, and Pittsburgh: C.H. Kay, 1846; 319 pages). In her book *Davy Crockett* (1934), Constance Rourke cites the 1846 *National Songster: Embellished with Twenty-five Splendid Engravings, Illustrative of the American Victories in Mexico. By an American Officer. New York*, which is said to contain a number of songs about Crockett and others alluding to him, probably taken from the *Crockett's Free and Easy Songbook*.

POMPEY SMASH

(Published in 1846) "Pompey Smash." This is another anonymous early minstrel song that mentions Crockett. Although the earliest known published version appeared in 1846, the song may have originated earlier. By the 20th century, the "Pompey Smash" title was largely discarded and the song became known as "Davy Crockett." Many versions were published and recorded:

(1846) — *The Negro Singers Own Book, Containing Every Negro Song That Has Ever Been Sung or Printed* (Philadelphia) includes "Pompey Smash - The Everlastin and Unkonkerable Skreamer." The same version was included in *Lloyd's Ethiopian Song Book* (London, 1847).

(1864) "My Polly Ann" (Written and Sung with the greatest success by Dave Reed; Music by T. McNally; Wm. A. Pond & Co., 547 Broadway). This Civil War era song relates a romantic chapter in Pompey's saga, but does not mention Crockett.

(c. 1860s; collected 1950) "Pom Smash," a version that includes all of the Crockett verses, was discovered by Mr. Warren Wilhite of Sherwood, Arkansas.

(1900; published 1925) A version found in Knott County, Kentucky, by Josiah E. Combs, but not published until 1925.

(1906) The first published version of the song under the title "Davy Crockett" was collected by C. H. Williams and consisted of a single stanza.

(1917) A more complete version, titled "Davy Crockett," with thirteen verses was discovered in 1917 by John Harrington Cox in Harrison County, West Virginia and published in 1925.

(1927) A version collected by Julia Beazley, titled "The Ballad of Davy Crockett," is said to be the most widely printed version of the song. A recording of it, credited only to "Mrs. Melton," was released in 1964 under the title "The Ballad of Davy Crockett" on the LP *A Treasury of Field Recordings* (Candid Records No. 8026).

(1930) A version titled "Davy Crockett" was collected by F. M. Goodhue of Mena, Arkansas on May 23, 1930, which he'd gotten from an "old woman who lived in the hills west of Mena."

(1931) "Davy Crockett" — Three stanzas performed by Mrs. Samuel Leake, Harrisonburg, Va.

(1931) 78 rpm single "Davey Crockett"/"His Parents Haven't Seen Him Since" — Chubby Parker (Conqueror Records No. 7895); first commercial recording of the song; recorded October 15, 1931.

(1936) "Pompey Smash" — David Rice (non-commercial recording made in Springfield, Mo., by Sidney Robertson. Library of Congress No. 3208 B1 and B2).

(1937) "Davy Crockett" — Mrs. Minnie Floyd (non-commercial recording made by John A. Lomax in Murrells Inlet, S.C.; Library of Congress No. AFS 2305 B1).

(1938) "Davy Crockett" — Lester Wells (non-commercial recording made by Alan Lomax in Traverse City, Mich.; Library of Congress No. 2305 B1).

(1938) "Davy Crockett" — Mrs. Pormola Eddy (non-commercial recording made by Louis Watson Chappell in Daybrook, Monongalia County, W.V.; WVU Archive disc 362).

(1938) "Pompey Smash and Davy Crockett" was published in *Texas Folk Songs* by William A. Owens from a version sung by Lemuel Jeffus.

(1939) "Davy Crockett" — Worthy Perkins (non-commercial recording made by Louis Watson Chappell in Wirt County, W.V.; WVU Archive disc 160).

(1939) "Davy Crockett" — spoken by Finley Adams (non-commercial recording made by Herbert Halpert in Dunham, Ky.; Library of Congress No. 2772 B2). Listed in *The Folksongs of Virginia* by Bruce A. Rosenberg, spoken by Finley Adams in 1939, collected by John Taylor Adams.

(1939) "Davy Crockett" — by Elmer Barton (non-commercial recording made by Alan Lomax and Helen Hartness Flanders in Quebec, Vt.; Library of Congress No. 3694 B1).

(1939) "Davy Crockett" — An updated version found in *America Sings* by Carl Carmer.

(1940) "Zip Coon" — Tom Whit (non-commercial recording made by Louis Watson Chappell in Mingo County, W.V.; WVU Archives disc 422). Although this song is titled "Zip Coon," it bears a very close resemblance to "Pompey Smash," including the story of Crockett going coon hunting without a gun.

(1941) "Davy Crockett" — Pearl Brewer (non-commercial recording made by Vance Randolph at an unknown location in the Ozarks; Library of Congress No. 12036 B23).

(1941) "Davy Crockett" — Mrs. Will Redden (non-commercial recording made by Vance Randolph at an unknown location in the Ozarks; Library of Congress No. 13131 B3).

(1954) 10-inch LP *Ballads of the Civil War* — Hermes Nye (Folkways Records FP 5004, FP 48-7/8). Includes the Beazley version of "Davy Crockett," plus some Crockett bragging narrative, and the 19th century sea song "Santa Anna." Both recordings also were released in 1960 on the CD *American History in Ballad and Song, Vol.1* — Various artists (Folkways Records - FW05801).

(1958) LP *Songs Inane Only* — Oscar Brand (Riverside RLP 12-835). Includes a version titled "Davy Crockett."

(1963) "Davy Crockett" — Adela Grostete Cook (unreleased a cappella field recording made in Sands, New Mexico; (CD #61, track 19, in the collection of J. D. Robb Field Recordings, Zimmerman Library, Center for Southwest Research, University of New Mexico, Albuquerque; http://www.unm.edu).

(1965) LP *Girl of Constant Sorrow* — Sarah Ogan Gunning (Folkways Records FSA-26). Includes an abbreviated reworking of "Davy Crockett," also released in 1976 on Gunning's *Silver Dagger* album (Rounder 0051).

(1982) LP *Tennessee: The Folk Heritage, Vol. 2: The Mountains* (Tennessee Folklore Society TFS 103). Includes a recording of "Davy Crockett" by Dee Hicks of Fentress County, Tennessee. Recorded in 1978 by Bobby Fulchjer.

(1982) LP *Make the Wildwoods Ring* — The MacArthur Family (Front Hall FHR-027). Includes a version titled "Davy Crockett."

(1992) Audio cassette *Folksongs and Ballads, Vol 4.* — Clyde Case (Augusta Heritage AHR 010). Includes a version titled of "Davy Crockett."

(1996) CD *Land of Yahoe — Children's Entertainments from the Days Before Television* — Various artists (Rounder 8041). Includes an a cappella version of "Davy Crockett" by Hobert Stollard.

(2002) CD *Davy Crockett's Fiddle* — Dean Shostak (Coastline Music DS 0151). A collection of authentic period fiddle tunes including "The Legend of Davy Crockett," a medley that includes "Remember the Alamo"

(Durriage), "Davy Crockett," and Disney's "The Ballad of Davy Crockett."

Other minstrel songs of the mid-19th century period that mention Crockett:

(Date Unknown) "Jim Crow" (Sold by L. Deming, at the sign of the Barber's pole; Hanover St., Boston, and at Middlebury, Vt.). Includes a reference to Crockett.

(Date Unknown) "Gumbo Chaff" (Sold and published by Leonard Deming, No. 61 Hanover Street, Boston MA. and at Middlebury, Vt.) and "Dinah Crow's abolition, or, The grand rumpus at the Bowery Theatre," (Chatham Chapel, 5 points, Tappan's, &c L. Deming, No. 62, Hanover Street, 2d, door from Friend Street, Boston.; publisher: L. Deming) both songs include the phrase "A sin to Crockett."

THE TEXAS REVOLUTION (1835-1836)

(1835/1836) "The Texian Grand March" (Edwin Meyrick). Written for piano forte and "Respectfully dedicated to Genl. Houston and his brave companions in arms."

(1836) "The Texan Song of Liberty" (M.A. Holley & Wilhelm Iucho). Dedicated to General Houston. (New York : Dubois & Bacon, 1836).

(1836) "San Jacinto" (Anonymous). The lyrics appeared in the 1848 *Rough and Ready Songster* (see below). Carl Peterson set this poem to the popular Scottish tune "Hey Tutti Taitie" (aka "Scot's Wha Ha'e") and recorded it for his 2001 CD *Scotland Remembers the Alamo*, where it is titled simply "San Jacinto."

(1836-37) "The Alamo, or the Death of Crockett" (Robert T. Conrad). The original lyrics appeared in the 1848 *Rough and Ready Songster* as "The Death of Crockett," but the song clearly dates from just after Crockett's death. It was recorded by Carl Peterson for his CD *Scotland Remembers the Alamo*.

(1839) "Go Ahead" (Anonymous). Another song from the 1839 edition of *Crockett's Free-and-Easy Song Book*, this one commemorates David's familiar slogan "Be sure you're right, then go ahead."

(1839) "The Yankee Volunteer" (Anonymous). This song also appears in the 1839 edition of *Crockett's Free-and-Easy Song Book*, but may well pre-date it.

(1839) "Colonel Crockett: A Virginia Reel" (George P. Knauff; published in Baltimore 1839 by George Willig, Jr.). Commercial recordings were released by Captain M. J. Bonner, under the title "The Gal on the Log" in 1925 (Victor 19699); by the Carter Brothers and Son in 1928 as "Jenny on the Railroad" (Vocalion 5297); and as "Colonel Crockett/Jenny on the Railroad" in 2001 by Jim Taylor on CD *Civil War Collection* (Volume 2) (Gourd Music).

(c. 1844) "The Song of Texas" (Anonymous; to the tune of "Lucy Neale.")

MEXICAN WAR (1846-1848)

(c. 1846) "Uncle Sam to Texas" (Anonymous; to the tune of "Yankee Doodle").

(1846) "The Alamo: Song of the Texan Ranger" (written & composed for the piano forte by John H. Hewitt. Published by Frederick D. Benteen, Baltimore 1846).

(c. 1847) "Wave, Wave, the Banner High" (Anonymous; to the tune of "March to the Battle Field.")

(c. 1848) *Rough and Ready Songster* (aka *General Taylor's Old Rough and Ready Songster*). This was a typical collection of period song lyrics with suggested tunes to which they should be played. *Rough and Ready* includes several songs with Alamo references, all of which date from the Mexican War:

"All For Texas! Or, Volunteers For Glory" (Anonymous).

"To the Field, Freemen" (Anonymous; to the tune of "Draw

the Sword, Scotland") raises the cry to extend the American flag over Texas and dislodge it from Mexico.

"Texas, The Young Tree of Freedom" (Anonymous; to the tune of "Harry Bluff"). Another Mexican War rallying cry that foresees the "Liberty tree" extending over Texas.

"Remember the Alamo" (T.A. Durriage) The song was recorded by Carl Peterson for his 2001 CD *Scotland Remember's the Alamo*. An adaptation by Rich Dehr and Terry Gilkyson, in a more modern, rousing, uptempo arrangement, was recorded by Terry Gilkyson and the Easy Riders for their 1960 LP *Remember the Alamo*. Dean Shostak included about a minute of the melody only, which is the same as that used by Petereson, as part of his medley "The Legend of Davy Crockett" on the CD *Davy Crockett's Fiddle*.

"Yankees Light the Fires Bright" (Anonymous; to the tune of "Gray Goose").

"Zachary Taylor" (Anonymous). A recording of the song appears on the 4-CD set *Moving West Songs* by Keith & Rusty McNeil.

"Liberty and Texas" (Anonymous; played to the tune "The Satty Fair").

"Freedom and Texas" (Anonymous; played to the tune "Banks of Aberfeldy").

"Uncle Sam and Mexico" (Anonymous; to the tune "Old Dan Tucker").

(1847) "Santa Anna's March" (Arranged for the piano forte by William Ratel; published in Philadelphia by George Willig & in Lexington, Ky., by Bodley & Curd).

(1847) "Santa Anna's Retreat from Cerro Gordo" (Published by W. C. Peters, Louisville, and Peters Field & Co., Cincinnati).

Carl Peterson's recordings of the above two songs were released in 2001 on the CD *Scotland Remembers the Alamo*.

(1847) "Santa Anna's Retreat" (Anonymous). Also known as "Johnny Cope," "Shay's March," "Quick March," "Nights of Gladness Quadrille," and "Spring Old-Time, Breakdown."

(1847) "Buena Vista" (Anonymous).

(c. 1847) "The Leg I Left Behind Me" (Anonymous) — A very brief recording of the song is included on the CD *Moving West Songs* by Keith & Rusty McNeil with a short narration.

(c. 1847-1848) "Santa Anna's L.E.G. from Illustrations of the Mexican War" (John H. Hewitt; published by F. D. Benteen, Baltimore; W.T. Mayo, New Orleans).

(c. 1847-1848) "Way Down in Mexico" (Anonymous).

(c. 1847-1848) "The Texas War-Cry" (Anonymous; to the tune of "The Star-Spangled Banner," aka "Anacreon in Heaven"). A recording of the song by Keith & Rusty McNeil is found on the CD *Moving West Songs.*

(1848) "Santa Ana's Retreat from Buena Vista" (Stephen Collins Foster; arranged by Robert L. Leist; 1962 printing published by Beekman Music, Inc.). Another instrumental march celebrating the U.S. victory at Buena Vista.

(c. 1848) "Santy Anno" or "Santy Anna" (Anonymous). There are many recorded variations:

(1935) "Santy Anno" — John M. (Sailor Dad) Hunt. Whitetop, Va., (non-commercial recording made by John A. Lomax, 1935; LOC 652 B). Hunt was recorded performing this song again in 1939 by Herbert Halpert (see below).

(1938) "Santy Anna" — James M. Connolly. N.Y., (non-commercial recording made by Herbert Halpert, 1938; LOC 3632 A1).

(1939) "Santy Anna" — Capt. Richard Maitland. Recorded at Sailors' Snug Harbor, Staten Island, New York, N.Y., (non-commercial recording made by Alan Lomax, 1939; LOC No. 2519 B).

(1939) "Santy Anno" — John M. (Sailor Dad) Hunt. Marion, Va., (non-commercial recording made by Herbert Halpert, 1939; LOC 2839 B1; 2840 A1).

(1954) "Santa Anna" — Hermes Nye. 10-inch LP *Ballads of the Civil War* (Folkways Records FP 5004, FP 48-7/8).

(1960) "Santy Anna" — LP *Whaling and Sailing Songs from the Days of Moby Dick* — Paul Clayton (Tradition Records; released on CD in 1997; also on CDs *Sailing & Whaling Songs of 19th Century* (1994; Legacy) and *Whaling and Sailing Songs: The Tradition Years* (2005; Empire Musicwerks).

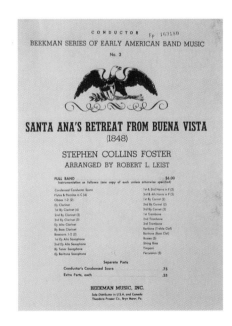

(1961) "Santy Anny-O" — Jimmie Driftwood. Released in 1991 on CD boxed set *Americana* (Bear Family).

(1978) "Santa Anna" — CD *Sea Chanties and Forecastle Songs at Mystic Seaport* - Stuart M. Frank, Stuart Gillespie and Ellen Cohn (Folkways Records - FW37300).

(1981) LP *Leave Her Johnny, Leave Her: The Stories and Shanties of Hjamar Rutzebeck, Clark Branson and Morrigan* (Folkways Records - FW38550). Includes the fol-

lowing suite: Cheerlio / Santa Anna / Clackmannanshire Mutiny / Leave Her Johnny, Leave Her / Jumping Ship with the Mate's Clothing and Money / Rio / Clackmannanshire Cook's Demise / A Sailor's Wife His Star Shall Be.

(1987) "Aweigh, Santy Ano." — CD *The Weavers Classics* (Vanguard Records).

(1993) "Santy Ana" — CD *The Tin Angel* — Larry Mohr, Odetta (OBC Records).

(1994) "Santy Anna" — CD *Time to Leave Her* — Shanty Choir Bremerhaven (SOB Records).

(1994) "Santy Anna" — CD *Folk Song America, Vol. 3* (Folk Song America: A Smithsonian Collection Series) — A. L. Lloyd and Ewan MacColl. Perhaps the most authentic version of "Santy Anna," the recording is also found on CD *Sailors' Songs & Sea Shanties* (2004; Highpoint).

(1999) "Santy Anna" — *Sea Shanties* — The Men of the

Robert Shaw Chorale (RCA). Performed at a slower tempo than most folk arrangements, which sounds more true to the original as sung by sailors.

(2001) "Santy Anna" — CD *High Seas and Lowlands* — Orpheus Male Chorus (no label info). This is a unique reworking by Alice Parker and Robert Shaw.

(1849) "Look Up on That Banner" — (R. Horace Pratt, esq.; music adapted and arranged by J. H. Hewitt; Dedicated to Lieutenant Colonel Dixon S. Miles, U.S.A.).

SECOND HALF OF THE 19TH CENTURY

(1850) Sam Houston Campaign Song (Untitled) (G. W. Pearce); sung to the tune of "Oh, Susannah!" In 1850 Sam Houston was being touted as a possible Democratic candidate for President, a short-lived movement that motivated the writing of this campaign ditty on his behalf.

(c. 1860-1874) "The Leaving of Liverpool" (Anonymous). The song mentions the clipper ship *David Crockett*, although it is referred to as "Davy Crockett." Several recordings have been released:

(1964) LP *The First Hurrah!* — The Clancy Brothers and Tommy Makem (Columbia CS 8965).

(1965) LP *A World of Our Own* — The Seekers: (Capitol T 2369). This truncated version omits the verse that refers to the ship.

(1973) LP *International Ambassador of Country Music* — George Hamilton, IV (RCA Victor LSP-4826).

(2003) CD *Gaelic Storm* — Gaelic Storm (Higher Octave Music SDA 88710).

(2005) CD *Kick It!* — Off Kilter (no label information). The band plays regularly at EPCOT's Canadian pavilion in Walt Disney World.

(1874) "Davy Crockett March" — (Composed by George Loesch; Arr. for Piano-forte by T. P. Ryder; Boston: White, Smith & Co.). Instrumental from Frank Murdock's play *Davy Crockett; Or, Be Sure You're Right, Then Go Ahead*, starring Frank Mayo. Sheet music notes that the march was "played by the orchestra between the 4th and 5th acts of the *Exquisite American Idyl, Davy Crockett*."

(1875) "Davy Crocket's (sic) Motto 'Be sure you're right, then go ahead'" (words: Sam Booth; music: Charles Schultz). Like the "Davy Crockett March," this snappy ditty was motivated by the successful play *Davy Crockett; Or, Be Sure You're Right, Then Go Ahead* and is "respectfully dedicated to Mr. Frank Mayo," who starred in the play. Some eighty years later a song of the same title, "Davy Crockett's Motto — Be Sure You're Right (Then Go Ahead)," would emerge from another Crockett dramatic production — Walt Disney's "Davy Crockett" television series. That later tune would be written and recorded by Fess Parker and Buddy Ebsen, who starred in the TV series.

(1878) "Davy Crockett Polka" (Mrs. T. A. Wilson; copyright by George W. Hagans, Manager of California Music Publishing Co., San Francisco). Sheet music for this instrumental features a postcard-size daguerreotype of Frank Mayo, in formal dress, rather than his Crockett costume. The sheet music also bears the dedication "To Frank Mayo," thus adding a third musical tribute to the actor and his portrayal of Crockett.

(1879) "The Alamo March" (Francis Muench; Published: New York: William A. Pond). Instrumental.

(1879) *The Fall of the Alamo* (Professor Francis Nona; the full title of the published work is *Patriotic Texan Hymns from "The Fall of the Alamo."*). A folio of music from the play includes the songs "Hymn of Texan Liberty," "Col. Crockett's Song," "Hymn of the Lone Star Flag," "Prayer Before Battle," "Anthem of the Alamo," "Mexican Battle March" and "Hymn of Victory."

(1882) "San Jacinto Memorial March" (William Amende; published by A. W. Perry & Son, Sedalia, Mo.). Instrumental.

(1883) "Alamo Grand March" (Gabriel Katzenberger; published by Read & Thompson, San Antonio, Tx). Instrumental.

(1884) "The Texian Heroes' Song" (Words by Mary Hunt McCaleb; music arranged and harmonized by G. P. Warner; Published by Mrs. M.A.C. Wilson, Austin, TX. 1885; by Texas Publishing Enterprises, Houston, TX., 1975; sung to "Auld Lang Syne"). A recording by Carl Peterson is on the CD *Scotland Remembers the Alamo*, where it is titled "Texas Heroes."

(1895) "The Alamo" (words: Mrs. Jennie Myers; music: Miss Ella Rodeffer). Sheet music cover features a photograph of the Alamo.

(19th or early 20th century): "The Texas Song" (Anonymous). A cowboy trail song that makes passing reference to the Alamo. A recording by Gordon Bok and Ann Mayo Muir was released in 1977 on the LP *Bay of Fundy and Other Songs* (Folk-Legacy Records FSI-54).

(Undated; 19th century): "The Texas Cowboy and the Mexican" (Anonymous). A transcription of the song appears in the 1919 *Songs of the Cattle Trail and Cow Camp* by John A. Lomax, a collection of authentic 19th century cowboy songs.

EARLY 20TH CENTURY

(1900) "Be Sure You're Right" (Serio Comic Song) (words: Capt. P. Kelly; music: F. Younker; published by C. H. Ditson & Co., New York).

(1902) "In the Shadow of the Sacred Alamo" (words: Thomas M. Bowers; music: W. H. Matchette). The sheet music features Jean Louis Theodore Gentilz's 1885 painting *Fall of the Alamo* on the cover and the notation that the song is "sung by E. L. Weston of the Olympia Opera Co."

(1903) "Flag Song of Texas" (Lee C. Hardy & Aldridge B. Kidd; © Daughters of the Republic of Texas). Lyrics include a references to Travis, Bowie, Crockett, and the war cry "Remember the Alamo!" shouted by Texian troops at San Jacinto.

(1903) "Texas — A Patrioic Song" (C. Appleyard, M.A. & Edmund Ludwig; published by Wm. von Rosenbert, Jr., Austin, Texas). Mentions San Jacinto, but not the Alamo.

(1903) "My Alamo Love" — One of several songs from a three-act musical play *The Tenderfoot* (lyrics by Richard Carle; music by H.L. (Harry Lawson) Heartz; published by M. Witmark & sons, New York).

(1904) "The Alamo March" (two step) (C. Forsiello; published by Thos. Goggan & Bro.). An instrumental "Dedicated to Miss Clara Driscoll," the celebrated "savior of the Alamo." The sheet music features Jean Louis Theodore Gentilz's 1885 painting *Fall of the Alamo* on the cover. A recording of the song was released in 1936: 78 rpm single "Alamo March"/ "Golden Wedding Anniversary Waltz" — The Paradise Entertainers (Decca 5221).

(1906) "Alamo" (words by Edward Madden; music by Dorothy Jarden).

(1907) "San Antonio" (words by Henry J. Breen; music by George Botsford). Recordings: (1927) Roy Harvey & Posey Rorer (Columbia unissued); (1929) Lowe Stokes & His North Georgians (Columbia unissued); (1929) The Highlanders; vocal by Roy Harvey (Paramount 3177 & 3267; also Broadway 8288); (1930) Smoky Mountain Ramblers (Vocalion 5422); (1930) Asa Martin (Gennett unissued); 1936 W. Lee O'Daniel & His Hillbilly Boys (Vocalion 03248).

(c. 1907) "Crockett's Honeymoon" or "Honeymoon Reel." (Anonymous fiddle tune). Recordings: LP *Heatin' up the Hall* (1989) — Yankee Ingenuity (Varrick 038), where it is part of a medley, with "Yellow Rose of Texas," used to back a square dance caller; CD *American Fogies*, Vol. 1 (1996) — Various artists (Rounder Records CD 0379) as part of "Three Reels," a medley by the Clayfoot Strutters; and CD *Dreamer's Waltz* (1996) — Scott Nygaard (Rounder Records ROUN0397).

(1908) "Remember the Alamo" Words and music by Jessie Beattie Thomas (Thomas and Davis Lyric and Music Publishers, 409 St. Louis Globe-Democrat Building, St. Louis, Missouri). Dedicated to Adina de Zavala.

(1908) "My Dream of the USA."(Leonard Chick, Charles Roth, & Ted Snyder; published by Ted Snyder).

(1909) "In the Shade of the Alamo" (lyrics: Mr. and Mrs. Thomas W. Mollaly; music: Adolph Rosenbecker). Another Alamo love song; from an original romantic operetta titled *In the Shade of the Alamo.*

(1910) "Alamo Rag" (Ben Deely & Percy Wenrich; published by Jerome H. Remick & Co., N.Y. & Detroit). Recording by Dolly Connolly released on Edison cylinder and 78 rpm single. An a-cappella rendition by The Allies was released in 2007 on the CD *2007 International Barbershop Quartet Contest — Final Round — Volume 2* (Naked Voice Records).

(1914) "Heroes of the Alamo" (words: Chris Quinn; Music: James C. Quinn). The composers dedicated this World War I-era Alamo tribute "To our Friend Hugh C. C. McClung."

(1914) "San Jacinto — Song Hymn" (poem by Laura Maverick; music by Carl Hahn). "Written for the Carnival Association of San Antonio, Texas, commemorating the anniversary of the battle of San Jacinto."

(1914) "When It's Moonlight on the Alamo" (Alfred Bryan & Fred Fischer). The first recorded song with reference to the Alamo, a tenor duet by Albert H. Campbell and Irving Gillette (aka Henry Burr) with orchestra accompaniment, was released on a Wax Cylinder in 1914 (Edison Blue Amberol wax cylinder 2422); also released in 1917 on 78 rpm single "Do You Remember"/"When It's Moonlight on the Alamo" — Frederick Wheeler & Reed Miller (Victor 17591).

(1914) "In the Shadow of the Alamo" (Will Callahan and Neil Moret; published by Jerome Remick).

(1914) "Alamo Blues — The Famous Blue Note Melody — One Step" (P. L. Eubank). Instrumental written for piano; sheet music cover features a contemporary photo of the Alamo.

(1915) *Martyrs of the Alamo*. The musical accompaniment to this silent film, published by G. Schirmer (New York; 84 pages) and arranged by Joseph Carl Breil, is held in the collections of the Library of Congress's Music Division. No recordings of this music have been found. However, the film was restored and released in 1993 on *Alamo Classics* (Old Mill Books, 1993), a VHS compilation of three restored silent films about the Alamo: *The Immortal Alamo* (1911), a lost film that was reconstructed through surviving still photographs, which included new music composed by Michael Boldt; *Martyrs of the Alamo* (1915) and *With Davy Crockett at the Fall of the Alamo* (1926), each with new music composed and performed by Dean Mora. In 1999 a new edition of *Martyrs of the Alamo* was released on VHS (Windmill Group, Inc. WGV-1202) with an entirely new score composed and performed by Boldt. The film also was released on DVD in 2004 (Delta 82 755).

(1916) "Somewhere in Mexico (Remember the Alamo)" (Francis J. Lowe; arranged by E. L. Jaco).

(1918) "In the Glow of the Alamo Moon" (George L. Cobb & Jack Yellen; published by Walter Jacobs, Boston, MA.). A ragtime tune about a romantic encounter at the "dreamy" Alamo.

(1922) "On the Alamo" (Isham Jones, Gus Kahn, Joe Lyons). One of the most oft-recorded songs that casts the Alamo as the backdrop for a romantic ballad. Later musical arrangements were written by many artists and numerous recordings of the song exist. Perhaps the first recording was made by Harry Raderman's Jazz Orchestra (4563 Edison Blue Amberol wax cylinder), released in 1922, which listed Jones and Harry Raderman as the co-composers, probably reflecting Raderman's arrangement. Other recordings include: (1922): 78 rpm single "On the Alamo"/"Mister Gallagher and Mister Shean" — Nathan Glantz's Orchestra (Pathe 020742), recorded in April 1922; (1941): 78 rpm single "Who Calls"/"On the Alamo" — Alvino Rey & Orchestra; vocals by Bill Schallen (Bluebird Reocrds B-11319); (1953) 45 rpm single "On the Alamo"/"Don't Worry 'Bout Me" — The Dave Brubeck Quartet (Columbia B-465-3); (1954) 45 rpm single "On the Alamo"/ "Mood Indigo" — Norman Petty Trio (Felsted 45-8647); (1958)

45 rpm single "On the Alamo"/"No Greater Love" — Hugo Winterhalter & His Orchestra (RCA Victor WP 296 47-3856); A-side also released on EP *No Greater Love* (RCA Camden 426); (c.1961) Charles Dant and His Orchestra on LP *Your Musical Holiday in The Golden West* (Decca DL8480).

(1923) "San Jacinto March" (Joseph Ricci). An instrumental tribute to the Texan victory.

(1924) "San Antonio" (Mattie Craig Carnathan & A. R. Walton). Popular song that includes a sketch of the Alamo on the sheet music cover.

(1925) "Sam Houston March" (Victor Alessandro). Instrumental.

(1926) "A Thought in the Alamo" (John M. Steinfeldt). The composer dedicated this song "to my friend Pompeo Coppini," who designed the Alamo Cenotaph. The sheet music directs that the song be played "slow with great dignity."

(1926) "Hymn to Texas" (words: Vivia M. Steinfeldt; music: John M. Steinfeldt). Repeats some lines from John M. Steinfeldt's "A Thought in the Alamo," suggesting that Vivia Steinfeldt may have had a hand in writing both songs.

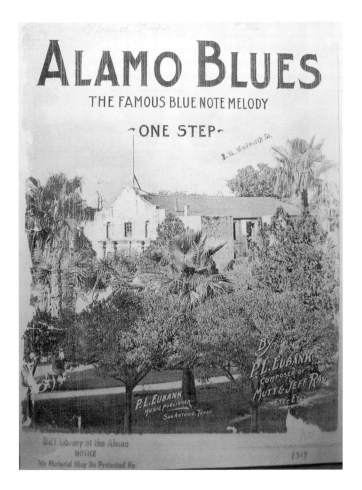

entry below).

(1934) "Alamo Schottische" (Anonymous) — Original title "Nightingale Clog"; recorded under several titles; released in 1948 on 78 rpm single "Alamo Schottische"/"Green Meadow Waltz" — Adolph Hofner (Imperial 1140).

(1934) 78 rpm single "A Heel and Toe Polka"/"Alamo Waltz" (Anonymous) (Vocalion 2769). Another song titled "Alamo Waltz" was written by Cynthia Jeanne Gayneau.

(1935) *Tejas* — An historical opera with libretto by May Abney Mayes and Willie Megee; music by Theophilus Fitz.

(1936) "Spirit of the Alamo" (Cal Cohen; arranged by Lee Zahler).

(1936) "Dear Texas" (Fern Jay Smith & Alta Lee Smith).

(1936) "The Texas Centennial Waltz" (Basil Bell).

(1936) "San Jacinto Tango" (S. S. Gay and Harve' Le Roy; Scored by Harve' Le Roy; unpublished).

(1936) "Empty Saddles" (Billy Hill) — This cowboy standard, which includes a passing reference to the Alamo, was sung by Bing Crosby in the 1936 film *Rhythm on the Range* and recorded by countless other artists.

(1937-1938) *Davy Crockett* (Kurt Weill & H.R. (Hoffman Reynolds) Hays; published by European American Music). Released in 2000 on CD *Kurt Weill: Marie Galante/ Davy Crockett* — Orchestra of St. Luke's; Victor C. Symonette, conductor; Joy Bogen, soprano, Thomas Hrynkiw, piano (Germany: Koch/Schwann 6592). Unfinished musical play about Crockett including the songs "Song of the Trees," "Hillbilly Narrative; Davy and Sarah's Marriage," "The Hand is Quicker than the Eye," "The Death of Josh Hawkins," and "Time Is Standing Still." Earlier drafts by Weill included music, but no lyrics for a piece called "Letter to Davy Crockett," which was eventually incorporated into the finished songs. The CD, which also includes music from *Marie Galante*, was later reissued as *Joy Bogen Sings Kurt*

(1927) "My Texas" (Patti Morriss Anderson). Sheet music cover is a picture of the Alamo with "A Shrine of Liberty" printed under it.

(1929) "Texas Our Texas" (Gladys Yoakum Wright & William J. Marsh). Texas' official state song.

(c. 1930) "San Antonio" (J. Frank Davis, Alva R. Willgus, Mrs. Alva R. Willgus). Sheet music cover features a sketch of the Alamo.

(1930) "Alamo March" (Charles Kama; published by Peer International Corporation). Instrumental.

(1933) "Beautiful Texas" (W. Lee O'Daniel). Recorded by Willie Nelson for LP *Texas in My Soul* in 1967 (see full 1967

Weill (no label identification or serial number; inner CD rim reads: CC1257 Joy Bogen Digirom 96966-2). The booklet from that CD includes lyrics to the *Marie Galante* songs, but not the *Davy Crockett* songs.

(1938) "Alamo Serenade" (Eileen Pike). Although the sheet music cover features a sketch of the Alamo, this is a love song with no relevance to the battle. It refers instead to the Shrine as a place where one can find serenity and peace.

(1938) "Seguin" — A Centennial Song (words: Jennie Hollamon; adaptation & music by Rev. L. J. FitzSimon). The song is an indirect tribute to Juan Sequin, one of the Alamo's couriers and the most noted Tejano hero of the Texas Revolution. "Seguin" actually celebrates the centennial of the Texas town of that name, which had been founded in 1838 as Walnut Branch, Texas, but changed to Seguin a year later to honor the man.

(1940) 78 rpm single "New San Antonio Rose"/"Bob Wills' Special"- Bob Wills and the Texas Playboys (Columbia 37014). "San Antonio Rose" was originally recorded by Wills as an instrumental in 1938, backed with "The Convict and the Rose" (Vocalion 04755); the record was later re-released by Columbia (Columbia 37009). This version added lyrics, including a reference to the Alamo.

(1941) 78 rpm single "Down by the Old Alamo"/"A Gay Ranchero" — Roy Rogers (Decca 5987).

(1942) "The Alamo" (J. Meredith Tatton; arranged by David Stevens).

(1942) "Alamo Polka" (Darrell Kirkpatrick; published by Peer International Corporation). Instrumental.

(1942) "Remember the Alamo" (words & music: Lucille Garland Puett). Another Alamo love song.

(1944) "Fightin' Flo from the Alamo" (Lou Breese and the Baers). A unique song about a most outrageous female, who fights her own battle at the Alamo. The song was introduced

in The Toodle Family comic strip, created by the Baers.

(1946) "Sam Houston"(David Stevens & Oscar J. Fox; published by C. C. Birchard & Company, Boston).

(1946) 78 rpm single "Rose of the Alamo" (George Lomas and Sophie & Julie Murray)/"A Lonely Cowboy's Dream" — Dick Thomas with the Sante Fe Rangers (National- NRC Records 5014). Neither song has anything to do with the battle or with Moses/Louis Rose; the A-side is a country and western love song.

(1946) 78 rpm single "Rose of The Alamo" (Billy Hughes)/ "The California Polka" — Tex Williams and His Western Caravan (Capitol 302).

(1946) 78 rpm single "Rose of the Alamo" (Billy Hughes)/ "Me Go Where You, Amigo" — Rosalie Allen & the Black River Riders (RCA Victor 2021).

(1947) *The Alamo* (Don Gillis). A tone poem composed by Gillis, who recorded it with the New Symphony Orchestra; released in 1950 on 10-inch mono LP *Symphony 5 1/2 (a Symphony for Fun)/The Alamo* (U.S.: Decca DRL 289; U.K.: London LPS.177); "The Alamo was part of a trilogy that also included "Portrait of a Frontier Town" and "Symphony No. 7 — Saga of a Prairie School"; Gillis' recording of the full trilogy was released on CD in 2002 (Vocalion CDLK 4163). A new stereo recording of the trilogy by Ian Hobson conducting the Sinfonia Varsovia was released in 2006 on CD *Don Gillis* (Albany Records TROY833). An early version of the work was performed in 1942 by the Baylor University Band of Waco, Texas, led by Gid Waldrop. The piece underwent substantial revision before reaching its final form and premiered on March 6, 1949, performed by the San Antonio Symphony Orchestra, conducted by Dr. Max Reiter. An unreleased 1961 recording of the piece by Dr. Joseph E. Maddy and the National High School Symphony Orchestra of Interlochen is housed at the North Texas State University library.

(1947) 78 rpm single "Across the Alley from the Alamo"/"No

Greater Love" — Woody Herman accompanied by The Four Chips (Andy Lambert, Gene Sargent, Dick Kane, Don Lamond) (Columbia 37289). One of many recordings of this perennial favorite.

(1947) 78 rpm single "Across the Alley from the Alamo" (vocal by June Christy)/"There Is No Greater Love" (vocal by The Pastels). — Stan Kenton & His Orchestra (Capitol 387).

Other artists who recorded "Across the Alley from the Alamo" include: Asleep at the Wheel, the Mills Brothers, the Starlighters, Hank Thompson, Bob Wills & the Texas Playboys, and the Three Suns.

(1947) "Santa Ana — Canción Rítmica" ("Santa Anna — Rhythmic Song") (Ricardo Fábrega). Text entirely in Spanish.

(1947) "Defense of the Alamo" — August 1947 episode from the radio series *CBS Is There*. In 1967 the program was rebroadcast by Armed Forces Radio and distributed on 33 1/3 rpm discs retitled *You Are There* (Program #47; Armed Forces Radio & Television Service; RU 26-7-71B). The program, a forerunner of TV's *You Are There*, featured modern correspondents reporting on the events of March 6, 1836.

(1948) "The Alamo" (words by James N. Cooper; music by J. Schatenstein; published by Nordyke Music Publications, Hollywood, Ca).

(1948) "The Alamo" (words by Evantha Caldwell; music by Oscar J. Fox; published by Southern Music Co., San Antonio).

(1948) 78 rpm single "Alamo Steel Serenade" (James A. Clark; published by Peer International Corporation)/"Swing with the Music" — Adolph Hofner and His San Antonians (Columbia 37817). Another of several tunes Hofner recorded with the word "Alamo" in the title.

(1949) 78 rpm single "Waltz of the Alamo" (Erwin King; aka Pee Wee King)/"The Color Song" — Pee Wee King and his Golden West Cowboys; vocal by Redd Stewart (RCA Victor 21-0015).

(1949) 78 rpm single "Waltz of the Alamo"/"Rainbow" — Ray Smith (Columbia 20583). Another recording of Pee Wee King's composition.

(1949) 78 rpm single "Rose of the Alamo" (Billy Hughes) — Chet Atkins with the Carter Sisters and Mother Maybelle. Released in 2006 on CD *Chet Atkins With The Carter Sisters And Mother Maybelle 1949* (U.K.: Country Routes 37).

(1949) 78 rpm single "Beside the Alamo" (Charles Leont) — The 101 Ranch Boys (Columbia).

(1950) Release of feature film *Davy Crockett, Indian Scout*, starring George Montgomery as Crockett's nephew, with musical score composed by Paul Sawtell; score not released on disc.

(c. 1950) 78 rpm single "Natalia"/"Desvelado" — Conjunto Alamo (Alamo Records 4991-1). Conjunto is a unique Texas-based musical form that originated in the 19th century, was popular in the 1940s and 1950s and is still played today. Although this trio is named Conjunto Alamo and recorded on the San Antonio-based Alamo label, which bore a drawing of the Alamo church, the music itself has nothing to do with the Alamo.

(1951) 78 rpm 4-disc set *Sing-a-Song of Pioneers and Explorers* — The Happy Students (Record of Knowledge. Album #1: ROK 1, includes discs 1001 and 1002; Album #2 ROK 9, includes discs 1003 and 1004). Contains songs about David Crockett, Samuel Houston, Daniel Boone, Buffalo Bill, Lewis & Clark and others. Written by Bob Weil and Dick Morros; music and arrangements by Arnold Holop; produced and directed by Richard B. Morros under the personal supervision of the Metropolitan Opera star Nanette Guilford.

(1951) *The Fall of the Alamo* — (Samuel E. Asbury). A planned stage musical that would have featured several songs from a fictional *Song Book of Davy Crockett and His Minstrels*, including "Gentlemen of Virginia," "The Valley of Humiliation" and "James Butler Bonham's Carolina Carol." The work remains unfinished.

(1952) Release of feature film *The Iron Mistress*, starring Alan Ladd as Jim Bowie, with musical score composed by Max Steiner; score not released on disc.

(1953) 45 rpm single "Within This Broken Heart of Mine"/"Beside the Alamo" (Charles Leont) — Jimmy Collett (A-side with Helen Kennedy) (Arcade 45-AR-101).

(1954) 10-inch LP *Ballads of the Civil War* — Hermes Nye (Folkways Records FP 5004, FP 48-7/8). Features "Davy Crockett," "Santa Anna" and other songs. Includes a 32-page booklet with background information on both characters, but none on the songs.

"THE BALLAD OF DAVY CROCKETT"

(1954) 45 and 78 rpm single "The Ballad of Davy Crockett" (Tom Blackburn & George Bruns)/ "Farewell" (music: Bruns) — Bill Hayes (Cadence 78 rpm CCS-1 (children's series with picture sleeve); also 1601; 45 rpm 1256; also CCS-1X). The A-side also appears on 45 rpm EP *Great Pioneers of the West* (London RE-A1051), on 1998 CD release *Treasury of the West Volume 2* (Sony/BMG/Time Life TCD 815 R1 24-08) and elsewhere. Single also released as "Die Ballade von Davy Crockett" (Cadence 1422).

(1955) 6-inch 45 rpm single "Davy Crockett and His Friend" (Disneyland). Commemorative record featuring Fess Parker singing portions of "The Ballad of Davy Crockett." Sold at Disneyland.

(1955) 45 rpm promotional single "Davy Crockett"("The Ballad of Davy Crockett") — Unreleased promo version — 1:47)/"Lonely" — Fess Parker & the Gus Norman Singers (Promo — Gusto 900). This promotional single contains an otherwise unreleased Parker recording of "The Ballad of Davy Crockett," which was issued to radio stations as a promotion for the Disney Crockett TV series, which starred Parker, who later recorded three released versions of the song. "Lonely," written by Parker, also was not released commercially.

Nearly 100 artists have recorded "The Ballad of Davy Crockett," including four that reached the upper echelons of the *Billboard* charts: The Walter Schumann Voices (#14), "Tennessee" Ernie Ford (#7), Fess Parker (#5), and Bill Hayes (#1); others included Buddy Ebsen, Tex Ritter, Rusty Draper, Karen & Cubby (Mouseketeers from Disney's *Mickey Mouse Club* TV series), Jiminy Cricket (aka Cliff Edwards), Dottie Evans & Johnny Anderson with the Merry Makers, the Disneyland Band & Vesey Walker, O Mickey Where Art Thou?, Burl Ives, Patti Page, Eddie Fisher, Johnny Horton, Mannheim Steamroller, Max Bygraves, Jo Ann Castle, Richard Hayman and his Orchestra, Longines Symphonette Society, The Cliff Adams Singers, Dean Shostak, The Sons of the Pioneers, Eddy Arnold, Tommy Scott, Gabe Drake and the Woodsman, Mac Wiseman, the Norman Luboff Choir, the Irving Fields Trio, Guy Chookoorian, Jack Andrews & the Rhythm Boys, The Rhythmaires, The Forty-Niners, the Tony Mottola Orchestra, Tex Stewart & the Sons of the Alamo, Jim Hendricks, Bob Towers with the Peter Pan Orchestra, Jack Richards with the Corwin Group, Bill Ruff and the Four Jacks, Vincent Lopez, Mitch Miller & the Sandpipers, The Wellingtons, Bill Hart and the Mountaineers with Orchestra, Paul DeWitt & the Songsters, Slim Boyd & His Range Riders, James Brown & the Trail Winders, Bob Campbell with the Ritchie Brothers, Moose and the Pelicans, Stephen Bishop, Doug Sahm, Gary Miller, The Ted Maksymowicz Orchestra, Stuart Anderson, Ronnie Ronalde, Captain Captain and the Kindygarten Kids, Mr. Mountain Dew, Seymour (a puppet), Wade Holmes, Asleep at the Wheel, the Kentucky Headhunters, the Riders in the Sky, The Phabulous Pheromones, unidentified artists listed only as "Let's All Sing," the English Chamber Orchestra, Lawrence Welk & Orchestra, David Timson & Martin George, The Mellomen, who recorded all of the verses for the TV series, theatrical films and Disney story records, and the unlikely Louis Armstrong, Steve Allen, Tim Curry, Diana Ross and the Supremes, and Buddy Hackett. Olivier Jeanes recorded the song in French, as did Chantal Goya, Serge Singer, Annie Cordy, Jacques Helian and His Orchestra, Claude

Jordan, Douchka, Patrick Simpson Jones, and Your Television Mates. Three Norwegian versions were recorded, one each by Ronald, Arne Bendiksen, and Vidar Lønn-Arnesen; Martine Bijl and Bobbejaan Schoepen and the Chicos recorded the song in Dutch; both the group Mörbyligan and Cacka Israelsson with Putte Wickmans Orkerter waxed the song in Swedish; Kauko Kayhko recorded a Finnish-language version; and Kazuya Kosaka recorded it in Japanese. Even Dick James, who later became the Beatles' music publisher, recorded a British release of the song, and Punch Miller recorded a blues arrangement called "Davy Crockett's Blues"; They Might Be Giants recorded an updated version called "The Ballad of Davy Crockett (In Outer Space)."

(1955) 10-inch 33 1/3 LP *Davy Crockett Autobiography Read by Bill Hayes — Bill Hayes* (Folkways Records — FC 7125). Reading of portions of Crockett's autobiography by Hayes; includes the following tracks: "Early Childhood," "The Creek Indian War," "The Bear Incident," "Electioneering," "Congressman," "Farewell," "The Alamo." Also released with a different cover under the title *The Real Davy Crockett — From the Frontier Hero's Authentic Autobiography "Davy Crockett's Own Story"* (Folkways FP 205). A new edition of *Davy Crockett's Own Story* had been re-printed by Citadel Press and this version of the record album carried prominent mention of the book (the earlier edition mentioned the book only on the record label, not on the cover). The book actually combined material from Crockett's authorized autobiography and other material, much of it fictional or not written by Crockett.

(1955) 45 and 78 rpm single "The Ballad of Davy Crockett" (Parker version 1 — 1:44; duet version with unidentified singer)/"I Gave My Love (Riddle Song)" — Fess Parker (Columbia red label 40449; also released on special yellow label with picture sleeve J4-242).

(1955) 45 and 78 rpm single "Farewell"/"I'm Lonely My Darlin' (Green Grow the Lilacs)" - Fess Parker (Columbia 40450; also issued as a promotional 45 rpm 4-40450; white label with red typeset). This is perhaps the only release of

"Farewell" that does not credit Davy Crockett as co-author of the song; it is credited to Blackburn and Bruns).

(1955) 45 and 78 rpm single "The Ballad of Davy Crockett"/ "Farewell" — "Tennessee" Ernie Ford (Capitol 78 rpm: CAS-3229 & CL 14506; 45 rpm F-3058 & CASF-3229).

(1955) 45 rpm EP *Tales of Davy Crockett* — "Tennessee" Ernie Ford (Capitol DAP1-3235). Includes Ford's recordings of "The Ballad of Davy Crockett" and "Farewell," plus his rendering of three Crockett tall tales, billed as "Stories from the Journal of Davy Crockett:" "The Death Hug," "A Sensible Varmint," and "Crockett's Opinion of a Thunder Storm." The EP was reissued in 2006 on the CD *Lusty Land (Including the Tales of Davy Crockett)* (Jasmine Music B000FEBVYA).

(1955) 45 & 78 rpm single "The Ballad of Davy Crockett"/ "Danger, Heartbreak Ahead" — Mac Wiseman (DOT 1240).

(1955) 6-inch 78 rpm single "The Ballad of Davy Crockett" (Part I and Part II) by The Sandpipers with Mitchell Miller and Orchestra (Little Golden Records D197). Also re-leased in 1962 on LP *A Golden Treasury of Songs About Heroes* (Golden Records GLP 42), with the song listed as "Davy Crockett."

(1955) 7-inch 78 rpm promotional single "The Ballad of Davy Crockett"/"I'm Lonely My Darlin' (Green Grow The Lilacs)" — The Sandpipers with Mitchell Miller & Orchestra (Peter Pan Peanut Butter premium disc DF100). Sold by Peter Pan Peanut Butter/Derby Foods by mail order only.

(1955) 45 & 78 rpm single "The Ballad of Davy Crockett"/"The Grave Yard Filler of the West" — The Sons of the Pioneers. (RCA Victor ; 78: BY-25; 45: 6055 & WBY-25).

(1955) 78 rpm single "Ballad of Davy Crockett"/"Robin Hood" — Gary Miller; Tony Osborne Orchestra and Beryl Stott Chorus (U.K.: Pye/Nixa N.15020). A-side also released on 45 rpm EP *Four Big Hits* (U.K.: Nixa Records NEP-24013).

(1955) 78 rpm single "The Ballad of Davy Crockett"/"Blue Shadows on the Trail" — Arizona Boys Choir (Decca DB-3707).

(1955) LP *Home on the Range #1* — Various Artists (Netherlands: Philips P 13009 R). Includes "De Ballade Van Davy Crockett" ("The Ballad of Davy Crockett" sung in Dutch) by The Chicos.

(1955) 45 rpm EP *Wade Holmes* — Wade Holmes (Blue Ribbon Records 3S-66A/B). Includes "The Ballad of Davy Crockett" and five other songs.

(1955) 45 rpm single "Jet Zoomy"/"Davy Crockett Boogie" — Stepin' Fetchit (Hollywood 1037).

(1955) 45 & 78 rpm single "The Ballad of Davy Crockett"/Cowboy Favorites (medley: "Polly Wolly Doodle," "She'll Be Coming 'Round the Mountain") — Gabe Drake and the Woodsmen directed by Maury Laws (Cricket C-51 — 45 & 78 rpm). A-side also released on the LP *Davy Crockett and Other Western Favorites* (Happy Times Records/ Pickwick International Inc. HT-1022), and LP *Songs from Walt Disney and Others* (Happy Time HT-1004), but the artist

is not credited on either album.

(1955) 78 & 45 rpm single "The Ballad of Davy Crockett"/"I've Been Thinkin'" — Rusty Draper (Mercury 78 & 45: 70555). A-side also on LP *Sing-a-long With Rusty* (Mercury Playcraft PLO-1302).

(1955) 45 and 78 rpm single "The Ballad of Davy Crockett"/ "Goober Peas" — Burl Ives (Decca 78 87322; K147 & 29423; 45: 9-29423 & 88184).

(1955) 45 rpm single "The Ballad of Davy Crockett"/"Windy Bill" — The Forty-Niners (Columbia J-4-752). A-side also released on the LP Songs from *Walt Disney's Magic Kingdom*.

(1955) 78 & 45 rpm single "The Ballad of Davy Crockett"- Jack Richards and the Corwin Group/"Bimbo"- Texas Jim and The Ranch Boys (Broadway 296).

(1955) 78 & 45 rpm single "The Ballad of Davy Crockett"/"He's a Rockin' Horse Cowboy" — James Brown & the Trail Winders (MGM 78 & 45: 11941). Brown is best remembered for his role as Lt. Rip Masters in the 1950s television series *The Adventures of Rin Tin Tin*.

(1955) 78 rpm single "The Ballad of Davy Crockett"/"Sky Chief" — Ted Maksymowicz Orchestra (Pavillion 691-A).

(1955) LP *Davy Crockett* — The Royale Singers & Orchestra (Tops in Pops Records 1801 G). Includes "The Ballad of Davy Crockett," titled "Davy Crockett."

(1955) 45 rpm single "The Crazy Pancho" (Medley): 1. "Say Si Si"; 2. "La Cucaracha"/"Davy Crockett Mambo" — Irving Fields Trio (Fiesta Records 45-049).

(1955) 45 rpm single "When Davy Crockett Met the San Antonio Rose" (Dave McEnery)/"The Night Before Xmas, Caramba!" — Red River Dave (McEnery) (Decca 9-29680; also released on TNT 1017). The recording includes a statement that the song was "recorded with the original authentic *Davy Crockett fiddle*, courtesy of the Witte Memorial Museum" (also see 2002 CD release *Davy Crockett's Fiddle* by Dean Shostak and K. R. Wood's 2007 CD release *Davy Crockett's Fiddle Plays On*).

(1955) 78 & 45 rpm single "Davy Crockett's Motto — Be Sure You're Right (Then Go Ahead)" (F. Parker & B. Ebsen)/"Old Betsy (Davy Crockett's Rifle)" (G. Bruns & G. George) — Fess Parker & Buddy Ebsen.(Columbia 40510; also J-254; Australia: CBS Coronet Records KK 018).

(1955) 78 & 45 rpm single "Davy Crockett's Motto — Be Sure You're Right (and then go ahead)"/"Old Betsy" — Burl Ives with Ray Charles Chorus (Decca 78: K-115 & 29549; 45: 9-29549).

(1955) 78 rpm single "Be Sure You're Right"/"Old Betsy" — Jimmie Dodd & the Frontier Men (Columbia 78 & Little Golden Records 6-inch 78: D-213).

(1955) 78 & 45 rpm single "A Whale of a Tale"/"Old Betsy" — Sons of the Pioneers (RCA Victor Bluebird Children's Records BY-27/WBY-27).

(1955) 45 rpm single "The Ballad of Davy Crockett"/"Very Square Dance" — Steve Allen (Coral 9-61368).

(1955) 45 rpm single "Old Betsy"/"Goo-Goo Doll" — Steve Allen; orchestra directed by Dick Jacobs (Coral 9-61445).

(1955) 45 rpm single "Old Betsy"/"Be Sure You're Right" — Tex Williams (Decca 9-29578).

(1955) 78 rpm single "Old Betsey"/"Be Sure You're Right" — Hollywood Recording Guild Orchestra (HRG 2003).

(1955) Dramatic recordings of the three Disney Davy Crockett television episodes, with Fess Parker and Buddy Ebsen recreating their original roles, were issued as 3 separate 78 and 45 rpm 2-record sets; "Davy Crockett: Indian Fighter" (Columbia 78: C-516; 45: B-2031; also issued as 2-record 78 rpm set in Australia; Philips Junior Series D21730/1H); "Davy Crockett Goes to Congress" (78: C-517; 45: B-2032); and "Davy Crockett at the Alamo" (78: C-518; 45: B-2033). Ebsen sings a bit of "The Ballad of Davy Crockett," the Mellomen add several more verses, and Parker and Ebsen sing a unique recording of "Farewell" during the Alamo episode. Boxed and paper gatefold cover editions were issued, each with several scenes from the television series. The same 3 recordings were issued in 1955 on the LP *Walt Disney's Davy Crockett: King of the Wild Frontier* (Columbia CL-666), which featured a head & shoulders photo of Fess Parker holding a prop-made pistol (from a sawed-off trapdoor Springfield Model 1873 rifle) on the cover. The album was reissued by Disney in 1958 in a gatefold edition as *Walt Disney's Three Adventures of Davy Crockett* (Disneyland WDA-3602), which included a black and white photo booklet with scenes from the TV series and a cover photo of Parker holding a rifle above his head from "Davy Crockett: Indian Fighter." Disney reissued the album with the same cover photo, but without the photo insert, in 1963 (Disneyland ST-1926), in 1968 (Disneyland DQ 1315 w/white border on cover), and around 1971 (Disneyland 1315 w/ yellow border). The recordings were released again in 2004 on the CD *Walt Disney's Davy Crockett King of the Wild Frontier! and Gene Autry Western Adventures* (Sony/DRG 19063), which features a copy of the original 1955 Columbia LP cover, with the original LP title, but part of the "Davy Crockett Goes to Congress" episode was omitted on the CD; also includes two 1950s Gene Autry story records.

(1955) *The Legend of Davy Crockett on Records* (Mattel/Rainbow 528-98). Set of 5 78 rpm, 7-inch plastic-coated cardboard cutout picture discs tied into the Disney Crockett TV series; the five records contain stories titled: "Davy Crockett — Hunter; Indian Fighter; Frontiersman; Goes to Congress; Alamo Defender." The records were sold as a set in an accordion type folder or booklet.

(1955) LP *Davy Crockett Indian Fighter* — Scotty MacGregor with The Plymouth Players; written by I. T. MacGregor (Palace PST-765) (B side is "Saddle Songs" by Cowboy Slim). Includes "The Ballad of Davy Crockett."

(1955) LP *Davy Crockett in Congress* — Scotty MacGregor with the Plymouth Players (Palace M-764; also Plymouth P12-133) (B side is "Cowboy Slim Sings Cowboy Songs"). Includes "The Ballad of Davy Crockett" and the story of Crockett in Congress. The same recording was released in 1956 on LP *Stories of the West*, credited to the T.V. Theater Players (I. T. MacGregor) (Canada: Masterseal MS-203), which includes "The Story of Daniel Boone." Another edition by the T.V. Players appeared on the Little Chip label (Little Chip KLP 1).

(1955) LP *Davy Crockett at the Alamo* — Scotty MacGregor with The Plymouth Players (Palace PST-763; also M-763; also Plymouth P-12-132) (B side is Cowboy Slim "Songs of the West"). Includes "The Ballad of Davy Crockett" and a dramatization of Crockett at the Alamo. Also released as *Stories of the Pioneers* (Little Chip Records KLP2).

(Above three discs also were issued in 45-rpm format without the songs that appear on the B-side of each LP; *Davy Crockett Indian Fighter* (Plymouth Records PEP-52); *Davy Crockett Goes to Congress* (PEP-53), and *Davy Crockett at the Alamo* (PEP-51).

(1955) 78 & 45 rpm single "Old Betsy (Davy Crockett's Rifle)"/"The Davy Crockett March (Westward!)"(Roy Freeman) — Paul DeWitt & the Songsters; Orchestra directed by Russ Haddock (Cricket C52; 45 & 78 rpm editions). The B-side also was released as "Davy Crockett Pioneer March" in 1955 on the LP *Davy Crockett and Other Western Favorites* (Happy Times Records/Pickwick International Inc. HT-1022), which also included "The Ballad of Davy Crockett" and eleven other sing-along traditional songs performed by Paul DeWitt & the Songsters, who are uncredited; "The Ballad of Davy Crockett" also appears on the LP *Songs from Walt Disney and Others* (Happy Time HT-1004), where it is titled "Davey Crockett."

(1955) 45 & 78 rpm single "The Ballad of Davy Crockett"/"Let's Make Up" — The Walter Schumann Voices (RCA — 6041; 45 & 78 editions).

(1955) 78 rpm single "Old Betsy"/"Shoeless Joe from Hannibal, Mo." — The Walter Schumann Voices (RCA — 6125 45 & 78 editions).

(1955) 45 rpm single "Davy Crockett Blues"/"Red Lipped Girl" — Red Kirk (Republic Records 7120). A-side is a novelty tune lamenting some household negatives to the Crockett craze.

(1955) 45 & 78 rpm single "The Ballad of Davy Crockett"/"Open Up" — Vincent Lopez (Sparton 133R; Waldorf 213).

(1955) 45 rpm single "Davy Crockett" (Disney "Ballad")/"Go to Bed" — Seymour and the Champagne Brothers (Bellaire B-110). Seymour is a hand puppet!

(1955) 45 & 78 rpm single "Pancho Lopez"/"I'll Never Let You Go" — Lalo Guerrero (Real Records REAL 1301); A-side is a parody of "The Ballad of Davy Crockett."

(1955) 45 & 78 rpm single "Duvid Crockett"/"Tweedle Dee" — Mickey Katz & His Orchestra (U.S. 78 & 45 rpm: Capitol EAP 1-647 & F-3144; U.K. 78 rpm Capitol C.L. 14579 b/w "Keneh Hora"). Yiddish-flavored parody of "The Ballad of Davy Crockett;" also released on LP *Mickey Katz* (Capitol T 298).

(1955) 45 rpm single "The Ballad of Ole Svenson"/"Lonesome Loverboy" — Yogi Yorgesson (Capitol F3089). Scandinavian parody of "The Ballad of Davy Crockett."

(1955) 78 & 45 rpm single "The Ballad of Davy Crewcut"/"Homer and Jethro's Pickin' and Singin' Medley No.1" — Homer & Jethro (RCA Victor 78 rpm: 20-6178; 45 rpm: 47-6178). Hillbilly parody of "The Ballad of Davy Crockett."

(1955) 45 rpm single "Dizzy Crockett"/"Six-Wheeler Rock" — Bob Campbell with the Ritchie Brothers Trio (Kryslar Records KR-5571).

(1955) 78 & 45 rpm single "Woody Woodpecker Meets Davy Crockett" (parts 1 & 2) — Mel Blanc (Capitol 78/45: CAS/CASF-3236; also on one-sided 45 rpm: Capitol DAP 58). Story record built around unlikely meeting of these two characters.

(1955) 78 & 45 rpm single "The Ballad of Davy Crockett" (parts 1 and 2) — Fred Waring and the Pennsylvanians (U.S.: Decca: 12-inch 78: DU-1011; 45: ED-1011; U.K.: Brunswick OE 9194 BFF.76 & BFF.77). The full 9-minute, 20-verse version of the famous "Ballad," also released the following year on LP *A Visit to Disneyland*. — Fred Waring & the Pennsylvanians (Decca DL 8221).

(1955) 78 rpm & 45 rpm single "The Ballad of Davy Crockett"/"Red River Valley" (Peter Pan Records 403). A side sung by Bob Towers with the Peter Pan Orchestra and Chorus; B side features vocalist Jack Arthur; both sides directed by Vicky Kasen.

(1955) 45 & 78 rpm single "The Ballad of Davy Crockett" — Bill Hart w/Mountaineer Boys & Orch./"Songs for Bronco Busters" — Jimmy Blaine w/ Guild Orch. (Record Guild of America, Inc. 78: 5-356; 45: FF 356).

(1955) 78 rpm single "The Ballad of Davy Crockett"/"The Tenderfoot" — Jack Andrews & the Rhythm Boys (Hollywood Recording Guild 2001).

(1955) 78 rpm single "The Ballad of Davy Crockett"/"The Golden Bracelet" — Guy Chookoorian (Lightning Records 17A).

(1955) 45 rpm single "Farewell"/"Jim, Johnny & Jonas" — Bing Crosby (Decca 29483).

(1955) 45 rpm single "The Ballad of Davy Crockett"/"A Good Idea, Son" — Max Bygraves (U.K. HMV Records 7M 357).

(1955) 78 & 45 rpm single "The Ballad of Davy Crockett" — Tex Stewart and Sons of the Alamo/"The Crazy Otto" — Buddy & His Pals (Bell Records 1091).

(1955) 45 & 78 rpm single "The Ballad of Davy Crockett" — Bill Ruff with the Four Jacks; "The Crazy Otto Medley" — Piano-Roll Thompson (Gateway Records 1111).

(1955) "Alamo Rag" — Instrumental rag written by Emil Hofner; recorded under the name Adolph Hofner, one of many instrumentals by Hofner with the word "Alamo" in the title. "Alamo Rag" also was released on the CD *South Texas Swing*.

THE MOVIE AND T.V. SOUNDTRACK ERA

(1955) *The Last Command.* Film score soundtrack composed by Max Steiner. A soundtrack album was released in 1980 (Citadel CT 7019), which included an 18-minute suite of music from the film on side one and music from the film *Come Next Spring* on side two. A European CD edition was released in 1995 (Best Records Nr. 9109W), which included the same 18-minute suite and other Max Steiner film music. The film's theme, "(What a Man Was Six-Foot-Six) Jim Bowie" (Max Steiner, Sidney Clare, Sheila MacRae), was performed by Gordon MacRae and the soundtrack version was released on the *The Last Command* album. A second recording by MacRae was released on a 45 rpm single "Jim Bowie"/"Why Break the Heart That Loves You" in 1956 (Capitol F 3191). That recording also was included on the 1999 CD *Wand'rin Star* (Bear Family Records BCD 16166 AR) and was a bonus track on the 2006 *3 Sailors and a Girl* soundtrack CD (Sepia Records). Another song from the film, "Consuela," was released on the LP *Great Love Themes from Motion Pictures* by Max Steiner and his orchestra (RCA LPM 1170). The film also included the song "Yo M'alegro de Haber," sung by Anna Maria Alberghetti, which has never been released on disc.

(1955) "Davy Crockett's March" (Scott Watson). Instrumental sheet music for piano (early grade) published by R. D. Row Music Company, Boston.

(1955) *Davy Crockett: An American Operetta in Two Acts* (book, lyrics and music by Charles George; published & copyrighted by T. S. Denison & Co., Minneapolis).

(1955) "Remember the Alamo" (Jane Bowers; nee Jane Gardner Riley; original title "Legend of the Alamo"). First recorded by Tex Ritter and released in 1956: 45 rpm single "Remember the Alamo"/"Gunsmoke" (Capitol F3230). Label notes that the A-side is "From the Warner Bros. Production 'Down Freedom Road'." The film, released in 1956, was actually titled *Down Liberty Road*, although it also appeared under the title *Freedom Highway*, and starred Ritter and Angie Dickinson. The single was issued in England with "The Searchers (Ride Away)" as the B-side (Capitol 45-CL 14605). The single version of "Remember the Alamo" was also released on Ritter's 1957 LP *Songs from the Western Screen* (Capitol 971; issued in U.K. in

1958 on Stetson label; HAT 3041), which included the correct movie title (*Down Liberty Road*). Ritter later re-recorded "Remember the Alamo" and his second version appears on several albums, including *Sweet Land of Liberty* (1967; Capitol ST 2743), CD *High Noon* (1992), and compilation CD *Ridin' West* (1995). Recordings of this popular Alamo song by many artists are listed below under their year of release.

(1955) 78 rpm single "Davy, You Upset My Life" (Tex-Glover)/"Band Of Gold" — The Hi-Fi Four (King K8623). A-side is an R&B swing parody of the ongoing Crockett Craze. The Hi-Fi Four included Doug Harman, Jack McNicol, John Van Evera, and Don Wainman.

(1955) 78 rpm single "Davy, You Upset My Life"/"Come in This House" — Joe Tex (King 4840).

(1955) 45 rpm single "W-O-M-A-N"/"That's All" — Etta James (Modern 972). A-side includes a reference to the ongoing Crockett craze. Also available on the album *The Definitive Collection*.

(1955) 10-inch LP *Songs from Walt Disney Famous Films Plus Other Favorites* — Various Artists (Waldorf Music Hall MH 33-137). Includes "The Ballad of Davy Crockett." The track was reissued in 1959 on the 10-inch LP *Children's Favorites* — Various Artists (Waldorf Music Hall MHK 33-1252).

(1955) 78 & 45 rpm single "The Ballad of Davy Crockett"/"It May Sound Silly" — The Rhythmaires (78 & 45 rpm: Tops R-254-49). The A-side also was released on a 10-inch 78 rpm EP with three songs ("Dance with Me Henry," "It May Sound Silly" and "Malaguena") by Sherri Lynn (45 & 78 rpm Tops R 254).

(1955) LP *Songs from Walt Disney's Magic Kingdom* — Dottie Evans, Johnny Anderson & the Merry Makers (spelled "Merrymakers" on label); arranged & conducted by Ray Carter (Columbia CL-672). Includes "The Ballad of Davy Crockett," by the Merrymakers. The LP was reissued in 1959 under the title *All Time Favorite Walt Disney Songs* (Harmony 9503), and again in 1993 on CD *All Time Favorite Walt Disney Songs* (Austria: Columbia/Sony Kids' Music 472783 2). Both the 1959 LP and the 1993 CD credit "The Ballad of Davy Crockett" to The Forty-Niners with Tony Mottola Orchestra; the original 1955 LP credits the song to The Merrymakers, but all three discs include the same recording. In 1955, the songs from the original LP also were issued on three separate EPs, each with the same title as the LP (Volumes 1, 2 & 3; Columbia B-6723, 6724, 6725).

(1955) 78 rpm EP *Davy Crockett and the Indians* (A Magic Talking Book) — Bernard Geis (John C. Winston Co. & T-19). Book and record set with a children's story about Crockett on a green vinyl record that is actually part of the book cover, thus the book could be read or placed on a record player and heard.

(1955) "Davy Crockett" — The Solitaires (Old Town Records). This original R&B song, inspired by the Disney television series, was recorded during an autumn 1955 session that included the song "Later For You Baby," but remained unreleased until 1985, when it appeared on the LP *Best of the Solitaires* (Murray Hill Records 0040). It also was released in 2000 on the CD *Spotlight on Old Town Records, Vol. 2* and in 2002 on the CD box *Spotlight on Apollo Records*, both on the Collectables label.

(1955) 45 & 78 rpm single "Sixteen Tons"/"Ballad of Davy Crockett" — Larry Cross and the Canadians (Embassy WB160).

(1955) Eddie Fisher sang "The Ballad of Davy Crockett," during a radio broadcast, as part of a medley, with "A Woman in Love" and "I'll Never Stop Loving You." The recording was released in England in 2000 on the CD *Eddie Fisher in Performance: Makin' Whoopee* (Jasmine JASCD 361).

(1955) *Walt Disney's "Davy Crockett King of the Wild Frontier" Official Souvenir Song Book.* Folio of sheet music for six songs from the Disney Crockett series, including "The Ballad of Davy Crockett," "Be Sure You're Right, and Then Go Ahead," "Old Betsy (Davy Crockett's Rifle)," which includes more lyrics than the recorded versions, "Farewell," and two additional songs: "I'm Lonely, My Darlin' (Green Grow the Lilacs)" and "I Gave My Love (The Riddle Song)." The folio includes five pages of photos from the film, posed production shots and stills of the series' star, Fess Parker.

The same year, Disney's Wonderland Music Company issued *The Ballad of Davy Crockett and Songs of the Period*, another folio of sheet music, this one containing eleven songs arranged for early grade pianist by Kenneth

Kimes. It includes "Ballad of Davy Crockett," "Farewell," and "Old Betsy" (again with additional lyrics), a traditional arrangement of "Old Zip Coon (Turkey in the Straw)" that makes no mention of Crockett, and "Old Rosin, the Beau," "Woodman, Spare That Tree," "I'm Lonely My Darlin' (Green Grow the Lilacs)," "The Old Oaken Bucket," "I Gave My Love (The Riddle Song)," "Rock of Ages," and "Home Sweet Home." Each song includes a different photo from the television series.

Before the year was out, a third Disney Crockett songbook appeared, *Walt Disney's The Ballad of Davy Crockett and Songs of the Period*, with sheet music arranged for pre-set and spinet model Hammond organ. Arranged by Lou Leaman, it features the same cover photo of Fess Parker used for the "Ballad of Davy Crockett" sheet music. The 12-page folio includes the same songs as *The Ballad of Davy Crockett and Songs of the Period*, except "Zip Coon."

(c. 1955) 45 rpm EP *Annie Cordy* — Annie Cordy (France: Columbia ESRF 1077 7TCL543). Includes "La Ballade de Davy Crockett" ("The Ballad of Davy Crockett," sung in French).

(c. 1955) 45 rpm single "Balladen Om Davy Crockett"/"Billy Boy" — Cacka Israelsson with Putte Wickmans Orkerter (Sweden: Odeon Records SD-5855). The A-side is "The Ballad of Davy Crockett" sung in Swedish.

(c. 1955) 45 rpm EP *Davy Crockett Roi des Trappeurs* — Claude Jordan (France: Vogue EPL 7224). Includes French language recordings "La Ballade de Davy Crockett" ("The Ballad of Davy Crockett"), "Pan! Quand je Tire" ("Old Betsy"), "L'enfant des Montages" ("Farewell") and "Je Vais Revoir Ma Blonde" ("The Yellow Rose of Texas").

(c. 1955) 45 rpm EP *La Ballade de Davy Crockett* — Serge Singer (France: RCA 75 092). Includes French-language recordings "La Balladed de Davy Crockett" ("The Ballad of Davy Crockett"), "Pan! Quand je Tire" ("Old Betsy"), "Sois Sur de Toi" ("Be Sure You're Right") and "L'enfant des Montages" ("Farewell").

(c. 1955) 78 rpm single "Davy Crockett Polka"/"Expressway Polka" — Ted Lach & Orchestra (Star Records 345-B).

(c. 1955) 45 rpm EP *C'era una volta Davy Crockett (There Was Once Davy Crockett)* (Italy: Baby Records BE 304). A story record with two Crockett tales, performed by a group of actors in Italian: side one, "L'orso Grigio" ("The Gray Bear") involves Crockett, a vicious bear and a damsel in distress; it includes an Italian adaptation of "Oh, Susannah" with lyrics adapted to include references to Crockett; side two: "L'assedio al Forte" ("In the Besieged Fort"), appears to be an account of a fort under siege, but not the Alamo, since Crockett manages to survive and even performs an original song about himself in Italian.

(c. 1955) 45 rpm single "The Ballad of Davy Crockett" (sung in Japanese)/"Montana Moon" — Kazuya Kosaka (Japan: Columbia Records).

(c. 1955) 45 rpm single "Davy Crockett"/"Clementine" — Bill Wilson and the Nat Charles Orchestra (Toys For Tots Records V535).

(c. 1955) 45 rpm EP (untitled) — Bobby Powers and his "Hits-A-Poppin" Orchestra (Parade 4510-A). Includes "The Ballad of Davy Crockett" and 5 other songs.

(c. 1955-56) LP *TV Western Themes* — Slim Boyd & His Range Riders (Coronet CXS 208). Includes a recording of "The Ballad of Davy Crockett;" also released as (Coronet CXS 175). The same recording appears on the LP *Songs of the West* by Tex Johnson and His Six Shooters (Diplomate 5015), suggesting that the identity of this group was somewhat amorphous.

(1956) 45 rpm EP *Great Pioneers of the West* — Bill Hayes (London RE-A 1051). Includes Hayes' recordings of "The Ballad of Davy Crockett" and "Farewell."

(1956) 78 rpm single "The Ballad of Davy Crockett"/"Robin Hood" — Dick James (U.K. Parlophone R.4117); also released in Japan (Angel Records OM1015). The A-side was released in 2007 on the CD *Big Hits and Highlights of 1956, Vol. 4* (Blue Orchid).

(1956) 45 rpm single "The Ballad of Davy Crockett"/"Hair of Gold" — Ronnie Ronalde (Columbia DB 3705; U.K.: Columbia SCM 5214; New Zealand: Columbia DNZ 10011).

(1956) 45 & 78 rpm single "Rock It Davy Crockett" (Jerry Gladstone & Bill Bellman)/"Hello" — Paul Williams & His Band featuring Jimmy Brown (45 & 78: Capitol 3205). Also found on the 1986 compilation CD *Battin' The Boogie* (Charly Records CRB 1127); compilation CD *Bang Bang Shoot'em Up* (Dead Dog Records CP-1111a); and on CD *Paul Williams — the Complete Recordings Volume 3 — 1947-1952* (Blue Moon Blues Series BMCD 6025).

(1956) 78 rpm single "Rock It, Davy Crockett"/"Please, Pretty Baby" — Billy Larkin and His Mello-Cats (Melody House Records 78 & 45 rpm: MH103).

(1956) 45 rpm single "Rock It, Davy Crockett"/"The Big Bear" — Patty Ross (Aardell Records AAPR-108).

(1956) 45 rpm EP *Vive Le Far-West* — Jacques Helian and His Orchestra (France: Trianon Records 4436). Includes "La Ballade de Davy Crockett" ("The Ballad of Davy Crockett") sung in French by an unidentified group of vocalists, backed by Helian's orchestra. The recording also is found on the 1956 EP *Jacques Helian* (France: Pathe 190), on an untitled 1984

French EP by various artists, billed as Jacques Hélian et ses cowboys (France: Trianon 4500), and on the 1997 CD release *Jacques Helian Et Son Orquestre* (EMI/Disques Pathe).

(1956) 10-inch LP *Davy Crockett de Walt Disney (Walt Disney Davy Crockett)* — Grand Prix Du Disque 1956 (France: Petit Ménestrel ALB.16/ALB-351). Record packaged in a spiral bound booklet. French-language adaptation of the three original Disney "Davy Crockett" stories, read by Francois Perier with Serge Reggiani in the role of Davy Crockett, Jacques Provins as Georgie Russel, Michel Mery as Norton and Christian Gentil as Jackson; music composed by Maurice Jarre. Includes a French-language rendition of "The Ballad of Davy Crockett" ("La Ballade de Davy Crockett") by Olivier Jeanes, which also was released on the 45 rpm EP *Moustache et Son Dixieland Jazz Band* — Various artists (France: Vega 45P-1650). The album was issued in Canada in 1967 as a 12-inch LP with two different covers; one with an original drawing of Crockett, the other with the same photo of Fess Parker used on the U.S. Disneyland LP *Walt Disney's Three Adventures of Davy Crockett* (Canada: Disneyland DF-1005). Also released in a 45 rpm edition, with 24-page book (France: Disneyland LLP-467F).

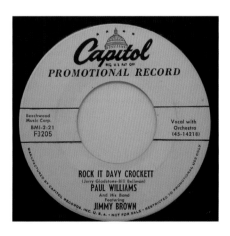

(1956) LP Disneyland Band Concert — Disneyland Band & Vesey Walker (Disneyland WDL 3002). Contains a march version of "The Ballad of Davy Crockett."

(1956) 45 & 78 rpm single "King of the River"/"Yaller Yaller Gold" — Fess Parker with Thurl Ravenscroft (uncredited) (Columbia 40568; also J4-260; Australia: CBS Coronet Records KK 018).

(1956) 45 & 78 rpm single "Yaller Yaller Gold"/"King of the River" — Lou Monte & Hugo Winterhalter Orchestra (RCA - 6246; 45 & 78 editions).

(1956) 78 & 45 rpm single "Yaller Yaller Gold"/"Give Me a Band and My Baby" — Gary Crosby (Decca 78 & 45: 29692).

(1956) 78 & 45 rpm single "King of the River"/"Yaller Yaller Gold" — A-side: George Bruns, Tommy Cole, Quincy Jones Orchestra; B-side: Mike Stewart (Hansen 78 & 45: 102).

(1956) 45 rpm single "King of the River"/"Yaller Yaller Gold" — Sons of the Pioneers (RCA 6276).

(1956) 6-inch 78 rpm single "King of the River (Mike Fink)"/"Yaller Yaller Gold" — The Frontier Men (Little Golden Records D-238).

(1956) 78 rpm 2-record set and 45 rpm EP *Walt Disney's Original Davy Crockett and Mike Fink: Their Great Keelboat Race and Their Fight with the River Pirates* — Dramatized recordings of the two Crockett-Mike Fink TV programs, with Fess Parker, Buddy Ebsen and Jeff York recreating their original roles, although only Parker is credited. Thurl Ravenscroft sings "King of the River" and Mort Mills portrays other characters, but neither performer is credited, nor is the performer who sings "Yaller Yaller Gold," which includes some alternate lyrics. The orchestra and chorus are conducted by George Bruns (Columbia 78: J-261; 45: B-2073). Gatefold cover includes still photos from the TV shows. The two stories were released on separate 78 rpm records in Australia: *Walt Disney's Original Davy Crockett and Mike Fink — "The Great Keelboat Race"* (Australia: CBS Coronet KK-023); *Their Fight with the River Pirates* (CBS Coronet Records KK 024).

(1956) 45 rpm single "Remember the Alamo" (Bowers)/ "Livin' It Up" — Johnny Bond (Columbia 4-21448).

(1956) 78 rpm single "Davy Crockett"/"Doe het nog een keer" ("Do It Again") — Bobbejaan Schoepen (Netherlands: Decca/Omega 4978-2; 35.550 25595). A-side is a Dutch-language rendition of "The Ballad of Davy Crockett."

(1956) "Jim Bowie" (aka "Natural Man, Jim Bowie," and "Jim Bowie, Adventurin' Man" (Kenneth Lorin ("Ken") Darby)). Theme from The *Adventures of Jim Bowie* television series, sung by The King's Men. Two commercial recordings of the song were released: a 1956 45 rpm single "Jim Bowie — Adventurin' Man"/"Old Chisholm Trail" by the Prairie Chiefs (RCA Bluebird 45: WBY-73; 78: BY-73; also issued as H2WW-0793); the A-side also is on the LP *Wyatt Earp, Cheyenne and Other TV Favorites* (RCA Victor Children's Bluebird Records LBY-1004). A different version was released in 1957 as "Jim Bowie Theme Song" on the 45 rpm EP *TV Favorites* by The Sandpipers with Mitch Miller & Orchestra (Golden Records EP 467) and on the LP A *Golden Treasury of Cowboy Songs* (Golden Records GLP 35), later reissued as *Hooray for Cowboys* (GLP 132). This is a livelier, uptempo arrangement of the song and it adds an additional verse not heard in any other recorded version. The 1956 TV pilot included a different version of the song, titled "Natural Man, Jim Bowie." Darby wrote additional music for several episodes, including "One Night in Tennessee," from a 1958 episode about a fictional early meeting between Bowie and Davy Crockett (played by George Dunn), and "Ursula" for an episode about Bowie meeting his future wife in Texas.

(1956) 78 rpm single "Davy Crockett is Helping Santa Claus" (Connor & Stanton)/"There's a Little Bit of Irish"- Joe Lynch (U.K. Beltona BE.2668). One of the odder songs of the Crockett craze era, which teams Davy with Santa on Christmas Eve.

(1956) "March Triumphant" (John Parker Collins). A march, originally envisioned as a tone poem by the composer, denoting the last few days of the Alamo siege, March 4-6, 1836. The sheet music includes a hand-written letter by the composer, dated April 21, 1956 — San Jacinto Day — addressed to "The Daughters of the Alamo" transmitting a copy of the

MUSIC OF THE ALAMO

music "composed by me to pay homage and honor the heroes and martyrs of the Alamo." The letter notes that the march had been played for Queen Elizabeth II of England and the Royal Family by the Scots Guard Band at Buckingham Palace on March 28, 1956.

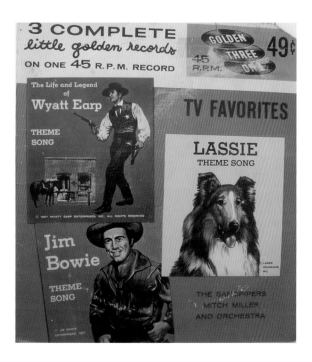

(1956) "Col. William Barrat (sic) Travis" (Robert L. (Bob) Travis). Unpublished ode to the Alamo commander and, quite possibly, the single worst-written song about the Alamo. The composer even managed to misspell Travis' middle name, which was Barret.

(1956) LP *Walt Disney Takes You to Disneyland — A Musical Tour of the Magic Kingdom* (Disneyland WDL-4004). Contains music from the original score written for the Disney "Davy Crockett" TV series and film productions to underscore the "Frontierland" segment of this orchestral suite framed as a tour of Disney's famed theme park, with Walt Disney himself speaking a few lines to introduce each segment. The "Frontierland" suite includes George Bruns-com-

posed themes from the series, such as the opening fanfare, the Davy Crockett theme, the Tennessee Homestead/Polly theme music, "Old Betsy," the "Farewell" theme, and music that accompanied Santa Anna's army, as well as the theme from *Westward Ho the Wagons*, which also starred Fess Parker. The album was reissued in 1959 as *Walt Disney Takes You to Disneyland (Musical Tour of Disneyland)* (Disneyland WDL-3042). Individual segments were issued in 1956 on 7-inch 45 rpm EPs, including *Walt Disney Takes You to Frontierland* (Disneyland DEP-4004C). The same recordings were issued in 1956 as *Your Trip to Disneyland* (Mattel/Rainbo 529), a set of five cut-out plastic-coated cardboard 78 rpm 7-inch picture discs, each with a different segment from the 1956 LP ("Introduction to Disneyland," "Tomorrowland," "Fantasyland," "Frontierland," and "Adventure- land"). The album also was re-edited to include new narration by Jiminy Cricket (aka Cliff Edwards) and his introductions of Disney's short openings, superimposed over the previously released musical segments. Jiminy also sings a bit of "The Ballad of Davy Crockett." It was released in 1958 as *A Day at Disneyland (With Walt Disney and Jiminy Cricket)* (Disneyland ST 3901), a "Record and Picture Book" for children. The original *Walt Disney Takes You to Disneyland — A Musical Tour of the Magic Kingdom* album was released on CD in 2005 (Walt Disney Records 61346-7).

(1956) 45 & 78 rpm EP *Johnny Appleseed* — read by Buddy Ebsen; music by William Lava (Disney Mickey Mouse Club DBR-60). Ebsen reads the story as Georgie Russel, the character he played in Disney's "Davy Crockett" series. He even refers to Crockett and his rifle "Old Betsy." The same recording was released in 1958 on the LP *The Littlest Outlaw and Three Other Disney Stories with Music* (Disney Mickey Mouse Club MM-26), which also was issued on 78 and 45 rpm discs (DBR 60).

(1956) "The Shotgun Rock and Roll" (Confrey Phillips, Len Phillips and Terry Arthurs). From the musical production "Adventures of Davy Crockett." This mid-tempo rock song was published in England by Mills Music Ltd., London.

TIGER TAIL

CHILDREN'S RECORDS

TIG-2011

Davy Crockett
And Around The U.S.A.

Davy Crockett
Red River Valley
Camptown Races
Down In The Valley
Dixie

Little Brown Jug
Erie Canal
Yellow Rose of Texas
Carry Me Back To Old Virginia
There's No Place Like Home

Polly Wolly Doodle
Blue Tail Fly
Arkansas Traveler
Let's Go To The Zoo

IMPORTANT MESSAGE
The back of this record container is a beautiful full color jig saw
puzzle. A wonderful gift for the wonderful children in your life.

TIGER TAIL CHILDREN'S RECORDS

A Product of AUDIO FIDELITY RECORDS, New York, N.Y.

(c. 1956) LP *Davy Crockett and Around the U.S.A.* — No artist listed (Tiger Tail Records TIG 2011). Children's album includes "The Ballad of Davy Crockett" and other folk songs. The back cover is a jigsaw puzzle of the album's front cover, created by George Buckett, featuring a cartoon of Davy surrounded by forest animals as he, rifle in hand, triumphs over a giggling bear. The album was also released on the Panda label (Panda PAN-3015), but without the jigsaw puzzle.

(c. 1956) 78 & 45 rpm single "The Ballad of Davy Crockett"/"Mambo Rock" — Tommy Scott & Prom Orchestra (Prom Records 78: 1109; 45: 45-1109).

(c. 1956) 45 rpm EP: *L'il Davy* — Mickey Mouse (Mouseketeer Records GM 104B). Includes "L'il Davy," a children's song about Crockett.

(1957) LP *Yarns and Songs* — Fess Parker (Disneyland WDL-3007). Includes "The Ballad of Davy Crockett" (Parker version 2 — 2:53; solo acoustic guitar) and "Farewell." Many songs from this LP, including this version of "The Ballad of Davy Crockett," were recycled on the 1969 Parker/ Disneyland album *Cowboy and Indian Songs*. *Yarns and Songs* was issued again in 1959 as *Yarns and Songs of the West* (Disneyland WDL-1007). Most of the songs were also released in 1964 on Parker's album *Walt Disney's Pecos Bill and Other Stories and Songs Including "Noah's Ark."* A selection of the songs appeared in 1959 on the EP *Stories in Song of the West* (Disneyland DBR-40).

(1957) "The Ballad of Davy Crockett" (Parker version 2)/"Farewell" — Fess Parker (Promo — Buena Vista Records F-426).

(1957) LP & 45 rpm EP *Lawrence Welk and His Champagne Music Play the Music of Walt Disney* — Lawrence Welk & Orchestra (LP: Coral CRL-57094; EP: EC 82033). Includes "The Ballad of Davy Crockett;" vocal by Larry Hooper.

(1957) 45 rpm single "Big Jim Bowie"/"Till My Baby Comes Home" — Chuck Bowers with the Anita Kerr Singers (Decca 9-30356).

(1958) 45 rpm single "The Ballad of Davy Crockett"/"Bidin' My Time" — Karen Pendleton & Cubby O'Brien (Disneyland F-112). The two singers were Mouseketeers on the Disney TV series *The Mickey Mouse Club*. Also released on *Moochie and Other Songs from the Mickey Mouse Club* (Mickey Mouse Club DBR-83).

(1958) LP *Songs About Zorro and Other TV Heroes* — Various Artists (Disneyland/Mickey Mouse Club MM-28). Includes "The Ballad of Davy Crockett" (Parker version 2), and "King of the River" performed by George Bruns (as Mike Fink) and Tommy Cole (as Crockett).

(1958) 45 rpm LP *Le Petit Michel Encyclopedisque* — Le Petit Michel (France: 7 RCA EGF 357). Includes "Davy Crockett" and seven other songs.

(c. 1958-60) "Davy Crockett's Jingle Bells" — Jo Jo Williams (Atomic-H Records). Mixes familiar Christmas music with some lyrics from "The Ballad of Davy Crockett." Also released in 1999 on CD *Chicago Ain't Nothin' But a Blues Band* — Various artists (Delmark 624). The album was originally issued as a vinyl LP in 1972, without Williams' recording and there is no record of its release prior to 1999.

(1959) 45 rpm single "De Guello (No Quarter)"/"Blue Safari" — Nelson Riddle Orchestra (Capitol F 4175; Japan: Capitol 7P-149). Instrumentals. A-side is billed as "From Warner Brothers Picture *Rio Bravo*" (Trumpet Solo by Manny Klein). Dimitri Tiomkin composed "De Guello" for the 1959 movie *Rio Bravo*, and then rearranged it for the 1960 film *The Alamo*. The A-side also appeared on the CD *Rio Bravo and Other Movie & TV Themes* (Bear Family BCD 16328 AR), released in 2000.

(1959) LP *The Kingston Trio at Large* — The Kingston Trio (Capitol T/ST-1199). Includes "Remember the Alamo" (Bowers). Also released on CDs *The Capitol Years* and *The Kingston Trio: Their Greatest Hits and Finest Performances*. The Kingston Trio also recorded a live version of the song in 1959, which was not released until 1994 on the CD *Live At Newport* (Vanguard 77009-2).

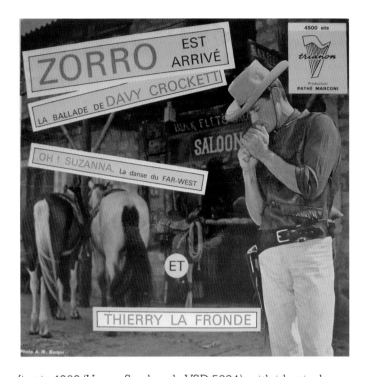

(1959) 45 rpm single "Remember the Alamo" (Bowers)/"At Last" — Rick Johnson (pseudonym of Gordon Ritter) (TNT Records; TNT-174). A-side also found on CD *The Best of TNT Records* (Collectables COL-CD-5555), released in 1995.

(1959) 45 rpm single "Grief in My Heart"/"Remember the Alamo" (Bowers) — Carl Butler (Columbia 4-41475).

(1959) "Sam Houston" (Elmo Kissee; pseudonym for Elmo Linn; "Kissee" appears in pencil on the sheet music and "Linn" is crossed out). Copyright by Westport Enterprises, Inc., Kansas City 11, Missouri.

(1959) LP *Thereby Hangs a Tale* — Eddy Arnold (RCA Victor LSP-2036). Includes "The Ballad of Davy Crockett."

(Late 1950s) LP *Songs of the Trail* — The Longines Symphonette Society (Living Sound SYS 5111/LWS 3811). Includes "The Ballad of Davy Crockett."

(Late1950s-early 1960s) 33 1/3 rpm 7-inch souvenir EP *The Alamo — A Visit in Sound Narration* — Narration by Rex Allen, written by Earl R. Martin (Rex Allen Tours America, San Antonio; no number); issued on red, blue and black vinyl. A dramatic account of the battle read by the western singer and film star.

(1960) LP *The Alamo* (Columbia mono CL 1558; stereo CS 8358; reel-to-reel 4-track stereo tape edition: Columbia CQ393; Japan: CBS LSS-5 24-C). Film soundtrack score composed by Dimitri Tiomkin with lyrics by Paul Francis Webster. Includes "Ballad of the Alamo" by Marty Robbins and "The Green Leaves of Summer" by the Brothers Four. Those tracks also were released as singles, the former b/w "A Time and a Place For Everything" (Columbia 41809); the latter b/w "Beautiful Brown Eyes" in both 45 and 33 1/3 rpm editions (Columbia: 45 rpm 4- 41808; 33 1/3 rpm 3-41808). The two songs were coupled on a 45 rpm single as well (Columbia LL-266). Robbins' recording also appears on the 1993 CD *My Rifle, My Pony and Me* (Bear Family Records BCD 15625 AH). Two CD editions of the soundtrack album were released, the

first in 1989 (Varese Sarabande VSD-5224), with identical contents and original liner notes by Patterson Greene, plus a few additional notes by Richard Kraft. An expanded 1995 CD edition (Columbia Legacy CK 66138) changed some of the track titles and added new notes, some voice tracks and previously unreleased music cues from the film including "Love Scene," a music cue leading into the LP track "David Crockett," which had been released in 1988 on the CD *Film Music of Dimitri Tiomkin* (Columbia/Sony CK 44370). Previously unreleased music on the expanded CD included "Cantina Music," which is actually from an early balcony scene between Crockett and Flaca originally titled "Old Mexico;" the Intermission, Entr'acte, and the erroneously mistitled "Finale," which is actually a choral reprise of "Tennessee Babe;" and "Exit Music," which is actually the movie's finale, a choral verse of "The Ballad of the Alamo," with orchestra; the original LP included an a cappella version. The film's real "Exit Music" was a reprise of the choral version of "The Green Leaves of Summer."

Parts of Tiomkin's score have been recorded by various orchestras. "The President's Country Suite," running nearly eleven minutes, includes music from Tiomkin's scores for *Duel in the Sun, Red River, High Noon, Giant, Rawhide,* and *The Alamo.* It was arranged for a small orchestra for the 1966 documentary film *The President's Country,* a salute to President Lyndon Johnson, narrated by Gregory Peck. A recording of the suite was released in 1985 on the LP *The Film Music of Dimitri Tiomkin,* recorded by the Royal College of Music Orchestra conducted by Sir David Willcocks (Netherlands: Unicorn Kanchanna DKP 9047). A half-hour suite from Tiomkin's *Alamo* score was arranged by Chistopher Palmer and released in 1995 on the CD *High Noon: Original Film Scores of Dimitri Tiomkin* — Various orchestras (RCA BMG Classics 09026-62658-2). This recording places "The Green Leaves of Summer" before the battle music. A different recording of the suite was released in 2004 on the 4-CD set *The Alamo: The Essential Dimitri Tiomkin Film Music Collection* by the City of Prague Philharmonic, conducted by Nic Raine, and the Crouch End Festival Chorus (Prime Time TVPMCD 811), but with "The Green Leaves of Summer" placed after the battle music. The CD set was also released as *Alamo: Dimitri Tiomkin — The Essential Film Music Collection* (Silva America 811). The LP *The Epic — Phase 4 Stereo Spectacular* — Stanley Black (London SP 4473) contains a shorter suite of Tiomkin's music running less than six minutes.

Music from the Film The Alamo, a 1960 LP by Tex Beneke and His Orchestra (RCA Camden CAL/CAS 655) is a tribute to Tiomkin's score and features some music from the film that was not included on the soundtrack album. These tracks include "Old Mexico" and "Reverie," a love theme from the morning scene between Crockett and Flaca. Beneke was a veteran big band musician who had once sung with Glenn Miller's band and he performs all four vocals on this album. *John Wayne "The Last American Hero,"* an LP released in Japan in 1979 (CBS 25AP 1583), features several cuts from The Alamo soundtrack, one misspelled "Davit (sic) Crockett."

(1960) 45 rpm EP *Frankie Avalon as "Smitty" Sings Songs of "The Alamo"* — Frankie Avalon (U.S.: Chancellor Records CHLA 303; U.K. EMI Records HMV 8632; France, as *Par le Vedette du film The Alamo,* President PRC 225). Avalon's recordings of four songs written for John Wayne's film *The Alamo,* in which Avalon played Smitty; "Ballad of the Alamo," "The Green Leaves of Summer," "Tennessee Babe (Oh, Lisa)" and "Here's to the Ladies." The first two titles were released as a single in Japan (Angel Records HM-111), Italy (Chancellor CH 02031), and Sweden (Sonet SXP-6029); also as a one-sided, 33 1/3 flexidisc, or "Discoflex," single in Spain (Chancellor S-21), where the songs are titled respectively "Cancion Del Alamo" and "Las Hojas Verdes." The other two titles were released as a single in Japan (Angel HM-1109). The recordings were released in 2000 on the CD *Rio Bravo and Other Movie & TV Themes* (Bear Family BCD 16328 AR).

(1960) 45 rpm single "Ballad of the Alamo"/"The Green Leaves of Summer" — Bud and Travis (Liberty F-55284).

(1960) 45 rpm and 6-inch 78 rpm single "Ballad of the Alamo" (Parts I and II on A and B sides, respectively) — The Sons of Texas (Golden Records 45 rpm: 636; 78 rpm: R836). Also released with artists listed as Michael Stewart & the Sons of Texas (Golden Records 636).

(1960) 45 rpm single "Ballad of the Alamo"/"Five Brothers" — Bob Cort (U.K. Decca F11285).

(1960) 45 rpm EP *Music of the Motion Picture The Alamo* — Nelson Riddle & His Orchestra (Capitol 1-20120; Japan: 7-149). Includes "The Green Leaves of Summer" plus songs from Riddle's soundtrack album from *The Untouchables* television series.

(1960) 45 rpm EP *El Alamo* — Nelson Riddle & His Orchestra (Capitol EAP 1-20142). Includes "Green Leaves of Summer" and "De Guello."

(1960) 45 rpm EP *Temas de Películas (Vol. 1)* — *El Alamo* — Hugo Montenegro & 20th Century Fox Orchestra and Chorus (Spain: 20th Fox Belter 50.401). Includes "Ballad of the Alamo" and "The Green Leaves of Summer"; cover is an original color painting by Bailestar modeled on the battle scene in John Wayne's movie *The Alamo*, showing Mexican cavalry charging in front of the Alamo.

(1960) 45 rpm EP *Alamo L'épopée du Texas (Alamo — The Epic Poem of Texas)* — Original soundtrack (France: Philips Medium 435.120 BE). Includes five tracks from the original *The Alamo* soundtrack album: "Overture," "The Green Leaves of Summer," "Here's to the Ladies," "Tennessee Babe (Oh, Lisa!)," and "Final."

(1960) 45 rpm single "Legend of the Alamo" (Russell, Johnston, Mellin, Johnston)/ "Gotta Travel On" — Bert Burns (Laurie Records 3074).

(1960) LP *Remember the Alamo* — Terry Gilkyson and the Easy Riders (U.S.: Kapp mono KL-1216; stereo KS-3216; U.K.: mono HA-R 2323; stereo SAH-R-6126). Includes "The Green Leaves of Summer," "Ballad of the Alamo," "Tennessee Babe" and "Here's to the Ladies," from the film *The Alamo*, a reworking of T. A. Durriage's 1848 composition "Remember the Alamo" in an uptempo folk arrangement, and other songs. The U.S. cover featured a color photo from Wayne's movie production, which was not used in the film, showing Mexican troops rushing the church building, but not an Alamo defender in sight, and a tractor-trailer truck, with a yellow cab (often wrongly identified as a bus, which may have given rise to false rumors that a bus could be seen during the film's battle sequences). The British cover, however, features a black and white photo of a scene from the film, looking in the opposite direction, showing Crockett and his men behind their impromptu barricade in front of the Alamo church, with the Mexicans advancing on them. The group also released a 45 rpm single "Ballad of The Alamo"/"The Green Leaves of Summer" (Kapp 355). The Easy Riders included Gilkyson, Dehr, Bernie Armstrong and Carson Parks.

(1960) LP *Remember the Alamo* — Narrated by Claude Rains; music composed by Tony Mottola. Designed and produced by Lyle Kenyon Engel; written by Michael Avallone. (Noble Records NOM 102). An audio dramatization of the Alamo story with segments devoted to Crockett, Bowie, Travis and Houston.

(1960) LP *Western Playhouse: Songs and Stories of the Great Wild West* — Featuring Bob Wilson (Lion 70103). Dramatic stories, adapted by Roberta Strauss, with music by Bill Simon and his Frontiersmen. Includes stories about Davy Crockett, Jim Bowie, Wyatt Earp, Bat Masterson, Daniel Boone, Kit Carson, and Wild Bill Hickok; part of a series of Lion LPs that were adapted from *Classics Illustrated* comic books.

(1960) LP *TV Western Themes* (no artists listed; Coronet Records CX 175). Includes a recording of "The Ballad of Davy Crockett," themes from various TV westerns and other songs.

(1960) LP *Theme from The Sundowners* — Billy Vaughn Orchestra (Dot DLP-3349). Includes "The Green Leaves of Summer."

(1960) LP *Great Motion Picture Themes* — Various artists (United Artists UAL 3122). Includes Nick Perito's instrumental arrangement of "The Green Leaves of Summer," also released as a 45 rpm single: "The Green Leaves of Summer"/ "Jennifer" (United Artists UA-262X; released in France; 7 EMF 238).

(1960) LP *Great Themes from Motion Pictures* — The 20th Century Strings (20th Century Fox Records FOX 1006). Includes an instrumental arrangement of "The Green Leaves of Summer."

Mantovani Plays the Theme from Exodus and Other Themes (Decca DFE 6671); and on CD *Instrumental Favorites: Mantovani* (Time Life R986-05).

(1960) LP *Film Hits* — Eddy Mers & His Concert Orchestra (Concert Hall M-980). Includes "The Green Leaves of Summer."

(1960) "Bowie Knife" (M. Oatman & E. Truman); released on LP *Hell Bent for Leather!* — Frankie Laine (Columbia CL 1615). This original song does not mention the Alamo or Jim Bowie, but celebrates the reliability of his famous knife in a tough spot.

(1960) LP *The President* — *A Musical Biography of Our Chief Executives* — Walter Brennan; the Patriots orchestra conducted by Joe Leahy; original music by Jerry Livingston; text and lyrics by Lenny Adelson (Everest SDBR-1123/LPBR-5123; also re-released by Liberty Records (LRP-3241/LST-7241); and as *The Presidents* — *A Musical Biography of Our Chief Executives* (Mark 56 Records 557). Includes anecdotes about several presidents and the original song, with the unoriginal title "Remember the Alamo" (Jerry Livingston/Lenny Adelson) sung by The Patriots, who are not credited on the album. The Patriots released a slightly longer version of the song on a single b/w "Andy Jackson" (Everest 19387).

(1960) *El Alamo* (Howard E. Akers). Instrumental concert march. Fillmore Music House Condensed Score and Parts (Fillmore Concert Band Series, C.B. 100). Copyright by Carl Fischer, Inc.

(1960) LP *Twelve Great Themes of the Soaring 60s* — The 20th Century Strings (i.e., the Fox studio orchestra) (20th Century Fox Records SFX 3043). Includes "The Green Leaves of Summer." The same recording was released again in 1961 on the LP *Great Themes from Motion Pictures* (20th Century Fox Records FOX 1006).

(c. 1960) 45 rpm EP *The Alamo* — *The History Makers* (Troubador Records IER 2-1052). Executive Producer: Joe Gallo; Producer/Engineer: Don Harris. Documentary recording.

(c. 1960) 45 rpm single "Green Leaves of Summer"/"Ballad of the Alamo" — Harry Simeone Chorale (20th Fox Records 227; also released in France; Fox V 45 P 2098).

(c. 1960) 10 inch LP *The Alamo* (Korea: National Records NL-36). Includes "Green Leaves of Summer" and "Ballad of the Alamo."

(1961) LP *El Alamo* — Lawrence Welk Orchestra (Argentina: Dot/Music Hall 12.149). Includes "The Green Leaves of Summer" ("Tema de 'El Alamo'"); also issued on EP *El Alamo* (Argentina Dot 45-E-100).

(1961) 45 rpm EP *4 Grandes Temas* — Las Cuerdas del Siglo (Argentina: 20th Century Fox/Music Hall MHALL 108). Includes "The Green Leaves of Summer" ("El Alamo").

(1961) 45 rpm EP *Alamo* — *Vepopée du Texas* — Various artists (France: Panorama 1241). Includes "The Green Leaves of Summer" ("Le Bleu de l'Ete") by Christian Juin, "Ballad of the Alamo" ("La Ballade d'Alamo") by Raymond Falgayrac, both sung in French, and two other songs. "La Ballade d'Alamo"/"Jesse James" released as 45 rpm single (France: Panorama — 2 NF MM 41).

(1961) 45 & 33 1/3 rpm single "Jimmy Martinez"/"Ghost Train" — Marty Robbins (Columbia 33 1/3: 3-42008; 45: 4-42008). The A-side is a rare tribute to a Mexican soldier, albeit a fictional one, who fought at the Alamo, the first serious song to take such an approach. The recording also was released in 1966 on Robbins' *Saddle Tramp* LP (Columbia Record Club D 237 — mono; DS 237 — stereo), and in 1995 on the 4-CD boxed set *Under Western Skies* (Bear Family Records BCD 15646).

(1961) LP *Exodus and Other Great Movie Themes* — The 101 Strings (Somerset SF 13500). Includes "The Green Leaves of Summer."

(1961) 45 rpm single "Davy Crockett's Blues" — Punch Miller. A blues arrangement of "The Ballad of Davy Crockett"; also released in 1993 on CD *Punch Miller & Louis Gallaud* (American Music Records AMCD-68).

(1961) 45 rpm single "Theme from 'The Alamo'"/"Where the Hot Winds Blow" — Clebanoff Strings (Mercury 71711).

(1961) 45 and 33 1/3 rpm single "Coward at the Alamo"/"You Are My Love" — Dave Gardner (RCA 7876). Comedian Gardner's attempt at Alamo humor.

(1961) 45 rpm single "Coward at the Alamo"/"TV Commercials" — Don Bowmen (La Gree Records 704). Another version of this comic Alamo offering.

(1961) "Alamo Rock" (Bill Bellman, Hal Blaine, Gordon Turner; published by Melody House Music Pub., San Bernardino, Ca.). Instrumental, described as having a "bright rock tempo;" no known releases.

(1961) EP *Walt Disney Presents Daniel Boone and Songs of Other Heroes* (Disneyland DBR-97). Includes "The Ballad of Davy Crockett," listed as "Davy Crockett," and songs from other Disney TV westerns.

(1961) LP *Viva Seguin* — Don Santiago Jimenez. Includes the instrumental polka "Viva Seguin," by Jimenez with his brother Flaco on bajo sexto. Issued on CD in 1995 (SCR Productions 742451854220). Another version was recorded

by Flaco Jimenez and released in 1989 on CD Arriba *El Norte* (Rounder Select 6032). There is no indication that the song has any connection to Juan Seguin, one of the Alamo couriers and a hero of the Texan Revolution, who fought at San Jacinto.

(c. 1961) (instrumental demo) "Davy Crockett Meets Mickey Mouse" — The Bel-airs. An instrumental, released in 1987 on CD *Origins of Surf Music* 1960-1963 (Goldr, Iloki ILCD1007).

(c. 1961) 45 rpm single "To Know You"/"Letter from the Alamo" (Elder, Cutchall and Devorzon). — Billy Elder (Capitol 4452). Rather than another reading of Travis' letter, this one is from an Alamo defender to his sweetheart, Jennie, written during the siege.

(1962) 45 rpm single "The Green Leaves of Summer"/"I'm Crazy 'Bout My Baby" — Kenny Ball and His Jazzmen (Pye Jazz Records 7NJ.2054).

(1962) 45 rpm EP *John William en Español* (Spain: Polydor 21 695 EPH). Includes a Spanish-language performance of "The Green Leaves of Summer" ("Las hojas verdes del verano").

(1962) "San Jacinto Valley" (Gracie George). A tragic ballad that takes place in California, not Texas, and has nothing to do with the Texas war or Sam Houston's victory over Santa Anna.

(1962) LP *Billy Edd and Bluegreass Too* — Billy Edd Wheeler (Monitor Records MF 367). Includes "Ballad of Sam Houston." Wheeler wrote the song after reading *The Raven*, a biography of Houston written by Marquis James.

(1962) 45 rpm EP *Pinky and Perky Out West* (Columbia SEG-8152). Includes "The Ballad of Davy Crockett."

(1963) LP *Walt Disney's Wonderful World of Color* (Disneyland DQ-1245). Includes "The Ballad of Davy Crockett" (Fess Parker version 1) and Parker's recording of "Farewell"; the two tracks were released as a single (Disneyland DBR-21; also F-426) with picture sleeve including lyrics on back.

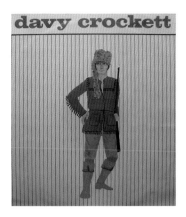

(1963) LP *Walt Disney Presents Folk Heroes* — Various artists (Disneyland ST-3921). Includes "The Ballad of Davy Crockett" and "King of the River" sung by the Wellingtons.

(1963) LP *Ring of Fire: The Best of Johnny Cash* — Johnny Cash (Columbia 2053); released on CD in 1995 (Columbia Legacy CK 66890). Includes "Remember the Alamo" (Bowers), first of three recordings Cash made of this song; also issued on 33 1/3 rpm single "Remember the Alamo"/"(There'll Be) Peace in the Valley (for Me)" (Columbia 3-8853). The recording is also found on the EP *Johnny Cash Sings The Rebel — Johnny Yuma* (Columbia B 2155).

(1963) LP *Davy Crockett: Tale Spinners for Children* (United Artists UAC 11030) — Denise Bryer & the Famous Theatre Company with the Hollywood Studio Orchestra. The same recording was released in England in 1965 as *Davy Crockett — The Adventures of the Great American Pioneer* (Beano BE12/001), which added the performers' names, collectively billed as The London Theatre Company, including Robert Hardy, Donald Pleasance, Marjorie Westbury, Paul Daneman and Derek Hart (above). No musician credit is given on the British disc.

(1963) LP *The Sounds of History*, Record 4: 1829-1849: *The Sweep Westward* — Narrated by Fredric March (Time-Life, Inc.). Side one features two brief literary passages: "Sam Houston and His Republic" (1846) by Charles Edward Lester, and "Davy Crockett: American Comic Legend" (1939) by

Richard M. Dorson. The Houston selection is a short comment the general made following his victory at San Jacinto; the Crockett selection is an abbreviated *Crockett Almanac* entry, "Crockett's Morning Hunt," about the frontiersman's successful effort to get the frozen earth moving on its axis with bear grease.

(1963) *Davy Crockett Hootenanny Song Album* — 30-page folio of popular folk songs published by Walt Disney; cover features a photo of Fess Parker, star of *Disney's Davy Crockett: King of the Wild Frontier*. Songs enjoyed some renewed popularity during a folk-revival then sweeping the country.

(c. 1963) LP *The Ballad of Jed Clampett* — Jo Ann Castle (Dot DLP 3511/2551). Includes "The Ballad of Davy Crockett."

(1963) LP *Music From Hollywood* — Various artists (Columbia CL2113). Includes "The Green Leaves of Summer" sung by Mahalia Jackson.

(1964) "The Alamo"— (Mort [Morton J.] Green & [Charles W.] Aldridge). Released on LP *Welcome to the Ponderosa — An Evening of Songs and Stories with Lorne Greene* — Lorne Greene (RCA Victor LPM & LSP 2843 RE); an original song done in spoken word with musical accompaniment and backing chorus. The song also was featured on the French EP *Lorne Greene* (France: RCA VICTOR 86.428).

(1964) LP *Walt Disney's Pecos Bill and Other Stories and Songs Including "Noah's Ark"* — Fess Parker (Disneyland DQ

1269). Includes "The Ballad of Davy Crockett" (Parker version 2 — 2:53; solo acoustic guitar), and other songs, most taken from the 1957 Parker LP *Yarns and Songs*. Parker's name and picture do not appear on the album's cover, which features Disney's animated Pecos Bill character from the film *Melody Time*; however, the singer's name and two pictures from the Davy Crockett series are featured on the back cover.

(1964) LP *Great American Heroes* — Fess Parker (RCA LPM-2973); reissued on CD in 1996 (Bear Family records BCD 16113 AH). Includes "The Ballad of Davy Crockett" (Parker version 3 — 2:16; uptempo fiddle arrangement) and "Jim Bowie," an original song about the knife fighter, and other historical figures, including the theme from Parker's *Daniel Boone* TV series. Includes 48-page booklet with background information. "The Ballad of Davy Crockett" and "Daniel Boone" also were issued as a 45 rpm single (RCA 47-8429), reissued in 1989 (Collectables 4572). This version of "The Ballad of Davy Crockett" also was released on the 1993 CD *My Rifle, My Pony and Me* (Bear Family Records BCD 15625 AH). The recordings on this album also were played during Parker's appearance on an Armed Forces Radio program around this time, which was distributed on disc (Armed Forces Radio W-1664).

(1964) 7-inch 3-LP set *Dr. Fun's Funhouse* — Various Artists (Columbia Record Club M3K 1003 MK 113 ZLP 76743). Includes "The Ballad of Davy Crockett" sung by Captain Captain and the Kindygarten Kids. Also sold as a six-disc, 12-inch LP set.

(1964) Untitled LP (Enrichment American Landmark Records 108). Side One: *Daniel Boone* (adapted from 1952 Landmark book by John Mason Brown); Side Two: *Sam Houston, the Tallest Texan* (adapted from 1953 Landmark book by William Johnson) Abbreviated renditions of the two books; the Houston recording includes mention of the Alamo and relates Houston's victory at San Jacinto.

(1964) LP *Hits from the Great Western Movies* — Kelso Herston & the Guitar Kings (Time Records S/2161). Includes "The Green Leaves of Summer."

(1964) 33 1/3 rpm single "Davy Crockett — Remember the Alamo" (General Electric Show 'N Tell Picturesound program — ST 131). Part of GE's Show 'N Tell library of classic stories for children. The record came with a vertical slide show of illustrations. The title track is a narration and musical bio of Crockett's life. The flip side, "Pioneer March," tells the story of a fictitious western wagon train led by Crockett.

(c. mid-1960s) 45 rpm EP *Musique Du Film Alamo* — Steve Sannard & His Orchestra (France: Musicdisc S-310). Includes "The Green Leaves of Summer", "Man of Mystery," "The Sound of Love," and "Song Without End."

(1965) *Remember the Alamo* (A tone poem by Julia Smith in collaboration with Cecile Vashaw; for symphonic band with optional narrator and optional chorus). Commissioned by Lt. Cmdr. Anthony A. Mitchell, leader of the U.S. Navy Band, for the band's inaugural concert of 1965. The ten-minute piece includes a reading of Travis's letter. The work was dedicated to President Lyndon B. Johnson on the occasion of his inauguration and premiered on January 15, 1965 in Washington, D.C.

(1965) LP *Catch the Wind* — Donovan (Hickory Records; LPM 123); includes "Remember the Alamo" (Bowers). The album was released on CD in 1996; the recording also appears on

CDs *Summer Day Reflection Songs, The Very Best of the Early Years* and *What's Bin Did and What's Bin Hid*; 45 rpm single "Remember the Alamo"/"The Ballad of Crystal Man" released in Holland (Pye 7N17088).

(1965) LP *I Believe* — Frankie Laine (Capitol (S)T-2277). Includes "The Green Leaves of Summer."

(1965) LP *Historic Music of the Great West* — Narration by Richard Boone (American Heritage Records). Produced as a companion to the book *The American Heritage History of the Great West*. It features such tracks as "El Deguello" and "Will You Come to the Bower."

(c. 1965) LP *Robinson Crusoe — Davy Crockett* (Storyteller/Mercury Records SLP 100). Each side of the album contains one story "dramatically enacted, accompanied by a 40-piece orchestra," according to the cover blurb. Side two features a 20-minute dramatization of Crockett's life.

(1966) LP *Woman* — Peter and Gordon (Capitol (S)T-2477). Includes "The Green Leaves of Summer."

(1966) 45 rpm single "Santa Anna" (actually "Remember the Alamo" by Bowers)/"Keep Me" — Gil Prather (Sims Records 329).

(1966) *The Alamo* (Robert Jager; copyright Elkan-Vogel Company, Inc., Phila.). An instrumental concert without lyrics, although, like Don Gillis' earlier symphonic work, clearly inspired by the historical events at the Alamo.

(1966) "San Antonio (The City of So Many Charms)" (Walter Jurmann). Sheet music cover is a photo of the Alamo and the lyrics mention the Alamo twice.

(1966) 45 rpm single "The Ballad of Pancho Lopez"/"Hall of Fame" — Trini Lopez (Reprise 0508). Spanish-language rendition of the 1955 Lalo Guerrero novelty parody of "The Ballad of Davy Crockett."

(1966) "Los Tejanos Escosis: The Scottish Texans" (Albert Irick Chandler). This instrumental is dedicated to natives of Scotland who died in defense of the Alamo, including John McGregor, who played the bagpipes during the siege, Isaac Robinson and David L. Wilson. Chandler, a retired Air Force master sergeant, was himself a piper.

(1967) LP *Sweet Land of Liberty* — Tex Ritter (Capitol ST 2743). Includes Ritter's second recording of "Remember the

Alamo" (Bowers) and "William Barrett Travis," a recitation of Travis's letter, which also was released as a single: "William Barret Travis: A Message from the Alamo" (adapted by Tex Ritter)/"A Working Man's Prayer" (Capitol 5966).

(1967) LP *Texas in My Soul* — Willie Nelson (RCA Victor LSP-3937). Includes "Travis Letter," a recitation of the Alamo commander's letter; Merle Travis received a writing credit for this track for the musical background. The album also includes "Remember the Alamo" (Bowers) and "Beautiful Texas," written in 1933 by W. Lee O'Daniel, which includes a reference to the Alamo. Released on CD in 2007 (American Beat Records 24122). Nelson's recording of "Remember the Alamo" also appears on the CD *Treasury of the West Volume 2*, released in 1998.

(1967) LP *Remember the Alamo* — Produced by Sonny Lester (United Artists True Action Adventure Series M22005). One of the lesser audio dramatizations of the Alamo story. None of the performers are credited on the album cover or disc.

(1968) LP *Disney Songs the Satchmo Way* — Louis Armstrong (Buena Vista STER-4044). Features Satchmo's treatment of "The Ballad of Davy Crockett"; reissued in 1971 as *The Wonderful World of Walt Disney* (Disneyland DQ/STER-1341). Also issued as a single "The Ballad of Davy Crockett"/"Chim Chim Cheree" (Buena Vista F-471; promo issued as Buena Vista WLP 45).

(1968) 45 rpm single "Remember the Alamony" (Noy-Burns-Fairchild)/ "Something Different" — Barbara Fairchild (Kapp K-925). The A-side is not an Alamo parody or novelty song, but rather a play on the word "ali-mony," and has nothing to do with the famous battle.

(1968) LP *Viva Max* — Film soundtrack composed by Hugo Montenegro and featuring Al Hirt (RCA Victor LSP-4275).

(1968) 45 rpm single "Viva Max March" — The 57th Street Orchestra (Commonwealth United Records C-3005).

(1968) LP *The Return of the Magnificent Seven and Other Great Western Themes* — The Bell Strings (Bell Records 6002). Includes "The Green Leaves of Summer."

(1968) "My Alamo Blue Bonnet" (Clayton A. Sanders). Written to commemorate the HemisFair '68, the World's Fair held in San Antonio. The song also was "Made for Vietnam and for Our Boys in Camps."

(c. 1968) LP *Six Flags over Texas* — The 50 Guitars of Tommy Garrett (Liberty LSS 14040/LMM 13040). Includes "The Green Leaves of Summer."

(1969) LP *Brave Words 'n' Fighting Talk* — The Gaberlunzie (Golden Guinea GGL 0435). Includes a version of "Remember the Alamo" (Bowers) under the title "The Alamo," complete with gunshot effects toward the end, ala Tchaikovsky's "Overture: 1812;" later reissued on CD.

(1969) *Cowboy and Indian Songs* — Fess Parker (Disneyland DQ-1336); reissued on CD in 2004 (also Disneyland DQ-1336). Contains previously released Parker recordings, most of them from his 1957 Disneyland album *Yarns and Songs*, including "The Ballad of Davy Crockett" (Parker version 2 — 2:53; solo acoustic guitar).

(1969) LP *The Story of the Love Bug* — Narrated by Buddy Hackett (Disneyland ST 3986). Audio recreation of the film story, with Buddy Hackett starting things off with a bit of "The Ballad of Davy Crockett."

(1969) 45 rpm single "Ballad of the Alamo"/"Save a Little Dream" — The Fortunes (U.S.: United Artists UA 27.019; U.K.: UP 35027).

(1969) "Davy Crockett: The Making of a Folk Hero" (written & recorded by Lowell Harrison). Recording released on album *Kentucky Folklore Record (#15)*.

(1969) "The Ballad of Richard Starr" (S. J. Flock & John Mason). Sheet music accompanied by a letter from Sidney J. Flock explaining that the song was inspired by a visit to the Alamo, where he noticed the name of Alamo defender Richard Starr of Liverpool, England, on a bronze tablet.

(1969) "Remember the Alamo" (Bowers) — Johnny Cash. Recorded live at Madison Square Garden, December 5, 1969, but not released until 2002 on CD *Johnny Cash at Madison Square Garden* (Columbia/Sony Legacy 5680). This is the second of three Cash recordings of the song.

(1969) LP *Big Western Movie Themes* — Geoff Love and his Orchestra (U.K.: Music For Pleasure MFP 1328). Includes "The Green Leaves of Summer."

(c. 1960s) 16-inch 33 1/3 rpm radio transcription disc "Davy Crockett"- Conrad Nagel (narrator); (Voice of the Army radio program 576). Issued to Armed Forces Radio; disc also contains program 575, "Ellington Moods," featuring Duke Ellington.

(c. 1960s) Internet download "Davy Crockett" — The Story Lady (Joan Gerber). This is one of many short sketches that Gerber performed as The Story Lady on Gary Owens' daily Los Angeles radio show. One of her comical sketches was called "Davy Crockett" (program 087), a humorous parody of the frontiersman's adventures. It has been available as a ringtone download on the AudioSparx website, although at 1:29 it is clearly too long for that purpose (http://www.audiosparx.com/sa/archive/Radio/Radioshows/Story Lady Davy Crockett/48446). It also is available from the Radio of Yesteryear website (CD-DH 0092) (http://www.originaloldradio.com/cddh0092.html); the Best Collection of 1930s 40s and 50s Radio website (http://www.bestoldtimeradio.com/story%20lady.htm), and other websites.

(1970) LP *American Tall Tales, Volume 2* — Read by Ed Begley (Caedmon TC 1319). Side one includes legendary stories involving Crockett; side two tells the tale of Pecos Bill. The album is part of an educational series that includes notes written by Adrien Stoutenburg, which describe how Crockett was elevated to mythical stature, and poses questions for students and teachers, such as "Why do people in this time, especially the young, enjoy stories about frontiersmen like Davy Crockett?"

(1971) 33 1/3 rpm EP *Walt Disney Presente Davy Crockett* — Narrated by Dominique Paturel; "The Ballad of Davy Crockett" sung in French by Olivier Jeanes (France: Disneyland LLP 360F). French-language Disney Crockett story record.

(1971) LP *Cub Creek Mulberry* — Gamble & Moore (Roger Gambill & Larry Moore) (AudioMedia AM-103). Includes "Remember the Alamo" (Bowers).

(1971) 33 1/3 rpm EP *Walt Disney's Story of Davy Crockett* — A-side narrated by Lois Lane; B-side by The Wellingtons (Disneyland 360). A 24-page read-along book and record set based on the December 15, 1954 TV episode "Davy Crockett, Indian Fighter." The B-side is the Wellingtons' recording of "The Ballad of Davy Crockett." A completely different version of the same story was issued in 1982 with the same title and Disneyland record number.

(1971) 45 rpm EP *Walt Disney presenta la Storia di Davy Crockett: Un Libro-Disco Della Disneyland (Walt Disney Presents the Story of Davy Crockett: A Disneyland Book-Disc)* — Narrated by Franco Morgan (Italy: Disneyland DSP 369). Italian-language Disney Crockett story record.

(1971) 45 rpm single "The Ballad of Davy Crockett"/"Whale of a Tale" — The Wellingtons (Disneyland promo DL 557; also Italy: DSP 218). The A-side also was released with Fess Parker's original version on the flip side (Disneyland VS-659F).

(1971) "The Alamo" (Tommy Brown & Micky Jones; published by E.G.G. Music France, Paris). Brown and Jones were reportedly British rock musicians based in Paris, where they penned this original song.

(1971) LP *Alamo* — Alamo (Atlantic SD 8279). Eponymous debut album by rock group Alamo. The cover, a rendering of the Alamo church by Barbara Sutherland Lewis, is the record's only connection to the Alamo.

(1971) "Alamo Cowboy" (Dick Campbell & Key Pashine). While the song begins as a familiar lament of a cowboy pining away for his lost love, we learn that he has left her to join the Alamo garrison, where he is personally welcomed by Crockett himself only moments before the final Mexican assault on the fort.

(1971) 45 rpm single "We Rockin'"/"The Ballad of Davy Crockett" — Moose and the Pelicans (Vanguard 35110). This group included Kenny Laguna, Bobby Bloom, Paul Naumann, Terry Marzano, Norman Marzano, and Sissy Spacek. Darlene Love provided backing vocals.

(1972) LP America *A 200 Year Salute in Story and Song* — Johnny Cash (Columbia KC-31645). Includes Cash's third recording of "Remember the Alamo" (Bowers), with a spoken introduction by Cash, who provides narration for the entire album, and songs by other artists; reissued in 1997 on CD and cassette *We the People* (Folk Era Productions FE 2055).

(1972) LP *The Wonderful Fantasy of Walt Disney* — Various artists (RCA Camden CXS-9014). Two-LP set, in "electronic stereo," includes "The Ballad of Davy Crockett" by Fess Parker and many other Disney songs by a variety of performers; reissued in 1976 by Candelite Music (RCA DPL-2-0165(e)).

(1972) LP *Southern Country Waltzes* (Rural Rhythm RRVC 236). Includes "Alamo Waltz" by Vassar Clements.

(1972) LP *Country Bear Jamboree* — Conducted by George

Bruns (Disneyland 3994). Includes a verse or two from "The Ballad of Davy Crockett."

(1972) LP *By Request* — The Hillsiders (U.K.: Polydor 2460 151). Includes "Remember the Alamo" (Bowers).

(1972) LP *Great Movies: They Went That-A-Way* — Stanley Black (RCA). Includes "Ballad of the Alamo."

(1972) 33 1/3 LP *Walt Disney Davy Crockett* — Piet Ekels (story); Martine Bijl (song) (Netherlands: Disneyland HLLP 360 w/ 24-page book). A Dutch-language dramatization of the Disney Crockett stories and rendition of "The Ballad of Davy Crockett."

(1973) "Santa Ana" (Bruce Springsteen). Written in late 1972 or early 1973, this song also has been referred to as "Hey Santa Ana," "Contessa," and "The Guns of Kid Cole." Although Springsteen recorded the song in May or June, 1973, during sessions for his album *The Wild, the Innocent, and the E Street Shuffle*, it was not officially released until 1998 when it appeared on the compilation boxed set *Tracks*. Springsteen had performed the song live in 1973 and again in 2005. The lyrics make no reference to the Mexican general or the Texas war.

(1973) "Santa Anna" (Jack Cortner; published by C. LO. Barnhouse Co., Oskaloosa, Iowa, under the title *New Dimensions for Jazz Band*). An instrumental composition; any connection to the Mexican general is left to the imagination.

(1973) *First Base* — Babe Ruth (Harvest SW-11151). British rockers perform "The Mexican," about one of Santa Anna's soldiers at the Alamo.

(1973) LP *The Boys at the Alamo Story* — The Rolling Stones. 2-LP bootleg album with a recording of the group's 1973 concert in Aarhus, Denmark. Cover of box has a photo of the band in front of the Alamo, but no other Alamo connection. A bootleg album titled *The Beatles at the Alamo* also appeared with an unauthorized recording of a Beatles concert.

(1974) 45 rpm single "The Ballad of Davy Crockett" (The Wellingtons)/"The Ballad of Robin Hood" (Elton Hayes) (U.K.: Disneyland Doubles DD20).

(1974) LP *Ragged Old Flag* — Johnny Cash (Columbia KC 32917). The title track of this LP, also written by Cash, is a spoken-word recording that describes an old American flag hanging from a county courthouse. Cash repeats what an old man told him about the flag and mentions that the stars and stripes flew at the Alamo along side the Texas flag. Neither banner, of course, flew at the Alamo during the 1836 siege. The recording also was released as a single b/w "Near Water" (Columbia 4-46028) and again in 1989 b/w "I'm Leaving Now" (Columbia, 38-69067); the album was issued on CD in 2001 (Columbia Legacy 505400). The recording also appears on the 2002 CD *The Essential Johnny Cash* (Columbia Legacy 86290), and the 2003 CD *America the Beautiful* (Sony 41224), which also includes "Davy Crockett's Speech" by John Wayne from *The Alamo* film soundtrack. Another recording of the song, by an unidentified narrator, was released in 2004 on the CD *Hero for Today* by the U.S. Army Band and Chorus (Altissimo Records 225577).

(1974) LP *Walt Disney presenta Tre Avventure Di Davy Crockett (Walt Disney Presents Three Adventures of Davy Crockett)* (Italy: Disneyland DQ 1315). Italian-language dramatization of the original three Disney TV Crockett stories.

(1975) 45 rpm 7-inch EP *Walt Disney's Davy Crockett and Songs of Other Heroes* (Disneyland Records 610). Disney studio recordings of "The Ballad of Davy Crockett" (Fess Parker version 2), "Zorro," "Johnny Tremain" and "Swamp Fox." Picture sleeve features a cartoon figure of Crockett facing off with a bear. Also released as a Mickey Mouse Club record (Disneyland LG 610).

(1975) LP A *Bicentennial Anthology of American Folklore* Julian Lee Rayford (Great American House of Folklore M1629). Folk album includes chants about heroes, including Davy Crockett and Sam Houston.

(1975) 6-LP set *Threads of Glory — 200 Years of America in Words and Music* (London Phase 4 Stereo; also released by Decca Records as *The American Spirit 1776-1976*). A retrospective in sound of U.S. history, including one track titled "The Alamo." This six-LP set was reissued as a 4-CD set in 2003 (Decca 289 475 201/202/203/204-2). The album is narrated by Lee Bowman and features Forrest Tucker as William Travis and Cesar Romero as President James K. Polk during the Alamo and Mexican War segments. Other Hollywood notables include Ronald and Nancy Reagan, Burt Lancaster, George Hamilton, Hugh O'Brian, Anne Baxter, Lorne Greene, Lloyd Nolan, Henry Fonda, Fred MacMurray, Susan Oliver, Rosalind Russell, Richard Carlson, Walter Pidgeon and William Bakewell. Vocal recitations are backed by traditional, classical and popular music performed by various orchestras and conductors.

(1975) 45 rpm single "De Guello" (from *Rio Bravo*)/"Mourir a Madrid" — George Zamfir (France: Philips 6042152). A-side is a rendition of Dimitri Tiomkin's composition played on the pan flute. The recording also was released in 1988 on Zamfir's LP *Romantic Dreams* and in 2006 on the CD *Gold*.

(1976) CD *The English Concertina* — Richard Carlin (Folkways Records — FW08845). Includes instrumental/concertina medley "Santa Anna's Retreat"/"Greasy Coat."

(1976) LP *Voulez vous Danser Grand mère* — Chantal Goya (France; RCA PL 37130). Includes "The Ballad of Davy Crockett," sung in French, under the title "Davy Crockett." The album was reissued in 1981 (France: RCA PW8746) and on CD in 1997 (France: Universal Records 539246). "Davy Crockett" also was released as a French single in 1976 b/w "C'est un Dernier Nuage" (instrumental) (France: RCA Victor PB 8005).

(1976) Neil Diamond sang "The Ballad of Davy Crockett" during a concert at the Convention Center Arena in San Antonio, Texas, on October 9, 1976. The song was not part of his regular concert repertoire, but he added it for the San Antonio audience. There are no known recordings.

(1977) LP *Bay of Fundy and Other Songs* — Gordon Bok (with Ann Mayo Muir) (Folk-Legacy Records FSI-54). Includes "The Texas Song," a cowboy trail song that makes passing reference to the Alamo. Bok's version also is found in his book *Time and the Flying Snow — Songs of Gordon Bok*.

(1977) LP *The Legend of Davy Crockett* — The Terrytowne Players (TIL Records TIL-498). A dramatization with music and effects, written by Scott Herbert; produced by Bob d'Orleans: "The Adventure": Part 1 and Part 2 (Crockett's name is spelled "Davey" on the record labels).

(1977) CD *Remember the Alamo* — Tom Bosley host/narrator (The Old Time Radio Club; 106). Dramatization of the Alamo story aired on CBS Radio's *General Mills Radio Adventure Theater*, June 5, 1977.

(1978) "The Alamo" ("Remember the Alamo" — Bowers) — John Otway & Wild Willy Barrett. Released on LP *Deep & Meaningless* — John Otway Wild Willy Barrett. Released on CD in 1993 as *John Otway Wild Willy Barrett & Deep & Meaningless*. This is a unique version of the Jane Bowers standard and includes cannon sounds and lyrics about a female Alamo courier!

(1978) 45 rpm single "Davy Crockett" ("The Ballad of Davy Crockett")/"Whoops a Daisy" — Humphrey Oceans (Stiff Records BUY 29B).

(1978) CD *Countryfest 3* — Various artists (Talent/Phonofile). Includes "The Ballad of Davy Crockett," titled "Davy Crockett," sung in Norwegian by Vidar Lonn-Arneson. The same recording appears on the compilation CDs *Norske Cuntrygutter* (2001) (Evigo/Phonofile) and *Melodibolgen 3* (2003) (Talent/Phonofile Godt Norsk Bellevue Entertainment 11864-2).

(1978) LP *Peter Rowan* — Peter Rowan (Flying Fish Records 071). Includes the song "Midnight Moonlight," with lyrics that refer to a rendezvous at the Alamo. Released on CD in 1992 (Flying Fish 70071).

(c. 1978) LP *Cowboys and Clowns* — Mr. Mountain Dew (Peter Pan Records 1119). Includes "The Ballad of Davy Crockett."

(1979) 45 rpm single "Heart of Glass"/"Return to the Alamo"- The Shadows (U.K. — EMI 5083). B-side is an instrumental composed by The Shadows (Welch, Marvin and Bennett).

(1979) LP *Deguello* — ZZ Top (Warner Bros. Records). Album title is taken from the bugle call reportedly played by the Mexicans during their attack on the Alamo.

(1979) 45 rpm EP *The Story of the Alamo* (Kid Stuff Records KSR 385). A story book record.

(1979) 2-LP set *Davy Crockett* (Illustrated Classics CBR 207) and *Moby Dick* (CBR 201). Record and comic book set; books adapted by Dr. Marion Kimberly; original Crockett story written by Elliot Dooley.

(c. 1970s) 45 rpm EP *Davy Crockett: The Man from Tennessee — Book and Recording* (Read & Hear Book & Recording; Peter Pan; PR 40); also released as *Davy Crockett — Read and Hear Book Recording* (Peter Pan Classics). Comic book and record set with often ludicrous, sketchy biography of Crockett, who is a very Arian blond, along with his buxom wives and their children; only the Indians

and Mexicans are dark. Sam Houston looks like Buffalo Bill, and the Alamo defenders are dressed in late 19th century U.S. cavalry uniforms. The Alamo includes only the church, as it appears now, and the U.S. Capitol also appears in its current form. The storyteller turns out to be Andrew Jackson, who actually hated Crockett and was staunchly opposed by him.

(1980) LP *Järtecken* — Mörbyligan (Sweden: Mistlur Records MLR 14). Includes this group's recording "Davy Crockett," a Swedish-language version of "The Ballad of Davy Crockett." The recording also was released in 1993 on the CD *Mörbyligan 1978-80* (Sweden: MNWCD 253).

(c. 1980) 45 rpm EP 4 *Chansons Vol. 4* — Tes Copains de la télé (Your Television Mates) (France: SFC 17104). Includes "La Ballade de Davy Crockett," a French-language rendition of "The Ballad of Davy Crockett," and three other television themes.

(1981) LP *Danny Joe Brown and the Danny Joe Brown Band* — Danny Joe Brown Band (Epic EPC 85122). Includes an original song titled "The Alamo;" issued on CD in 2004 (Wounded Bird Records 7385).

(1981) LP *Easy Listening Folk* — Various Artists (Readers Digest RD6A-065; RDK 5348). Includes "The Green Leaves of Summer" by Los Indios Tabajaras.

(1981) Audio cassette *Remember the Alamo* — Ken & Billie Ford (U.K.: VFM Cassettes Ltd. VCA 88). Includes Jane Bowers' "Remember the Alamo."

(1982) 33 1/3 EP *Walt Disney's Story of Davy Crockett.* — unidentified performers (Disneyland 360). A 24-page read-along record and book set based upon the 1954 *Disneyland* TV episode, "Davy Crockett, Indian Fighter." Side one and the first third of side two is a dramatized reading by unidentified narrator and performers with orchestral background music. Side two also includes "The Ballad of Davy Crockett" and "Polly Wolly Doodle" by unidentified sing-a-long male performers.

(1982) LP *Tug of War* (Parlophone PCTC 259) — Paul McCartney. Album features the song "Ballroom Dancing," which includes a reference to the 1950s Disney Crockett craze.

(1985) "The Alamo: A Song to Honor the Sesquicentennial of the Battle — March 6th 1836-1986." (Eric von Schmidt; ©Minglewood, 1985.); Von Schmidt, a painter-historian, composer and folksinger, penned this six-verse song in conjunction with his painting *The Storming of the Alamo*, which debuted the following year. In March, 1986, Von Schmidt performed his song live at the Alamo Village Cantina on *The Alamo* movie set in Brackettville, Texas. The performance was recorded, but never released.

(1985) LP *A Taste of the Phabulous Pheromones* — The Phabulous Pheromones (Gypsy Moth Records). This group's only album includes "Davy Crockett," a unique arrangement of the Disney "Ballad of Davy Crockett."

(1985) 45 rpm single "Davy Crockett" ("The Ballad of Davy Crockett" sung in French)/"Copain, Copain" ("Friend, Friend") — Douchka (France: Ibach Records 45T. 884 471-7). A-side includes audience sound effects; there is also a shorter edit without those effects available as an internet download.

(1986) LP *Remember the Alamo* — Donnie McCormick, Tommy Carlisle and Larry Bowie (Chiken Scratch Records CS-1836). McCormick (The Kings & Eric Quincy Tate) co-wrote, produced and recorded this album with Carlisle and Bowie (Back Alley Bandits) as a country & western tribute to the Texas sesquicentennial (all songs were written or co-written by the three artists; three (*) were co-written by Danny Smith. Songs include "Texas Fever," "No Dictators in Texas," *"Ol' Ben Milam," "Adios Señorita," "A Time for Reflection," "Men of the Alamo," *"No Quarter" (includes Travis' letter, read by Billy Joe Royal), "Santa Anna's Coming" "Lone Star" and *"Remember the Alamo."

(1986) LP *The Skies of Texas: A Sesquicentennial Salute* — United States Air Force Band of the West; Col. Benny L. Knudsen, conductor; narration by Gordon Jump, scripted by Bob MacNaughton. A promotional-only album distributed to

radio stations by the U.S. Department of Defense, recorded at the Scottish Rite Temple auditorium and the United Audio Recording Studio, San Antonio, Texas. The first of three pieces, "The Skies of Texas" is a musical work with narration that traces the history of Texas, particularly the Revolution, juxtaposing important events with the cyclical orbit of Halley's Comet, including its appearance shortly before the Alamo battle. The musical score includes "Ballad of the Alamo," "The Green Leaves of Summer," and "De Guello" from John Wayne's *The Alamo*, and the theme from *Giant*, all composed by Dimitri Tiomkin, excerpts from "Across the Alley from the Alamo" and "San Antonio Rose" and other "representative songs, folk tunes and popular hits." Side two features "Symphonic Dance No. 3 'Fiesta'" and "Zacatecas."

(1986) "Gentleman from the Cane" (Tony Marchese). Unreleased recording of a song written during the Texas Sesquicentennial and the bicentennial of David Crockett's birth. Joining Marchese on the recording were Jim Seagraves and Jeff Halle of the country band Southern Boulevard. Lyrics were published in *The Crockett Chronicle* (No. 3, Feb. 2003).

(1986) LP *Golden Movie Themes* — The 101 Strings Orchestra (Allshire). Includes "The Green Leaves of Summer."

(1986) Release of made-for-TV movie *Houston: The Legend of Texas* (later retitled *Gone to Texas*) starring Sam Elliot, with musical score composed by Dennis McCarthy; no known releases.

(1986) 45 rpm single "La Ballade de Davy Crockett" ("The Ballad of Davy Crockett" sung in French)/"La Marche du Trapeur" — Patrick Simpson Jones (France: AB Records 883.757-7).

(1987) — LP *The Never-Before-Released Masters* — Diana Ross and the Supremes. Includes the group's soulful rendition of "The Ballad of Davy Crockett," recorded in January 1967 as part of an unfinished album of Disney songs tentatively titled *The Supremes Sing Disney Classics or Heigh Ho*. The songs finally were released on this album, which was issued on CD in 1990, but both the LP and CD are extremely rare.

(1987) LP *Changing Rhythm* - Scott Lindenmuth (Dark Stream Records 226578). Includes "The Alamo," a jazz instrumental.

(1987) Release of made-for-TV movie *Thirteen Days to Glory*, with musical score composed by Peter Bernstein; no known releases.

(1988) 45 rpm single "Stout and High" (Monte Warden) — The Wagoneers. An uptempo song about the Alamo walls, released as a single and also on the group's debut album *Stout and High* on LP and CD. Asleep at the Wheel later covered the song in a slower arrangement on their CD *Remembers the Alamo*.

(1988) 33 1/3 rpm EP *Killer Klowns from Outer Space* — The Dickies (Rykodisc 5-song EP; Enigma DIE-73322). Includes the punk rock song "Jim Bowie," with virtually indecipherable lyrics, except for the clear mention of Bowie's name. Released on CD in 2005.

(1988) *Alamo...the Price of Freedom* — Merrill Jensen, composer. Film score from IMAX production. A soundtrack album was released on audiocassette in 1993 (Rivertheater

Associates Ltd; no number) and on CD in 1998 (Rivertheater Assoc. Ltd./Video West CD09723CD001). Includes the song "The Price of Freedom" performed by Sergio Salinas, which is not in the film.

(1988) CD *Great Adventures of Slick Rick* — Slick Rick (Def Jam 527359). Includes "Indian Girl," an off-color rap song that includes the refrain from "The Ballad of Davy Crockett" in its chorus, but has no other connection to Crockett or the Alamo.

(1989) Audio cassette *Remember the Alamo: Mexican and Texian Music of 1836* — Produced by Ray Herbeck, Jr. (Sound Great - Star Line Productions, Inc. SGC-5020). Recordings of songs from the 1830s played on period instruments, including "Come to the Bower," "La Cachuca," and "Deguello."

(1989) 4-CD set *Moving West Songs* — Keith & Rusty McNeil (WEM Records WEMCD 505). Contains ten songs related to the Texas Revolution and Mexican War including "The Texas Rangers," "The Texas War Cry," "Will You Come to the Bower?," "Zachary Taylor," and "The Leg I Left Behind Me" with narration; other musical themes are Territorial Expansion and Abolition, Minstrel Shows and the California Gold Rush, and Immigrants from China, Ireland and Germany.

(1989) single "We Didn't Start the Fire"/"House of Blue Light" (Columbia 7-3021) — Billy Joel. A-side mentions Davy

Crockett in reference to the 1950s Disney Crockett craze.

(1989) CD *Happy Trails (Round-Up 2)* — Erich Kunzel & the Cincinnati Pops Orchestra. (Telarc CD-8019). Includes "The Green Leaves of Summer" with vocal by the U.S. Air Force's Singing Sergeants.

(1990) 45 rpm single "The Ballad of Davie Crockett"/"The Unicorn" — Stuart Anderson (U.K.: Scotdisc ITV.7S527). Anderson, a Scottish youngster, gives a spirited performance, but the record and sleeve both misspell Crockett's name "Davie" and the song itself is credited to G. "Brouns" (instead of Bruns), T. Blackburn and the previously unknown Campbell Connelly, whose credit likely derived from his arrangement of the song; the recording was produced by Bill Garden.

(1990) CD *The Greatest Western Movie Themes* — The Ned Nash Orchestra (Delta/Laserlight 15055). Includes "Ballad of the Alamo."

(1990) 12-inch single "You Make Me Feel Brand New"/"The Alamo" — Lorraine McKane (Profile Records PRO-7290). The B-side is a disco-infused metaphor that employs Alamo imagery in support of a somewhat desperate sounding romantic quest.

(1990) CD *Schizoid* — Jeff Kollman (Marmaduke 30104). Includes an original rock instrumental titled "Remember the Alamo."

(1991) 45 rpm single "The Ballad of Davy Crockett"/"Smooth" — Kentucky Headhunters (Mercury Memory 868 122-7). An up-tempo rock arrangement of the famous Disney theme; also released on the group's album *Electric Barnyard*.

(1991) CD *For Our Children* — Various Artists (Disney 60616-2). Includes "The Ballad of Davy Crockett" sung by Stephen Bishop.

(1991) CD *The Disney Collection Vol. 2- Songs from Disney Movies* (U.S.: Walt Disney Records 60817-2; U.K.: Pickwick Music DST CD 454). Includes "The Ballad of Davy Crockett" (Fess Parker version 1).

(1991) CD *The Wild West: The Essential Western Film Music Collection* — The City of Prague Philharmonic (Silva Screen FILMXCD-315). Includes "The Alamo — Overture" from John Wayne's 1960 film.

(1992) 45 rpm single "Davey Crockett"/"Young Blood" — Thee Headcoatees (U.K.: Damaged Goods DAMGOOD 4). The A-side is an original Crockett punk-rock song performed by a female foursome backed by Billy Childish's trio. The song is based on the garage rock classic "Farmer John" and contains references to the Disney "Crockett" series, the Alamo and a Bowie knife. It also was released in 1999 on the LP *Sisters of Suave* by Thee Headcoatees (U.K.: Damaged Goods, DAMGOOD 161LP) and in 2006 on the CD *My First Billy Childish Album* by Billy Childish (U.K.: Damaged Goods DAMGOOD 264 CD).

(1992) "The Alamo" (Joey Berkley) — The Joey Berkley Quartet. A recording of this jazz instrumental was released in 2008 on the CD *More 'n Four* (Independent release; available as a download). The song was actually inspired by, and refers to, a sculpture in New York City's East Village. It sits in Cooper Union Square and was a landmark around which musicians performed for the public.

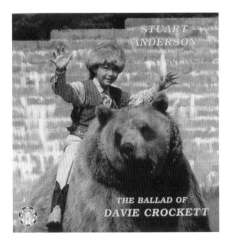

(1992) 3-CD boxed set *The Music of Disney: A Legacy in Song* (Walt Disney Records 60957-2). Includes "The Ballad of Davy Crockett" by the Mellomen, who sang all the verses of the song in the original Disney television episodes and the later theatrical film releases of them. The same recording was released in 1996 on CD *Television's Greatest Hits — Black & White Classics Volume 4* — Various artists (TVT Records 1600-2).

(1992) CD and audio cassette *Davy Crockett* — Nicholas Cage (narrator); music by David Bromberg (Rabbit Ears Productions — American Heroes and Legends; Cassette: 74041-70226-4 CD (1993): Rhino/WEA R2 70498). Children's dramatization of Crockett's adventures, produced by James Howard Kunstler. Bromberg's music includes "Davy Crockett," "Rampant," "The Death of Errol Flynn," "Emily," "Mike Fink's Asthma," "Sleepytime Song for Sam," "Ruth Rampant," "Jacob's Joy," "Rampant Redux," and "Buck Dancer's Choice." Cage also provided Crockett's voice in a TV adaptation of this production that was released on video in 1996, also by Rabbit Ears Productions.

(1992) LP *The Cowboy Album* — Various artists (Rhino R4 7043; CD R2 7043). Includes "The Ballad of Davy Crockett" by Fess Parker.

(1993) CD *Col. Bruce Hampton & The Aquarium Rescue Unit* — Col. Bruce Hampton (Capricorn Records). Includes the original rock song "Davy Crockett" (recorded live).

(1994) "Cold Texas Moon" (James Boylston; published by Perfect Heart Music, adm. by Bug Music, BMI). In 2000 the composer recorded a demo of this song about the Alamo battle, but no recording has been released to date.

(1994) CD *Songs for the Alamo* — Various artists (Stage Door Productions SD 03061836). Includes "Never, Never Forget," "Theme from 'The Texas Adventure'," a new recording of "The Green Leaves of Summer" by the Brothers Four, "Crockett's Dance," "Big Jim Bowie," "Dawn at the Alamo," "Sweet Texas Rain," "Travis' Theme" and other songs related to the Texas war.

(1994) CD *Voodoo Lounge* — The Rolling Stones (Virgin 7243

8 39782 2 9). Includes "Mean Disposition," which has a line about Crockett and the Alamo.

(1994) CD *...in Front of the Alamo* — Bryan Shumate (Tug Records TR 10394). The album includes one song called "Alamo," which is hard to understand, but shows all signs of involving a saloon called The Alamo, where the singer is lamenting something, perhaps a lost love.

(1994) "Crockett Waltz." — Adrian Legg; on CD *High Strung Tall Tales* — (Relativity Records).

(1994) CD: *Ses Vi I Slesvig* — Johnny Madsen (no label information). Includes an original song titled "Alamo," sung in Danish. (download at http://www.mp3sale.ru/release.php?ms_releaseid'70367).

(1994) CD *When You Wish Upon a Star* — Richard Hayman and his Orchestra (Naxos International 8.990032). Includes "The Ballad of Davy Crockett."

(1994) CD *Golden Age of the March* — The Washington Winds, Conducted by Edward Petersen (Walking Frog Records WFR101). Includes "Alamo March" by K. L. King, arranged by James Swearingen.

(1994) CD *Cancioneros* — Los Mier (Fonovisa). Includes "Recuerdos del Alamo," a ballad about a father's love and what the singer learned from him; nothing to do with the battle.

(1994) CD *Television Themes: 16 Most Requested Songs* (Sony/Legacy 53609). Includes "The Ballad of Davy Crockett" (Fess Parker Version 1).

(1994) CD *Leurs Plus Grands Succes* — Les Compagnons De La Chanson (France: EMI Records 828938). Includes "Le Bleu de L'Ete" ("The Green Leaves of Summer") sung in French.

(1995) "Memory of the Alamo" (William Pasqua, Michael Boldt and Tony Pasqua). This original song was performed live in the Alamo church on March 5, 1995, by Tony Pasqua and Boldt during the inaugural ceremonial meeting of the Alamo Defenders Descendants Association. It was performed there again at the group's ceremony on March 6, 2004, by Tony Pasqua and William Chemerka. A 2005 studio recording was released that year on the CD *At the Alamo*.

(1995) "Moses Rose of Texas" (Stephen L. Suffet; to the tune of "The Yellow Rose of Texas"). Recorded by Carl Peterson for his CD *Scotland Remembers the Alamo* in 2001. The song tells the tale of the one man at the Alamo who is said to have left the night before the final battle.

(1995) CD *New Western Dance* — Dave Sheriff (Stomp DS03). Includes "The Alamo," a song about a Line Dancing club near Preston, England, called "The Alamo." A line dance also was written to the song, but does not mention the battle or its heroes. The song also appears on Sheriff's CD *Best of Dave Sheriff Vol 1* (Stomp DS0045).

(1995) CD *Tom Feely's Crockett's Last Stand* (Alamo North Special Archive Recording). Music by Mike Boldt; narration by William Chemerka and Tony Peters-Pasqua (William B. Travis). This soundtrack accompanied the detailed 54-mm Alamo diorama that was at the entrance to the now-closed "Texas Adventure" attraction on Alamo Plaza in San Antonio.

(1995) 2-Disk CD-ROM set *The Alamo — "Victory or Death" — A Multimedia History of Early Texas featuring the Battle of the Alamo and the Texan Revolution* — Various artists (W.S. Benson and Company, Inc.). Marketed to schools with a teachers guide and billed as the first CD-ROM about Texas history and the Texas Revolution, the production features stories read by Dan Rather, Sissy Spacek, Charley Pride, Freddy Fender, Linda Gray and Tess Harper backed by period music recorded by Texans Pride, Fender and Robert Earl Keen.

(1995) CD *Plow United* — Plow United (Creep Records 10). Includes a nearly-incomprehensible 17-second track titled "Tour Guide at the Alamo."

(1995) CD and cassette 22 *Famous Western Film Themes* — Various artists (Star Inc. CD: 86005; cassette: 286005). Includes instrumental version of "Ballad of the Alamo."

(1995) CD *Righteous Pop Music Volume 2* — Mark Bradford (One Way Street DRP-02). Includes "David's Theme," a religious parody of "The Ballad of Davy Crockett," with the focus on the biblical David, rather than Crockett.

(1996) CD *Bibbidi Bobbidi Bach — More Favorite Disney Tunes in the Style of Great Classical Composers* — Various artists (Delos DE 3195). Contains fifteen Disney songs arranged in the style of various classical composers. "The Ballad of Davy Crockett" is performed by the English

Chamber Orchestra, conducted by Donald Fraser, in the style of Aaron Copland.

(1996) CD *Disney's Music from the Park* — Various Artists (Walt Disney Records 60915-7). Includes perhaps the most unique recording of "The Ballad of Davy Crockett," sung by Tim Curry.

(1996) CD *Classic Disney, Vol. 3: 60 Years of Musical Magic* — Various artists (Disney International 298244). Includes "The Ballad of Davy Crockett" by the Wellingtons.

(1996) CD *Here and Now* — Charlie Major (Imprint Records). Includes "Remember the Alamo" (Bowers).

(1996) 12-inch Maxi-single & CD promo "Fort Alamo" — Jean-Louis Murat (France: Virgin 12-inch: SAB-145; CD: 3792). The French poet-singer's recording compares a romantic relationship to the battle at "Fort Alamo," sung in French. The maxi-single offers eight different mixes of the song.

(1996) "Davy Crockett: A Folktale for Reading Out Loud" — Activated Storytellers! National Touring Theatre; L'Eau Theatre Productions. Podcast adapted from the stage production written by Dennis Goza. "In a section on Sally Ann Thunder Ann Whirlwind, Davy meets her at a barn dance where she said she would marry any man who could outdance her, and after dancing hard all night, Davy wears her out." From: http://www.ferrum.edu/applit/bibs/tales/crockett.htm; the recording can be heard at: http://www.activated_storytellers.com/folktales/davy_crockett.html.

(1996) CD *Lucky Man* — Charlie Major (Arista Records ARI30728; also on BMG 30728 2). Includes "Remember the Alamo" (Bowers).

(1996) CD single *Talula* — Tori Amos (Atlantic/WEA A8512CD2 7567-88511-2). Includes a song titled "Alamo," written and sung by Amos, that has no connection to the Alamo beyond one mention of the word.

(1997) CD *K. R. Wood's Fathers of Texas* — Various artists (Fathers of Texas Series; Texanna Records TXA 1-001). A 25-track assortment of songs, poems and narratives about the Alamo and the Texas war for independence, subtitled "A Texas musical expression of the independence, spirit, and commitment on which the State of Texas was founded." Artists include Townes Van Zandt, Tom T. Hall, Eliza Gilkyson, Red Steagall, Guich Koch, Gary P. Nunn, Delbert McClinton, Rusty Wier, Skeet Anglin, Gib Lewis, Steven Fromholz, Durango Ron Wood, Ray Wylie Hubbard, Reg Lindsey, John Guthrie, C.B. Stubblefield, Guy Clark, Steven Fromholz, Ricky Yanez, Alex Harvey, T. Gozney Thornton, Shake Russell, L. E. McCullouch, Johnny Boy Lee, Johnny Dee, Charles John Quartro and K. R. Wood.

(1997) CD *Real Black Rhythm* — Bob Roubain (Netherlands: Still 1156). Includes "Rock It, Davy Crockett."

(1997) CD: *The Alamo: A Line in the Sand* — Narrated by Rick Lance (Readio Theatre, LLC). Written by Wyman Windsor, produced and graphic design by Joe Loesch. Readio Theatre revised the production completely and re-wrote the script for a new edition in 2005 titled *Legend of the Alamo* (Topics Entertainment; produced by Creative License, Inc. for Readio Theatre, LLC), narrated by Benny Shipley, written by Jimmy Gray; produced by Joe Loesch. Released as part of Topics Entertainment's 3-CD set *Tales of America's Fallen Forts*, which also includes CDs about the siege at Fort Phil Kearny and the Little Big Horn (which was not a fort at all).

(1997) CD *Ridin' the Dreamland Range* — R. W. Hampton (available only online at http://www.rwhampton.com/Dreamland.html). Includes "Ballad of the Alamo."

(1997) 2-CD set *A Treasury of All-Time Favorite Children's Songs* — Various artists (Reader's Digest Music; Ardee Music Publisher, Inc.). Disc #1 is titled *Let's All Sing — Great Songs From Shows and Movies* and includes "The Ballad of Davy Crockett" by unidentified artists.

(1998) 2-CD *Liberty! The Siege of the Alamo* (a musical by Bernard J Taylor) (Logue Rhythm Productions). *Liberty!* is a stage musical retelling of the Alamo siege with an emphasis on the individual defenders — men, women, Anglo, Tejano, black and white — who chose to risk their lives. The show debuted in San Antonio at the Josephine Theatre in 1998 directed and choreographed by Missy Miller. The CD studio recording of music from *Liberty!* features an international cast with Michael Berlet, Richard Warren, Richard Austin, Jeffrey Jones-Ragona, Matt Elizondo, other soloists and members of the Capital City Men's Chorus of Austin, Texas.

(1998) CD *Treasury of the West Volume 2* — Various artists (Time Life R124-08; BMG Special Products TCD 815). Includes "The Ballad of Davy Crockett" by Bill Hayes and "Remember the Alamo" (Bowers) by Willie Nelson.

(1998) CD *Cowboy Nation* — Cowboy Nation (Coconut Grove Recording Co.). Includes "Remember the Alamo" (Bowers), also found on the group's CD *We Do As We Please*.

(1998) 45 RPM single "Remember the Alamo"/"True" — George Strait (MCA Nashville MCAS7 72063). A-side is a country and western love song that utilizes the famous battle cry of the title, and locates the two lovers by the old mission, but has nothing to do with Alamo history; also found on Strait's 1998 LP *One Step at a Time*.

(1998) CD *Alamo Suite* — Alamo Suite (LeRay Music B00005YHO5). Includes one track titled "Alamo Suite" played by this jazz-swing-blues band comprising Don Leady, Cliff Hargrove and Glenn Rios.

(1998) CD *Welcome to West Texas* — Alan Munde & Joe Carr (Flying Fish Records FF 669). Includes the song "San Jacinto Farewell," which commemorates that battle.

(1998) CD *Trippin' the Light Fantastic* — London Starlight Dance Orchestra (Dyna Music China). Includes a dance arrangement of "The Green Leaves of Summer."

(1998) CD *Reel Cowboys: Songs from Western Movies and TV Shows* — The Flying W Wranglers (Flying W Ranch Records; no number). Includes "Ballad of the Alamo."

(1999) CD *16 Tunes...and Whaddaya Get....A Songwriter's Portfolio* — Danny McBride (Cosmic Casual Co. CCC00001). Includes "Heroes (Davy Crockett)," an ode to the 1950s Disney series.

(1999) CD *American Tranquility* — Phil Coulter (Shanachie SH 53012). Includes "The Green Leaves of Summer."

(1999) Audio cassette *The Alamo* — Jerry Robbins & the Colonial Radio Players (Colonial Radio Theatre on the Air — AT 9901). Radio dramatization of the Alamo story, recorded in January, 1999, and released on cassette the following July; it was first broadcast on XM Radio in April 2006. The production was re-edited and enhanced with new sound effects in 2007.

(1999) "About to Give Out" — Tom Petty & the Heartbreakers; on CD *Echo* (Warner Bros. 47294). Includes lyrics referring to Davy Crockett in the chorus.

(1999) CD *Mannheim Steamroller Meets the Mouse* — Mannheim Steamroller (American Gramaphone). Includes "The Ballad of Davy Crockett."

(1999) CD *Sogna Ragazzo Sogna* — Robert Vecchiori (EMI). Includes a song called "Alamo," sung in Italian, that mentions the fort and General Santa Anna, but in the context of a somewhat convoluted love story.

(2000) CD *The Alamo Concert: Celebrating the Musical Crossroads of South Texas* — San Antonio Symphony, Christopher Wilkins, conducter with various artists. (NPR Texas Public Radio Alamo Classics 001). Recorded live September 15 & 16, 1997, in the Alamo Hall, San Antonio, Texas, the concert includes the "Overture and Prolog" from Dimitri Tiomkin's 1960 score for the film *The Alamo* and other songs related to or inspired by San Antonio.

(2000) 3-cassette set *David Crockett: Frontiersman, Soldier, and Man for the Ages* — Gary Wiles & Delores M. Brown (Birth of America Audiobooks; History as It Happens series; ISBN: 1889252069). Documentary recording of Crockett's life, read by Wiles & Brown, including excerpts from journals, letters and verified texts. Includes two maps on one sheet, pasted in the cassette container.

(2000) CD *Blue Collar Comedy Tour [Live]* — Jeff Foxworthy, Bill Engvall, Ron White, Larry the Cable Guy (Scream Marketing). Includes Foxworthy's comedy routine titled "Consider the Alamo," which mentions the famous shrine and battle.

(2000) CD *Sing Something Simple: Time After Time* — The Cliff Adams Singers (BBC 665390). Includes "The Ballad of Davy Crockett."

(c. 2000) CD *100% Texan* — David Price (DP-1001J). Contains "Remember the Alamo" (Bowers).

THE 21ST CENTURY

(2001) 2-CD set *Scotland Remembers the Alamo* — Carl Peterson (Darach Recordings 2001). Songs of the early 19th century played to authentic period tunes, including a few bugle calls, "Remember the Alamo" (Durriage), "Moses Rose of Texas," "Death of Davy Crockett" (original title "The Alamo, or the Death of Crockett"), "Will You Come to the Bower," "San Jacinto", "Freedom and Texas," "Texas War Cry," "Santa Anna's March," "Santa Anna's Retreat from Cerro Gordo," "Texas Heroes" (original title "The Texian Heroes' Song") and an instrumental version of Jane Bowers' "Remember the Alamo." Peterson released an accompanying book, *Now's the Day, Now's the Hour*, with more information on the songs and Scotland's contribution to the Alamo.

(2001) CD *The Eagle & the Snake: Songs of the Texians* — Brian Burns (Bandera Records). Includes a segment called "1836: Revolution" comprising "Travis' Letter," "Degüello," "Ballad of the Alamo," and Burns' original "Goliad."

(2001) CD *Get a Life* — Doug Sahm (Munich Records). Includes "The Ballad of Davy Crockett."

(2001) CD *Wild Wild West, Songs of the Silver Screen* — John Darnall (arranger and orchestra conductor) (Monarch Records MONA 1027). Includes "The Green Leaves of Summer."

(2001) CD *Salad Days* — Hermann Grimme (Mullet Records 42668). Includes "The Alamo," an original instrumental number with a Duane Eddy-like twangy guitar lead.

(2001) CD *Alamo Concert* — San Antonio Symphony Orchestra, Christopher Wilkins, conducter. Other performers: Olivia Revueltas, George Prado, Elisenda Fabregas, Timothy Jones, Mark Alexander (Alamo Classics).

(2001) CD *Disney's Greatest Volume 2* (Disney 860694). Includes "The Ballad of Davy Crockett" (Fess Parker version 2).

(2001) CD *Music from the Westerns* — South China Music Troupe (China Record Corporation; CRC Jianian Publishing). Includes the instrumentals "Alamo" (Actually "De Guello" by Dimitri Tiomkin, arranged by Shi Li), and "Ballad of the Alamo."

(2002) CD *Made in Texas* — Jimmy C Carpenter (Big Thicket Records BTR-040502CD). Includes "Alamo Moon Over Texas" (James Carpenter), a honky-tonk number that relates a young man's reminiscence of a happy time in modern San Antonio as he awaits his sweetheart's return.

(2002) CD *Davy Crockett's Fiddle* — Dean Shostak (Coastline Music DS 0151). A collection of authentic period fiddle tunes including "Turkey in the Straw or Old Zip Coon" and a medley titled "The Legend of Davy Crockett," which features parts of "Remember the Alamo" (Durriage), "Davy Crockett" (aka "Pompey Smash") and Disney's "The Ballad of Davy Crockett." Shostak recorded this album of fiddle tunes on what is purportedly Crockett's actual fiddle, although doubt has been raised as to the instrument's provenance, and to the oft-mentioned suggestion that Crockett played the fiddle.

(2002) "Jim Bonham's Last Ride" (Fabio Ragghianti) — The Low-Tech Boys; on CD *Country in This Country, Vol. 1* — Various artists (C.Y. CD-0100).

(2002) CD *The Dust of Davy Crockett (Imagining America)* — Doug McArthur (Tableaux Vivants tv 1112). Includes McArthur's "The Dust of Davy Crockett."

(2002) CD *K. R. Wood's The Crockett Chronicles* — Various artists (Fathers of Texas series; Texanna RecordsTXA 1-001). This 25-track collection features songs and narrations about

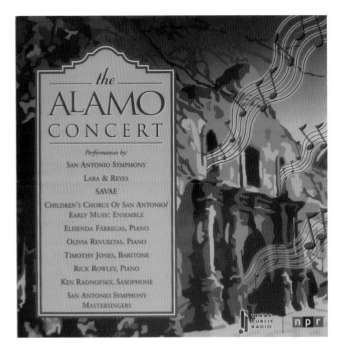

Crockett. Artists include K. R. Wood, Doug Taylor, Greg Lowry, Richard Bowden, J. B. Henry, Charlie Yates (as voice of Crockett), Terry Tex Tolar, Cara Cooke, Lloyd McShelby, Susie Yandell Wood, Elizabeth Gidden and Mary Hattersley. The CD includes the original Alamo song, "I Am With My Friends," written by Michael J. Martin and sung by Wood, who also sang it in the Alamo church on March 6, 2004, during annual ceremonies of the Alamo Defenders Descendants Association. A 2005 studio recording of the song by Tony Pasqua was released the same year on the CD *At the Alamo*.

(2002) *Gone to Texas* (musical production; book by Steve Warren, lyrics by June Rachelson-Ospa, music by Tom Masinter). Premiered April 5-14, 2002, at the Josephine Theatre, San Antonio, Texas. A recording of the show's songs was made during a 2003 performance, including: "Overture," "Gone To Texas," "Mi Casa Es Su Casa," "A Way With Words," "Take the Tex Out of Texas," "Master," "Urselita," "Davy and Me," "Texas Gals," "We Draw the Line," "Hand in Hand," "Happy Birthday George Washington," "Everyday Man," "With Love," "Last Shot," "Did You Ever Love Me?," "Brand New Day," "Count on the Stars," "Remember These Men."

(2002) CD *Deep in the Heart of Texas: Favorite Songs of the Lone Star State* — Craig Duncan, producer (Green Hill CHD5292). Contains instrumental versions of various Alamo-related songs.

(2002) CD *Famous Americans in History by Barnaby Chesterman* — read by Kerry Shale and Lorelei King; musical excerpts programmed by Nicolas Soames (Naxos Junior Classics/Audio Books NA 225812; 2 CDs). A children's audio book with profiles of several notable Americans, including "Davy Crockett (1786-1836) — The Spirit of the American Frontier," featuring two tracks: "Six Feet Tall and Dressed in a Coonskin Hat," and "Bear Hunting." David Timson and Martin George sing several verses from "The Ballad of Davy Crockett."

(2002) CD *98 to 1* — Heroes of the Alamo (Heroes of the Alamo 18924). There is no Alamo music here, but the name of the group does conjure images of the Alamo defenders. In fact, this New York rock group was formed in 1999 and took its name from a poster for the 1937 film *Heroes of the Alamo* that hung in an East Village shop. The group included Richard Brown, Todd Carlstrom, David Makuen and Kevin Slane.

(2002) "Alamo Waltz" (Cynthia [Jeanne] Gayneau) — Cynthia Gayneau. Released on CD *West of West Texas* (Botte Music). One more love song that reflects on a past rendezvous in the shadow of the old fortress, the first of its type in the 21st century.

(2003) "We Remember the Alamo" (William Chemerka). This original composition was performed live in the Alamo church by Chemerka and Tony Pasqua on March 1, 2003, during annual ceremonies of the Alamo Defenders Descendants Association. Chemerka's 2005 studio recording of the song was released that year on the CD *At the Alamo*.

(2003) CD *K. R. Wood's Los Tejanos* — Various Artists (Fathers of Texas Series; Texanna Records 1-003). A rare assortment of songs and narratives that focus on the Hispanic figures who played important roles at the Alamo and in the Texas Revolution. Each track is presented in Spanish and English. Artists include K. R. Wood, Ray Wylie Hubbard, Mary Welch, John Arthur Martinez, Ricky Yamez, John Murray Greenburg, Selena Hernandez; narrations read by Ernesta Vazquez Howell, John Authur Martinez, Leti Del Vega, Guich Kooch, Consuelo Samboro, and Selina Hernandez.

(2003) CD *Asleep at the Wheel Remembers the Alamo* — Asleep at the Wheel (Shout DK 31133). Includes "Remember the Alamo" (Bowers)/"Letter from Col. Travis," "Green Leaves of Summer" (featuring Tosca String Quarter), "Ballad of the Alamo," "Deguello," "The Ballad of Davy Crockett" (10 verses), "Stout and High," "Across the Alley from the Alamo," "New San Antonio Rose," "Yellow Rose of Texas," three fiddle tunes that were old enough to have been played at the Alamo during the siege ("Billy in the Low Ground", "Eight of January" and "Soldier's Joy"); plus the comic number "Don't Go There," which commemorates rock star Ozzy Osbourne's 1982 citation for urinating on the Alamo Cenotaph.

(2003) CD *Alamo — Extra Notes* — Joe Basquez (www.basquez.net; 2205 2127 4444). A collection of instrumentals built around the siege and fall of the Alamo, including: "Alamo," "Bowie's Wedding," "Crockett's Theme" and other original songs.

(2003) CD *Couldn't Have Said It Better* — Meat Loaf (Sanctuary Records 84653). Includes "Tear Me Down," which features a spoken-word interlude about the Alamo, read by Giselda Vachky.

(2003) CD *The Great American Storyteller Volume One* — Phil Thomas — (Story Records SA 001-00). Includes Thomas reading "Farewell to the Mountains (Poem by Davy Crockett — circa 1814)." This is the full poem, written by Richard Penn Smith, but erroneously credited to Crockett, as it originally appeared in print in 1836.

(2003) CD *O Mickey, Where Art Thou: The Voices of Bluegrass Sing the Best of Disney* — Various Artists (Walt Disney Records DIS-860083). Includes "Mickey Mouse Medley," an instrumental consisting of "The Mickey Mouse Club March" and "The Ballad of Davy Crockett" by a group billed as "O Mickey Where Art Thou?"

(2003) TV Movie *Sam Houston: The Volunteer Exile*. Emmy Award-nominated score composed by Michael Killen, who won an Emmy for his score from the TV film *Rachel and Andrew Jackson, A Love Story*.

(2004) CD *Riders in the Sky Present: Davy Crockett, King of the Wild Frontier* — Riders in the Sky. (Rounder 8123). Includes "The Ballad of Davy Crockett" (full 20-verse version; 6:44); "Be Sure You're Right, and Then Go Ahead," "King of the River," "Old Betsy," "Farewell" (full version; 4:30)," all from the 1950s Disney television production, and "Heading for Texas," "The Grinning Tale," "Colonel Crockett's Speech to Congress," and "Remember the Alamo" (Bowers).

(2004) CD *Rock, Bop, Folk and Pop Vol. 1* — Alan Leatherwood (Ohio Moon Records CD-790). Includes two versions of Jane Bowers' "Remember the Alamo"; Original & Tribute Versions. The Tribute Version features new lyrics by Leatherwood that add a reference to Osama bin Laden in place of Santa Anna.

(2004) "Ghost of the Alamo" (Bobby Boyd) — Bobby Boyd. Released on CD *The Honky Tonk Tree* (Boydroom BB-2883). Boyd had offered the song to the Walt Disney Studio for its 2004 film *The Alamo*, but was turned down. The CD appears to have originally been released in 2001 without "Ghost of the Alamo" and reissued in 2004 with the song added.

(2004) CD *The Alamo Remembered* — Various artists (St. Clair SHO 19572). Features new arrangements of "The Ballad of the Alamo," "Green Leaves of Summer," and "De Guello," from the 1960 film *The Alamo* and two tracks from the 2004 film of the same title ("The Battle of the Alamo Part 6" and "Flesh and Honor") and other songs that conjure images of old San Antonio.

(2004) CD *The Alamo* — Carter Burwell, composer (Hollywood Records 2061-62433-2). Film soundtrack; a far more somber and moody score than Dimitri Tiomkin's music from John Wayne's 1960 film of the same title. The 26-track collection includes six tracks on the battle as well as the memorable "Deguello de Crockett." The traditional composition "Listen to the Mockingbird Sing" was arranged by Craig Eastman.

(2004) CD *Western Adventures: Gene Autry; Davy Crockett: King of the Wild Frontier* (Sony/DRG 19063). CD reissue of the three recorded Disney adventures of Davy Crockett, originally released on a variety of records in 1955. However part of "Davy Crockett Goes to Congress" is missing on this CD, which also includes four Fess Parker 1950s singles: "The Ballad of Davy Crockett" (Parker version 1)/"I Gave My Love (Riddle Song);" "Be Sure You're Right (Then Go Ahead)" (with Buddy Ebsen)/"Old Betsy;" "Farewell"/"I'm Lonely My Darlin' (Green Grow the Lilacs);" and "King of the River" (with Thurl Ravenscroft)/"Yaller Yaller Gold." The CD also includes reissue of two Gene Autry 1950 children's story records.

Audio Tour of THE ALAMO
& OLD SAN ANTONIO OF THE WILD WEST

NARRATED BY THE GHOST OF
WILD BILL KEILMAN

THE MOST FAMOUS TOUR GUIDE IN SAN ANTONIO

(2004) CD *Every Now & Then* — Southwind (Oasis). Includes a version of "Remember the Alamo" (Bowers).

(2004) CD *The Alamo: A Musical Tribute to John Wayne's Epic Film* — Mike Boldt & various artists (SpyGuise). Cover versions of the following music from the 1960 film: "The Ballad of the Alamo," "Overture," "Deguello," "The Green Leaves of Summer" (vocal and instrumental versions), "Here's to the Ladies" and "Tennessee Babe"; also original background music for dramatic readings of three original Alamo documents: "I Am with My Friends" (from Crockett's last known letter, read by William Chemerka), "I Will Never Surrender or Retreat" (from Travis' famous letter, read by Tony Pasqua) and "A Parting Kiss" (from the recollections of Mrs. Susanna Dickenson, read by Nancy Boldt). The CD also includes seven original 1960 radio spots promoting Wayne's film.

(2004) 3-CD set *Spirit of the West* — The Silver Screen Orchestra (Stetson/Madacy Entertainment Group Ltd. ST2 50351). Includes "The Green Leaves of Summer." Also released in 2005 on 2-CD *Classic Country Favorites* (Madacy), where artists are listed as 101 Strings Orchestra, Silver Screen Orchestra and Singers.

(2004) CD *An Ardmore Afternoon* — Don Bridges (Working4U Music). Album includes "At the Alamo," an infectious uptempo love song, but this one is metaphorical and compares a romantic breakup at a Tex-Mex restaurant to the famous battle and even mentions Jim Bowie!

(2004) CD *En Kjuagutt Fra Bergen* — Arne Bendiksen (Norway: Triola/Phonofile TNCD2012). Includes "Davy Crockett (The Ballad of Davy Crockett)," sung in Norwegian.

(2004) CD *Love Is Worth It* — Silent Drive. Additional writing by Nick Branigan & Andrew Kyte (Equal Vision Records 92). Includes an original song titled "Davey Crockett," that has nothing to do with Crockett or the Alamo.

(2004) CD single "The Alamo" (12:37)/"The Alamo Narrative" (4:12) (both written by Terry Friend) — Terry Friend

& Cheryl Murphy, with Alter Ego (New Morning Recordings CDTHFO 11). An original epic song, which is presented in three distinct parts and was developed from a poem written years earlier by Friend. He re-recorded "The Alamo" in 2006, replacing most of Murphy's vocal with his own. The new version was released on the CD *Strange Journey: The Anthology Part 2: The CD Years* (New Morning Recordings CDTHFO15). Friend recorded a new version of the song in 2007 and released it on a CD single that year, backed again with "The Alamo Narrative" (New Morning Records CDTHFO17).

(2004) "The Ballad of Fess Parker" (C. Hodgkins) — Craig Hodgkins. Posted as a video on YouTube (http://www.youtube.com/watch?v'7SgBXr-l68M). A parody of both "The Ballad of Davy Crockett" and the theme from the "Daniel Boone" television series, both of which starred Fess Parker. Hodgkins composed the song and performed it before a live audience prior to an interview he conducted with Parker at the May 2004 Walt Disney Art Classics Convention in the Pacific Ballroom of Disney's Paradise Pier Hotel.

(2004) CD-BOOK SET *Davy Crockett: An American Hero* (Published in 2004 by Black Cat; book copyright is 1998 & 2003; CD says 2004; CD has number: ISRC CN-R08-03-0060-4). Children's book and CD for reading level 1, the lowest reading level. Book has Japanese and English writing on it. It is one of the dullest presentations about Crockett or the Alamo on record, read in a near-broken English monotone, slowly and methodically, as if by programmed computers. It also has a number of inaccuracies, including the year of Crockett's birth.

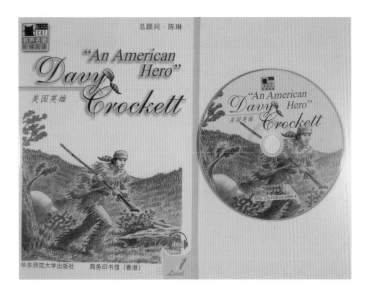

(2004) CD and Cassette: *The 13 Days of the Fall of the Alamo* — Written & narrated by Henry Guerra (WOAI Radio; Matson Creative; no number). An audio account of the siege and battle, originally broadcast on San Antonio radio station WOAI. Produced by George Rivera; bugle by Arnaldo Garza; guitar by Rick Guerra. The CD release by Matson Creative of San Antonio is titled *The Thirteen Days of the Alamo* and adds a PDF file with a program transcript.

(2004) CD *Audio Tour of The Alamo & Old San Antonio of the Wild West* — Narrated by Jimmy "Honest Texan" Roberts, billed as the Ghost of Wild Bill Keilman (Alamo Tours and Travel). An audio tour of the Alamo and San Antonio, which helps to guide visitors around the shrine and through the city, highlighting historical locations. The CD includes a 19 X 19-inch poster filled with original photos of characters and places described in the tour.

(2004) CD *La Marcha del Golazo Solitario* — Los Fabulosos Cadillacs (RCA International 6511321). Includes "Alamo," an instrumental by an Argentinian group.

(2004) CD L.A. *Was Our Alamo* — Pushstart Wagon (Pushstart Wagon 23423). This album's only connection to the Alamo is its title; it includes no Alamo-related songs.

(2004) "Alamo's Battle" (Gianfranco Plenzio). An instrumental that is not necessarily written about the Alamo, but is in a Tex/Mex style. The song was part of a library of music cues licensed for use on television or in films.

(2005) CD *At the Alamo* — Bill Chemerka, Tony Pasqua, Mike Boldt (BeeTee Music). Studio recordings of original songs that had been performed live in the Alamo church during annual ceremonies of the Alamo Defenders Descendants Association. "We Remember the Alamo" (Chemerka), "Memory of the Alamo" (Pasqua-Boldt-Pasqua), "I Am With My Friends" (Martin), bonus track: "Soldier" (Boldt).

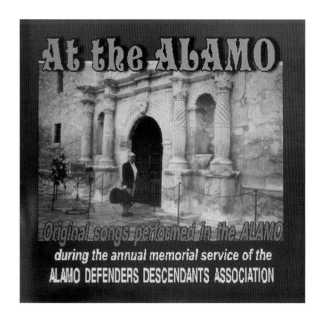

(2005) CD *Morrison Williams* — Morrison-Williams (Palo Duro Records PDR-0601). Includes "Good Day to Die (The Alamo Song)." Shayne Morrison and Clint Williams had unsuccessfully submitted the song for the soundtrack to the 2004 film, *The Alamo*. When producers chose to use an all-instrumental score instead, Morrison and Williams decided to record the song on their own.

(2005) CD *Tin Church* — Kevin Brown (Doodah Records DD04). Includes the blues number "Lancashire Blood on a Texas Floor," which honors Alamo defenders who came from Lancashire, Brown's home county in England.

(2005) 6-CD boxed set *A Musical History of Disneyland* — Various artists (Disney 861284). A collection of music heard throughout the Disneyland theme park, issued on the park's 50th anniversary. Two medleys include "The Ballad of Davy Crockett": 1) the Country Bear Jamboree track on Disc 2, and 2) the 50th Anniversary section on Disc 5.

(2005) "Alamo" — Peter Walker. The composer's recording of the song remains unreleased. The lyrics do not relate to the battle, but do include the refrain "Alamo."

(2005) CD *Rockabilly Box CD-56-60.torrent* — Various artists. This online CD includes and mp3 download of "I Won't Forget the Alamo" by the Rockabilly Rockets (CD 56-12; available at website: http://www.btmon.com/Audio/Unsorted/Rockabilly_Box_CD_56 60.torrent.html).

(2006) CD one-track single "Always Cross the Line" — Jim Wick (Resonance Audio Media PG 1200). Written as a theme for the Alamo Defenders Descendants Association and for its website (www.alamodescendants.org).

(2006) CD *Ronald 15* — Ronald (Norway: Talent/Phonofile; Busk Katalognr: BCD 255). Includes "The Ballad of Davy Crockett" sung in Norwegian.

(2006) David and Catherine Mocniak wrote new Alamo-related lyrics to several traditional Christmas carols. The songs were performed live on December 12, 2006, by the 2005-2006 Alamo Committee at the Alamo Hall in San Antonio and included "Alamo Jingle" and "Twelve Days at the Alamo." The songs were printed and titled *Alamo Staff Christmas Songbook*.

(2006) CD *Western Themes* — Jim Hendricks (Maple Street Music MS-2030-2). Includes instrumental versions of "The Ballad of Davy Crockett" and "Ballad of the Alamo."

(2006) CD *Way Out Yonder* — The Sons of San Joaquin (Dualtone Music Group 1213). Includes "Where the Very Same Cottonwoods Grow," a western tune that commemorates the place where the Alamo defenders died.

(2006) CD *20 Suosikkia / Mikki ja kumppanit* — Various artists (Finland: WEA). Includes "Davy Crockett" by Kauko Kayhko, a Finnish-language version of "The Ballad of Davy Crockett." Sold as MP3 download on several websites.

(2006) CD *Disney: The Music Behind the Magic* — Various artists (Disney 000000102). Includes "The Ballad of Davy Crockett" (Fess Parker version 2).

(2007) "Joan of the Alamo" (Jerry Hadley & Frank Thompson). The composers performed this song in honor of Joan Headley, a long-time Alamo patron and devotee, during her tenth annual party coinciding with the Alamo Society Symposium in San Antonio.

(2007) MP3 Download "My Alamo" (words & music: Mike Petee; ©Symmetry Point Music; BMI) — Elixir (Mike Petee, Chris Petee & Gerry Rensel). A unique view of Crockett only hours before the final assault, writing a letter to his wife, Elizabeth, conveying regrets about some of his actions. It makes the battle and Crockett's death nearly anticlimactic in its focus on his personal feelings and thoughts at that moment. Available through www.elixirsings.com or elixir_petee@hotmail.com.

(2007) CD *One More Midnight* — Hal Ketchum (Pid 670910). Includes "Alamo," with backup vocals by LeAnn Rimes. Also released as a CD single (Curb Records) under the title "In Front of the Alamo." Written by Gary S. Burr, this is another love song set near the Alamo.

(2007) CD *Tribute to Duane Eddy* — Riccardo Zara (Duck/The Orchard Records). Includes the Italian artist's instrumental rendition of "The Ballad of Davy Crockett."

(2007) "I Love the South" — Rocky Edwards (demo). This uptempo country song mentions Davy Crockett and other famous Southerners.

(2007) CD *K. R. Wood's Davy Crockett's Fiddle Plays On, Live in the Alamo* — Various artists (Fathers of Texas Series; Texanna

Records TXA-1-008). An assortment of fiddle recordings of Alamo tunes, including "Ballad of the Alamo," "Green Leaves of Summer," and a reading of Travis' letter.

(2007) CD *Texas Freedom* — Bill Ramsel (Star Eagle West/Silver Star Enterprises). Collection of original and older songs, including "13 Days of Glory" (actually "Ballad of the Alamo"), "The Men on the Alamo Walls," "Travis Letter," "Crockett's Ride," "Remember the Alamo" (Bowers) and related songs.

(2007) "The Alamo Is No Place for Dancing" (Eric Bowley & Andrew de Torres) — The Scene Aesthetic; on CD *The Scene Aesthetic* (Destiny Worldwide 22). A tear-in-the-beer ditty that has nothing to do with the Alamo, although one can't argue with the caution expressed in the title.

(2007) CD *American Music Legends Presents Walt Disney* (Walt Disney Records D000096202 CR02952; produced and manufactured for Cracker Barrel Old Country Store). Includes "The Ballad of Davy Crockett" by the Mellowmen, although the vocal group is uncredited. The CD was sold at Cracker Barrel restaurants.

(2008) CD single "The Ballad of El Pablo"/"Angelina's Song of the Alamo" (Paul Scheineman & Richie Williams) — Paul Scheineman (Independent release).

(2008) CD *K. R. Wood's Lone Star Legacy* — Various artists (Fathers of Texas Series; Texanna Records). The latest in this series of albums dedicated to Texas history includes "32 Men from Gonzalez," a tribute to the only relief force that reached the Alamo, "Alamo Joe," the first song about Travis' slave, who was among the Alamo survivors, "Juan Seguin — A Man Without a Country," which honors the most celebrated Tejano leader of the Texas Revolution, and other songs.

(2008) "The Ladies of the Alamo" (Major Gavin Stoddart, MBE, BEM). Instrumental pipe tune composed by the former director of the Army School of Bagpipe Music in Edinburgh; published by *pipetunes.ca* and McGillivray Piping. An MP3 download is available on the website http://pipetunes.ca.

(2008) CD *Disney Music Block Party* — Various artists (Disney 000068402). Includes an updated reworking of "The Ballad of Davy Crockett (In Outer Space)" by They Might Be Giants. In this version, Davy is a buckskin astronaut!

(2008) "The Alamo Song" (Keith Kubena). This 3:49 instrumental was recorded by Kubena as the theme for The Alamo Sentry website.

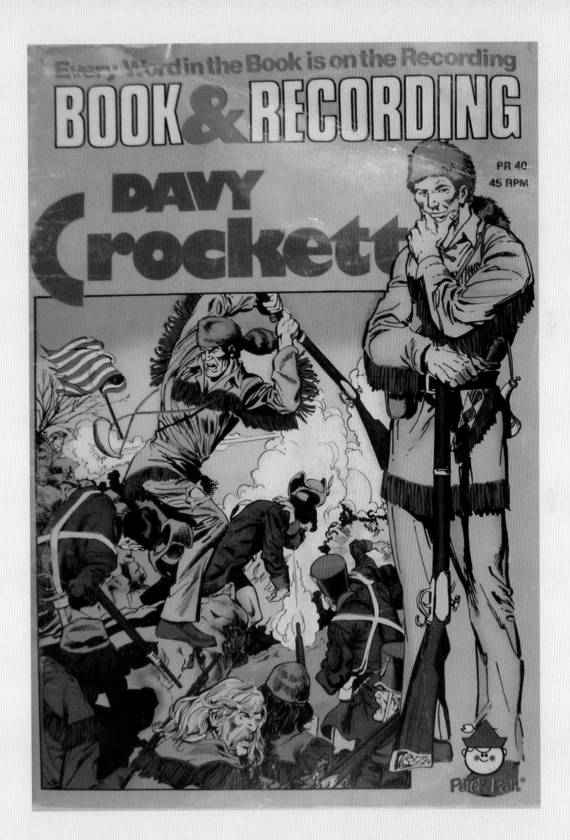

LOST ALAMO SONG TITLES AND RECORDINGS

The following song titles have been registered or published, but no information could be found regarding when they were composed or any recordings of them. The authors would welcome any additional information about these songs for future editions. Such information can be sent to the authors in care of the publisher.

"Alamo" by Olav Norstad & Fred Spannuth (publisher unknown)

"Alamo" by Robert Murray Jamieson; Publisher: Universal Music-MGB Songs

"Alamo" by Sean Craig Anta Naitis & Katrina Kelly Ford; Publisher: Magic Paw

"Alamo" by Kurt Dustin King; Publisher: King Catamount Productions

"Alamo" by Philippe Tristan Fragione; Publisher: Kobalt Songs Music Publishing

"Alamo" by Farina Mauro & Fabio Serra; Publisher: W.B.Music Corp.

"Alamo" by Don Charles Great (publisher unknown)

"Alamo" by David Charles Nevin (publisher unknown)

"Alamo" by Paul D. Wood (publisher unknown)

"Alamo" by Gordon Menzies; Traditional; Publisher: Cminor Music

"Alamo" by William James Sherman & Willam James Sherman, Jr. (publisher unknown)

"Alamo" by Allan Glenn Ellery & Raymond John Mussell (publisher unknown)

"Alamo" by Jimmy R. Hightower; Publisher: Jim Hightower Music Co.

"Alamo" by Chris Pattern, Mathew Peters, Darryl Shave (publisher unknown)

"Alamo" by Bruce Fields & Lorraine Findlay (publisher unknown)

"Alamo" by Matthew Charles Srader (publisher unknown)

"Alamo" by Sam Shepherd; Publisher: Inbetween the Blues Publishing

"Alamo" by Lafe Dutton & Mark A. Greenberg; Publisher: Upstreet Music

"Alamo" by J. Vincent Edwards, Jennings Colin Horton, & Patrick O'Donnell; Publisher: Universal Music Careers

"Alamo" by Josh Heineman & Michael Stein; Publishers: Big Truth Music

"Alamo" by Joshua Reino Timonen (publisher unknown)

"Alamo Showdown" by Don Julin; Publisher: First Digital Music

"Alamo" by Jon Paul Stirling (publisher unknown)

"Alamo" by Terrence Raymond Cuddy (publisher unknown)

"Alamo" (versions 1 through 4) by William Ashford & Alan Ett; Publisher: Music Et Al

"Alamo Sleeps" by Craig Garfinkle; Publisher: Zoo Street Music

"Alamo Song" by Paul Leslie Staggs (publisher unknown)

"Alamo Stands for Texas" by Mark Raymond Charron; Publisher: Points West Publishing

"Alamo Suite" by John Richard Handy III; Publishers: Hammerica Songs; & Hard Work Music

"Alamo Fiesta" by Elmer Stigman (also listed as performer; publisher unknown)

"Alamo March" by Peter Petroff (publisher unknown)

"Alamo Rag" by Elmer William Hoffnauer; Publisher: Anne-Rachel Music Corporation

"El Alamo" by Peter Taylor (publisher unknown)

"The Alamo" by Bobby Fischer (Fischer, Robert Warren), Danny Joe Mitchell (Mitchell, Pearly), Murray Kellum; Publisher: EMI

"The Alamo" by Tony Hiller, Lee Sheridan, Martin Lee; Publisher: EMI

"Bonham" by Benjamin Forrest Davis; Publisher: Heaven Meadow Music

"Bonham" by Ryan David Winkle; Performer: Van Deacon; Publisher: Genevieve Music

"Jim Bowie" by Joseph Davis Hooven & Jerry Winn (publisher unknown)

"Bowie" by James Fernando Ellis III; Publisher: Escape Velocity Publishing Company

"Crockett's Farewell" by Paul Driver; Publisher: Stephen Edward Hartz Mystery Ridge Publishing

"Davy Crockett" by Bruce Cowles Hampton & Charles Williams; Publishers: 1. Pulse Plus Music; 2. Three Bronson Bark Music; 3. Warner-Tamerlane Publishing Corp.

"Davy Crockett" by M. Brochetain; Publisher: EMI Unart Catalog Inc.

"Davy Crockett" by Michael Okrun; Publisher: Alpha Film Music

"Davy Crockett" by Dave Wall; Publishers: EMI Blackwood Music Inc.

"Davy Crockett's Honeymoon" by David Lynn Schnaufer; Publisher: Three Minute Movie Music

"Davy Crockett the Grinnist Man" by Dennis Olan Bassham; Publisher: Sound Two Thousand Publishing

"Remember the Alamo" by Joy Swinea (Wydner), Shane Decker, Phillip Douglas; Publisher: EMI

"Sam Houston" by Dan Bridges; Publisher: Gravenhurst Music

"Sam Houston" by James Alan Johnston; Publishers: 1. Cherry River Music Co.; 2. Stephanie Music Publishing Inc.

"Sam Houston" by Mark David Manders (publisher unknown)

"Santa Anna" by Richard Paul Iacona & Douglas A. Wood; Publisher: Franklin-Douglas Inc. (Omnimusic)

"Santa Anna" by Ronnie Thompson; Publisher: John Parker Music

"Santa Anna" by Bernard John Marsden & William Simon Pieter Webb; Publisher: Cypress Creek Music

"Santa Anna's Retreat from Buena Vista" by Hans Lengsfelder (publisher unknown)

"Santa Anna's Downfall" by Shelton G. Berg; Publisher: J.Fraser Collection LLC

"Santa Anna" by Frank Luther; Publisher: Embassy Music Corporation

"Santa Anna" by Pete Moore; Publisher: Songs of Universal Inc.

"Santa Anna" (writer unknown); Publisher: Alpha Film Music

"Santa Anna" by Meic Stevens; Publisher: Universal Music Careers

"Santa Anna" by Peter Michael Dircks (publisher unknown)

"Santa Anna" by Alan Albert Shacklock; Publisher: Ex Patriot Music

"Santa Anna at the Alamo" by Gene O'Bannon; Publishers: 1) Glad Music Publishing & Recording LP; 2) Pappy Daily Music LP

"Santa Anna Blues" by Josef Peters; Publisher: Mango Boy Music

"Santa Anna's Foot Soldier" by Richard Minus; Publisher: Rich Minus Music

"Santa Anna's Retreat" by David Lynn Schnaufer; Publisher: John Lomax III DBA; Three Minute Movie

BIBLIOGRAPHY

BOOKS

Armitage, Theresa, Peter W. Dykema, Gladys Pitcher, David Stevens and J. Lilian Vandevere. *Our Land of Song*. Boston: C. C. Birchard and Company, 1942.

Blair, Walter. *Davy Crockett — Legendary Frontier Hero*. Springfield, IL: Lincoln-Herndon Press Inc., 1986.

Bok, Gorden. *Time and the Flying Snow — Songs of Gordon Bok*. Sharon, Connecticut: Folk-Legacy Records, Inc., 1977.

Botkin, B. A., ed. *A Treasury of American Folklore*. New York: Crown, 1944.

Brunnings, Florence E. *Folk Song Index: A Comprehensive Guide to the Florence E. Brunnings Collection*. New York & London: Garland Publishing, Inc., 1981.

Carmer, Carl. *America Sings — Stories and Songs of Our Country's Growing*. New York: Alfred A. Knopf, 1942.

Cash, W. J. *The Mind of the South*. New York: Alfred Knopf, 1941.

Chemerka, William. *The Alamo Almanac and Book of Lists*. Austin: Eakin Press, 1997.

_____. *The Davy Crockett Almanac and Book of Lists*. Austin: Eakin Press, 2000.

Colcord, Joanna C. *Songs of American Sailormen*. New York: Oak Publications, 1938.

Cox, John Harrington, *Folk-songs of the South*. New York: Dover Publications, Inc., 1967.

Davis, Arthur Kyle, Jr. *Folk-Songs of Virginia*. New York: AMS Press, Inc., 1949.

Dolph, Edward Arthur. *"Sound Off!"* New York: Cosmopolitan Book Corporation, 1929.

Dorson, Richard, ed. *Davy Crockett: American Comic Legend*. Westport, CT: Greenwood Press, 1977.

Dykema, Peter W., Gladys Pitcher, David Stevens, and Lilian J. Vandevere, eds. *Sing Out!* Boston: C. C. Birchard & Co, 1946; 1947.

French, James Strange. *Sketches and Eccentricities of Col. Crockett of West Tennessee*. New York: Arno Press, 1974; New York, J. J. Harper, 1833.

Green, Jeff. *The Green Book*. Nashville: Professional Desk Reference, Inc., 2002.

Ives, Burl. *More Burl Ives Songs*. New York: Ballantine Books, 1966.

Lofaro, Michael A. ed. *Davy Crockett: The Man, the Legend, the Legacy, 1786-1986*. Knoxville: University of Tennessee Press, 1985.

Lofaro, Michael A. and Joe Cummings, eds. *Crockett at Two Hundred: New Perspectives on the Man and the Myth*. Knoxville: University of Tennessee Press, 1989.

Lomax, Alan. *The Folk Songs of North America — In the English Language*. London: Cassell & Co. Ltd., 1960.

Lomax, John A. *Songs of the Cattle Trail and Cow Camp*. New York: The Macmillan Company, 1919.

Lomax, John A. and Alan Lomax. American Ballads and Folk Songs. New York: Macmillan Co., 1934.

_____. *Cowboy Songs and Other Frontier Ballads.* New York: Macmillan Co., 1938.

_____. *Best Loved American Folk Songs.* New York: Grosset & Dunlap, 1947.

_____. *Folk Song U.S.A.* New York & Scarborough: New American Library, 1947.

_____. *Our Singing Country.* New York: Macmillan Company, 1949.

Lynn, Frank. *Songs for Swingin' Housemothers.* San Francisco: Fearon, 1963.

____. *Songs for the Singin.'* San Francisco: Chandler, 1961.

Meade, Jr., Guthrie T., et al. *Country Music Sources: A Biblio-Discography of Commercialy Recorded Traditional Music.* Chapel Hill, NC: Southern Folklife Collection, University of North Carolina at Chapel Hill Libraries in Association with the John Edwards Memorial Forum, 2002.

Murray, R. Michael. *The Golden Age of Walt Disney Records*: 1933–1988. Dubuque, IA: Antique Trader Books, 1997.

Owens, William *Texas Folk Songs.* Dallas: SMU Press, 1950; 1976.

Owens, William A. Musical arrangements by Willa Mae Kelly Koehn. *Texas Folk Songs.* Austin: Texas Folklore Society, University Press in Dallas, 1950.

Peterson, Carl. *Now's the Day and Now's the Hour.* Mexico Beach FL: Dream Catcher Publishing, Inc., 2004.

Randolph, Vance. *Ozark Folksongs.* Norm Cohen, ed. Urbana, IL: University of Illinois Press, 1982.

_____. *Ozark Folk Songs.* Columbia, MO: State Historical Society of Missouri, 1950.

Rios, John F., comp. and ed. *Readings on the Alamo.* New York: Vantage Press, 1987.

Rosenberg, Bruce A. *The Folksongs of Virginia: A Checklist of the WPA Holdings Alderman Library University of Virginia.* Charlottesville, VA: University Press of Virginia, 1969.

Rough and Ready Songster, The. New York and St. Louis, MO: Nafis & Cornish, 1848(?).

Rourke, Constance. *Davy Crockett.* New York: Harcourt, Brace & Company, Inc., 1934; Lincoln, NE: University of Nebraska Press, 1998.

Shackford, James Atkins. *David Crockett: The Man and the Legend.* Chapel Hill: University of North Carolina Press, 1956.

Shay, Frank. *American Sea Songs and Chanteys from the Days of Iron Men and Wooden Ships.* Freeport, New York: Books for Libraries Press, 1948; reprint 1969.

Silber, Irwin and Fred. *Folksinger's Wordbook.* New York: Oak Publications, 1973.

Silverman, Jerry. *Mel Bay Presents the American History Songbook.* Pacific, MO: Mel Bay Publications, 1992.

Smith, Richard Penn. *Colonel Crockett's Exploits and Adventures in Texas* (1836); 2003 edition, published as *On to the Alamo: Colonel Crockett's Exploits and Adventures in Texas.* New York: Penguin Classics, 2003, John Seelye, ed.

Spaeth, Sigmund. *Read 'em and Weep: The Songs You Forgot to Remember.* New York: Da Capo Press, 1979.

Tobitt, Janet E. *Sing Me Your Song!* New York, 1941.

Thompson, Frank. *The Alamo: A Cultural History.* Dallas: Taylor Trade Publishing, 2001.

Whall, W. B. *Sea Songs and Shanties.* Glasgow: J. Brown & Son, 1920.

Whitburn, Joel. *Joel Whitburn Presents The Billboard Pop Charts: 1955–1959.* Menomonee, WI: Record Research, Inc., 1992.

_____. *The Billboard Book of Top 40 Hits: 1955 to present.* New York: Billboard Publications, Inc., 1983.

ARTICLES

"A Mixture of Yarns about Davy Crockett." *The Ozarks Mountaineer* July/Aug 1992: 52–53.

Chemerka, William R. "'David Crockett' Bicentennial: Clipper Ship Launched 150 Years Ago." *The Crockett Chronicle* #2 (November 2003): 4–5.

_____. "The Leaving of Liverpool: 19th Century Tune Acknowledges 'Crockett' Clipper Ship." *The Crockett Chronicle* #13 (August 2006): 8–9.

Dienst Alex. "Contemporary Poetry of the Texan Revolution." *Southwestern Historical Quarterly* 21.2 (1917).

Dorson, Richard M. "The Sources of *Davy Crockett: American Comic Legend*." *Midwest Folklore* 8 (1958): 145.

Groneman, William III. "Fiddling with History: David Crockett and the 'Devil's Box'." *True West* 54-3 Mar. 2007: 58–61.

Kirkland, Edwin C. "A Check List of the Titles of Tennessee Folksongs." *Journal of American Folklore* 59-2 (1946): 423–476.

Von Schmidt, Eric. "The Alamo Remembered — From a Painter's Point of View." *Smithsonian Magazine* 16–12 Mar. 1986: 54–67.

_____. "Notes on the Song." *The Alamo — A Song to Honor the Sesquicentennial of the Battle* — March 6th 1836–1986. (© Minglewood, 1985); sheet music p. 4

Wolfe, Charles. "Davy Crockett's Dance and Old Hickory's Fandango." *The Devils' Box* 16 Sept. 1982: 34–41.

_____. "Davy Crockett Songs: Minstrels to Disney." *Davy Crockett: The Man, the Legend, the Legacy, 1786-1986*. Ed. Michael A. Lofaro. Knoxville: University of Tennessee Press, 1985: 159–190.

_____. "Crockett and Nineteenth-Century Music." *Crockett at Two Hundred: New Perspectives on the Man and the Myth*. Eds. Michael A. Lofaro & Joe Cummings. Knoxville: University of Tennessee Press, 1989: 83–96.

MUSIC OF THE ALAMO:

FROM 19TH CENTURY BALLADS TO BIG-SCREEN SOUNDTRACKS
NOTES ON THE BONUS CD

We thought it appropriate to include a small sampling of songs that are described in the book. Rather than include familiar movie themes and pop chart hits, the featured CD selections reflect a cross section of nearly forgotten 19th century tunes and more recent compositions about the Alamo and its heroes.

TRACK 1: "Remember the Alamo" (T. A. Durriage) — "The Ballad of Davy Crockett" (aka "Pompey Smash") (Anonymous) — Dean Shostak. These two 19th century songs originally appeared as part of a medley titled "Legend of Davy Crockett" on the CD *Davy Crockett's Fiddle* (©2002 Coastline Music, Dean Shostak).

TRACK 2: "Will You Come to the Bower" (Anonymous) — Carl Peterson. This tune, played at the battle of San Jacinto in 1836, is taken from Peterson's *Scotland Remembers the Alamo* CD (©2001 Darach Recordings).

TRACK 3: "Santa Anna's Retreat from Cerro Gordo" (Anonymous) — Carl Peterson. This musical celebration of the U.S. victory over Santa Anna during the Mexican war in 1847 also appeared on *Scotland Remembers the Alamo* (©2001 Darach Recordings).

TRACK 4: "The Day the Alamo Fell" (K. R. Wood) — John Guthrie. This tribute to the Alamo defenders captures the idea that there was ultimate victory for Texas in their defeat. Taken from *K. R. Wood's Fathers of Texas* CD (©1997 Texanna Records).

TRACK 5: "Women of the Alamo" (K. R. Wood) — Mary Welch. The vocal, delivered in both English and Spanish, describes the plight of the women who survived the Battle of the Alamo. An earlier version of this song was titled "Mother of the Alamo." From *K. R. Wood's Los Tejanos* CD (©2003 Texanna Records).

TRACK 6: "A Parting Kiss" (M. Boldt) — Nancy Boldt. A narration piece set to music that reflects the thoughts of Alamo noncombatant Susanna Dickinson. From Mike Boldt's *The Alamo: A Musical Tribute to John Wayne's Epic Film* (© 2004 Spy Guise Entertainment).

TRACK 7: "Memory of the Alamo" (W. Pasqua, T. Pasqua & M. Boldt) — Tony Pasqua (lead vocal), Mike Boldt and Bill Chemerka (backing vocals). A 1985 composition that captures the lasting impact of the struggle at the Alamo. From the CD *At The Alamo* (©2005 Bee Tee Music).

TRACK 8: "We Remember the Alamo" (W. Chemerka) — Bill Chemerka. This 2005 composition features lyrical commentary about both Anglo and Tejano Alamo heroes. From the *At the Alamo* CD (©2005 Bee Tee Music).

CD produced by Michael Boldt, William R. Chemerka and Allen J. Wiener at Alamo North Recording, Weehawken, NJ.